Academic Reading
with Active
Critical Thinking

Academic Reading
with Active
Critical Thinking

Janet Maker

Los Angeles Trade-Technical College

Minnette Lenier

Los Angeles Pierce College

Wadsworth Publishing Company

I(T)P™   An International Thomson Publishing Company

Belmont • Albany • Bonn • Boston • Cincinnati • Detroit • London
Madrid • Melbourne • Mexico City • New York • Paris • San Francisco
Singapore • Tokyo • Toronto • Washington

English Editor: Angela Gantner Wrahtz
Editorial Assistant: Royden Tonomura
Production: Robin Lockwood & Associates
Text Designer: *By Design* / Wendy LaChance
Cover Designer: Harry Voigt
Cover Photo: Chambered Nautilus by Lester
  Lefkowitz/Tony Stone Images
Print Buyer: Randy Hurst
Permissions Editor: Robert Kauser
Copy Editor: Robin Witkin
Compositor: G & S Typesetters, Inc.
Printer: Malloy Lithographing, Inc.

Printed in the United States of America
1 2 3 4 5 6 7 8 9 10—01 00 99 98 97 96

For more information, contact Wadsworth Publishing Company:

Wadsworth Publishing Company
10 Davis Drive
Belmont, California 94002, USA

International Thomson Publishing Europe
Berkshire House 168-173
High Holborn
London, WC1V7AA, England

Thomas Nelson Australia
102 Dodds Street
South Melbourne 3205
Victoria, Australia

Nelson Canada
1120 Birchmount Road
Scarborough, Ontario
Canada M1K 5G4

International Thomson Editores
Campos Eliseos 385, Piso 7
Col. Polanco
11560 México D.F. México

International Thomson Publishing GmbH
Königswinterer Strasse 418
53227 Bonn, Germany

International Thomson Publishing Asia
221 Henderson Road
#05-10 Henderson Building
Singapore 0315

International Thomson Publishing Japan
Hirakawacho Kyowa Building, 3F
2-2-1 Hirakawacho
Chiyoda-ku, Tokyo 102, Japan

Library of Congress Cataloging-in-Publication Data

Maker, Janet.
    Academic reading with active critical thinking / Janet Maker,
  Minnette Lenier.
      p. cm.
    ISBN 0-534-22020-7
    1. Study skills. 2. Critical thinking. 3. Reading comprehension.
  I. Lenier, Minnette. II. Title.
  LB2395.M33 1995
  378.1'7028'1—dc20   95-2648

In memory of Tom Nealon
who gave so freely of his time to make this a better book.

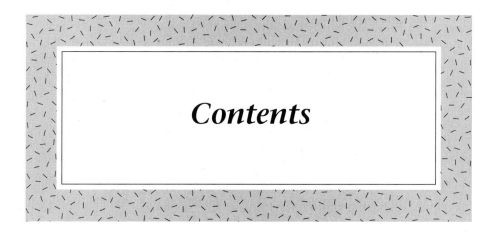

Contents

Unit Three: Textbook Reading   137

Unit Four: Advanced Application of ACT   249

Preface to Students

If you can already read college textbooks, but need improvement in critical reading and study reading, this book is for you. You may find yourself reading and rereading assignments without knowing how to identify which material is most important to learn. You might be trying to memorize too much. Even when this leads to good grades, the cost to you is too high, and often causes frustration and burnout. The purpose of the six-step ACT (Active Critical Thinking) system we use is to give you a method for handling college reading so that you can earn high grades while using your time efficiently.

The textbook material in this book is taken from a representative sample of current college texts. The critical reading material represents controversial issues often seen in the news and commonly the subject of college debate.

Unit One covers the prerequisite skills you will need to handle the reading selections in this book. Answers to the practice activities are in the Study Guide. If you have difficulty with Unit One, be sure you let your instructor know, so that he or she can assign some extra practice. Unit Two (critical reading) and Unit Three (textbook reading) each consist of ten reading selections with a preview of the vocabulary words and practice activities for the six steps of ACT. Answers to the practice activities and tests of comprehension and vocabulary for each reading selection are in the Study Guide. Unit Four consists of ten selections with vocabulary but without the practice activities. You will be designing the practice activities for critical and study reading yourself, as you will for your classes, and sample answers and tests are in the Study Guide. The Study Guide also contains short programs for vocabulary skills and reading flexibility.

Acknowledgments

We would like to thank the following reviewers for their excellent advice and suggestions: Hilda P. Barrow, Pitt Community College; Robin W. Erwin, Niagara University; Mary Jane Farley, Dyersburg State Community College; Kathryn M. Gardner, West Valley Community College; Carol Helton, Tennessee State Technical Institute; Joycelyn Jacobs, Lee College; Faye Jones, Nashville State Technical Institute; Marilee McGowan, Oakton Community College; Thomas E. Nealon, Nassau Community College; Wendy Paterson, Buffalo State College; Joyce Ritchey, El Paso Community College; Shirley Sloan, Evergreen Valley College; Karen Sookram, Doane College; Dorothy K. Wamsley, Bethany College; Brenda R. Williams, University of New Haven; and Lynda Wolverton, Polk Community College.

Academic Reading
with Active
Critical Thinking

Unit One

Reading
Fundamentals

I f you are an average full-time college student, you read about ten textbooks in an academic year, plus any outside reading you do for classes, work, or pleasure. Your challenge is to handle this load effectively, to learn as much as you can, and to earn high grades in the process. The techniques taught in this book will help you make the most of the time you have.

Active Critical Thinking: A Six-Step Process

Inefficient readers often read passively. Like sponges, they try to absorb all the information in their books and lecture notes. Finally, overwhelmed with information, they end up rereading the material, wasting time, and feeling frustrated. The goal of this book is to convert passive readers into active critical thinkers.

ACT is a six-step system for reading, thinking, and studying.

Step 1   Preread

You will use a prereading method that will give you an overview of all the major ideas in the reading and activate your background knowledge. This step will make you aware of what you know and don't know about a subject.

Step 2   Read

After completing the prereading step, you will be able to read actively, interacting with the material, with increased comprehension.

Step 3   Analyze What You Read

For critical reading, analysis will mean recognizing the author's point of view, arguments, and supporting details. This analysis will provide the basis for making your own judgments. For study reading, the analysis will mean deciding what to study, including predicting test questions and creating a study guide.

Step 4   Remember What's Important

You will decide what you need to remember and learn techniques to aid your memory.

Step 5   Make Use of What You Read

This step will help you use what you read in class discussions, written assignments, oral reports, and, most commonly, tests.

Step 6   Evaluate Your Active Critical Thinking Skills

You will be able to analyze the feedback you received in step 5. Feedback can come in several ways: a grade on a test, comments on a paper, or a response to an oral presentation.

You will be using the ACT system in Units II, III, and IV of this book. Unit I reviews the most basic skills prerequisite to active critical reading. The first skill—understanding the subject, the main idea, and supporting details—is used for informative writing. The second skill—understanding the point of view, the argument, and supporting details—is used for persuasive writing. All the techniques for study and critical reading in this book depend on your knowledge of these two skills.

Skill I: Understanding the Subject, the Main Idea, and Supporting Details

Identifying the Subject

Every sentence, paragraph, chapter, article, book, TV program, movie, class, lecture, or conversation has a subject. The subject is who or what the whole thing is about. For example, the subject of this book is active critical thinking. In a paragraph, every sentence must relate to the subject.

Paragraph 1

Males and females in our culture speak different body languages. Males use power cues, such as expanded limb positions and serious facial expressions to create an overall impression of power, dominance, high status, and activity. Females, on the other hand, use affiliative displays, such as smiles and head cants, to create an overall impression of submissiveness, subordination, low status, and passivity.[1]

Circle the letter preceding the subject of paragraph 1.

The subject is

a. body language in men and women.

b. men and women.

c. power and submission.

d. sexism.

The answer is *a*. The other three topics are too broad, since they extend to many more issues than body language.

Paragraph 2

The tricky aspect of inflation is that rising prices often result in lower real incomes for buyers who can't buy as much with their dollars. But from a seller's viewpoint, rising prices for their products and services mean higher incomes. (Of course, the sellers will probably have to pay higher prices for the resources they use.) Thus, the central problem with inflation is to identify who wins and who loses.[2]

Circle the letter preceding the subject of paragraph 2.

The subject is

a. the effects of unemployment.

b. the effects of recession.

c. higher costs of resources.

d. the problem with inflation.

The answer is *d*. Choice *a* is not mentioned in the paragraph. Choices *b* and *c* are too narrow; they cover only part of the paragraph.

Paragraph 3

Nature is the term for human genetic makeup or biological inheritance. Nurture refers to the environment or the interaction experiences that make up an individual's life. Some scientists debate the relative importance of genes and environment, arguing that one is substantially more important than the other to all phases of human development. Both are essential to socialization. Trying to distinguish the separate contributions of nature and nurture is analogous to examining a tape player and a cassette separately to determine what is recorded on the tape rather than studying how the two work together to produce the sound.[3]

Circle the letter preceding the subject of paragraph 3.

The subject is

a. the nature of socialization.

b. personality development.

c. scientific arguments.

d. nature and nurture.

The answer is *d*. The other choices are too broad.

Understanding the Main Idea

The main idea is the main point the author is making about the subject, the idea that the writer intends to prove. Circle the main ideas of paragraphs 1, 2, and 3.

The main idea of paragraph 1 is that

a. males and females in our culture use different body language.

b. males use power cues, such as expanded limb positions and serious facial expressions.

c. females use affiliative displays, such as smiles and head cants.

d. males want power, dominance, and high status, whereas females create an impression of submission, subordination, and passivity.

The answer is *a*. Choices *b* and *c* are too narrow; they cover only part of the paragraph. Choice *d* may or may not be true, but it does not mention body language—the subject of the paragraph.

The main idea of paragraph 2 is that

a. inflation raises the prices of resources.

b. rising prices result in greater profits for sellers.

c. rising prices often result in lower real incomes for buyers.

d. the problem with inflation is identifying who wins and who loses.

The answer is *d*. Choices *a, b,* and *c* are true, but they are too narrow to be the main idea. The main idea must be broad enough to include every sentence in the paragraph.

The main idea of paragraph 3 is that

a. nature refers to human genetic makeup or biological inheritance.

b. nurture refers to the environment or the interaction experiences that make up an individual's life.

c. both nature and nurture are essential to socialization.

d. scientists argue about the relative importance of nature and nurture.

The answer is *c*. Choices *a, b,* and *d* all lead to the conclusion that both are necessary.

More often than not, the main idea is at the beginning of a paragraph, but sometimes it is in the middle or at the end. Look back at paragraphs 1, 2, and 3.

1. In paragraph 1, is the main idea at the beginning, middle, or end?
   _____

2. In paragraph 2? _____

3. In paragraph 3? _____

The main idea is at the beginning of paragraph 1, at the end of paragraph 2, and in the middle of paragraph 3.

Finding the Supporting Details

The third part of each paragraph is support for the main idea. The author may give historical or scientific facts to support the main idea. He or she may give reasons to explain why the main idea is true. The main idea may be supported with examples. Expert (or not-so-expert) testimonials may also be used.

In paragraph 1 the author gives examples of expressions and postures used by males and females to create different overall impressions. The paragraph can be outlined as follows:

I. *(Main idea)* Males and females in our culture speak different body languages.
   A. *(Supporting example)* Males use power cues, such as expanded limb positions and serious facial expressions to create an overall impression of power, dominance, high status, and activity.
   B. *(Supporting example)* Females use affiliative displays, such as smiles and head cants, to create an overall impression of submissiveness, subordination, low status, and passivity.

In paragraph 2 the author gives reasons for the difficulty in identifying the winners and losers created by inflation. The paragraph can be outlined as follows:

I. *(Main idea)* The problem with inflation is to identify who wins and who loses.
   A. *(Supporting reason)* Buyers have lower incomes.
   B. *(Supporting reason)* Sellers have higher incomes.

In paragraph 3 the author gives a reason to support the main idea.

I. *(Main idea)* Both nature and nurture are essential to socialization.
   A. *(Supporting reason)* They work together (like a tape player and a cassette).

Implied Main Idea

Sometimes the main idea is implied rather than stated. You have to infer what the author is saying by reading between the lines. Circle the letter preceding the implied main idea of the following paragraph, and put it on the outline. Write the main idea next to the Roman numeral I, and write the supporting details on the lines beneath.

Paragraph 4

To get a clearer idea of what happens, imagine a woman with a family of three young children receiving Aid for Families with Dependent Children (AFDC). The father has disappeared. The mother receives assistance in the form of cash, food stamps, and medical care. If the woman finds a job, for every $100 she earns, she will have to pay $7 in Social Security taxes. Typically, she will lose about $35 in AFDC benefits and $25 worth of food stamps. Taxes (assuming no income tax) and lost benefits total $67; for every $100 she earns, she increases her net income by only $33. The marginal tax rate on work is thus 67 percent, a much higher rate than the maximum tax rate paid on earned income. (The maximum federal income tax rate on individuals, excluding Social Security taxes, is 28 percent.)[4]

Circle the implied main idea:

a. Welfare mothers don't want to work.

b. Welfare mothers don't get much for their work.

c. Welfare mothers should work.

d. Welfare mothers should get a lower income tax rate.

The answer is *b.* Choice *a* is not implied, although certainly people's motivation to work would be affected by how much pay they can keep. Choices *c* and *d* are not implied. The author does not make any recommendations; he leaves the reader to draw his or her own conclusions.

Outlining the Main Idea and Supporting Details

Outlining gives you a way to visualize the relationship between the main idea and the supporting details and therefore helps you understand what you have read. Outline paragraph 4 again. Note that there are two levels of supporting details: major and minor (the minor details support the major ones).

I. _____

   (Implied main idea)

   A. _____

      (Supporting fact/major detail)

      1. _____

         (Minor detail)

2. _____
     (Minor detail)

3. _____
     (Minor detail)

B. _____
     (Supporting fact/major detail)

Paragraph 4 should be outlined as follows:

I. Welfare mothers don't get much for their work.

    A. For every $100 they earn, they keep only $33.

        1. They pay $7 in Social Security taxes.

        2. They lose $35 in AFDC benefits.

        3. They lose $25 in food stamps.

    B. Their marginal tax rate is 67%.

You have already outlined paragraph 4. Now outline the following five paragraphs. Ask yourself who or what the paragraph is about (the subject), and what the main point is that the writer is trying to make about the subject. Write the stated or implied main idea next to the Roman numeral I, and the supporting major and minor details beneath. In Paragraphs 5 and 6 the details are filled in; you fill in the main ideas. In paragraphs 7, 8, and 9, the main ideas are filled in; you fill in the details.

Paragraph 5

Many underdeveloped countries have a contradictory policy of simultaneously promoting tobacco production (for economic reasons) and discouraging tobacco consumption (for health reasons). For example, China has revolutionized the healthcare of its people, and yet leads the world in tobacco production and consumption. In many third world countries (including Mexico), cigarette advertising and promotions overwhelm poorly funded anti-smoking efforts that go virtually unnoticed by the general public.[5]

I. _____

    A. China

    B. Mexico

Paragraph 6

American conservatives shrink from "welfare-state" policies for many reasons. Womb-to-tomb security, they fear, will reduce striving and discourage risk-taking. High taxes not only cut into venture capital, in their thinking, but reduce the individual's desire to work and his choices in the spending of income. A large social role for the government, conservatives fear, will discourage individual creativity and promote national uniformity.[6]

I. _____

   A. Reduce striving and discourage risk-taking

   B. Cut into venture capital

   C. Reduce individual's desire to work

   D. Reduce choices in the spending of income

   E. Discourage individual creativity

   F. Promote national uniformity

Paragraph 7

Unlike Western instruments, many non-Western instruments have remained remarkably stable over long periods. The Chinese *qin* (or *ch'in*, pronounced "chin") is a member of the zither family that dates back to at least the eighteenth century B.C. Today's instrument differs little from that of nearly four thousand years ago. The qin consists of a shallow wooden box with seven silk strings tuned to degrees of the pentatonic (five-note) scale (on our modern piano, about G-A-C-D-E-G-A). Its dimensions (3.65 Chinese inches, for the number of the days of the year) and shape (a convex soundboard to symbolize heaven; a flat bottom board to symbolize earth) are part of an elaborate symbolism. The qin's delicate plucked sound (including "sliding" tones that are possible on fretless instruments like this) is well suited to the expression of subtle moods.[7]

In the following outline, the main idea is given. Fill in the example that supports the main idea, and the details that support the example.

I. Many non-Western instruments have remained stable.

   A. _____

      1. _____

      2. _____

      3. _____

      4. _____

Paragraph 8

Coleman argues that because athletic achievement is widely admired, everyone with some ability will try to develop this talent. With regard to the relatively unrewarded arena of academic life, "those who have ability may not be motivated to compete." This reward structure may explain why top students in the United States have difficulty competing with top students in many other nations—the United States does not draw everyone who has academic potential into the competition.[8]

I. Top students in the United States have trouble competing with top students in many other nations.

    A. _____

       1. _____

       2. _____

Paragraph 9

Some sociologists have found that geographic separation virtually guarantees that family members will meet less frequently than if they live close to one another and that over time this spatial distance results in emotional distance as well. Other sociologists have found that although geographic separation hinders face-to-face interaction, it does not necessarily disrupt kinship relations because family members can keep in touch by phone or mail. In fact, this latter group of sociologists found substantial interaction despite distance and concluded that separation can enhance relationships. That is, separation teaches family members not to take one another for granted and to enjoy and appreciate the limited time available for interaction.[9]

I. Sociologists disagree about the effects of geographic separation on families.

    A. _____

    B. _____

       1. _____

       2. _____

Finding the Main Idea in Longer Selections

The following five selections are several paragraphs in length. However, you can find the main idea and support the same way you did in one-paragraph selections.

Selection 1

Most people, especially in affluent societies, have a *throwaway worldview,* also known as a *frontier worldview,* based on the idea that there will always be more. A modified version of this view is the *Spaceship–Earth worldview,* in which earth is viewed as a spaceship—a machine that we can understand, control, and change at will by using advanced technology.

    People with these worldviews see Earth as a place of unlimited resources, where any type of resource conservation or pollution prevention that hampers short-term economic growth is unnecessary. If we deplete or pollute the resources in one area, they believe we will find substitutes and control the pollution through technology. If resources become scarce or a substitute can't be found, we can get materials from the moon and asteroids in the "new frontier" of space. Even if we pollute an area, we can invent a technology to clean it up, dump it into space, move elsewhere, or live in space or on another planet. If we extinguish other species, we can use genetic engineering to create new and better ones.

According to these worldviews, continued economic growth and technological advances will produce a less crowded, less polluted, and more resource-rich world. It will also be a world in which most people will be healthier, will live longer, and will have greater material wealth.[10]

I. _____

    A. Earth has unlimited resources; conservation or pollution protection is unnecessary.

        1. If resources are depleted or polluted, find substitutes and control pollution through technology.

        2. If resources are scarce or substitutes can't be found, get materials from space.

        3. If we pollute an area, invent a technology to clean it up, dump it into space, move elsewhere, or live in space or on another planet.

        4. If we extinguish other species, create new ones.

    B. Continued economic growth and technological advances will produce a less crowded, less polluted, more resource-rich world where people will be healthier, will live longer, and will have greater material wealth.

Selection 2

A few squatter communities have organized to improve their living conditions. They gradually turn flimsy shacks into solid buildings, and work together to lay out streets, build schools, and bring water and electricity lines.

One example is Rio de Janeiro's Santa Marta slum, home for 11,500 of the city's 2 million squatters. Residents organized to establish a day-care program and to bring in water lines, electricity, health clinics, and drainage systems to prevent mud slides.

In Villa El Salvador, a squatter settlement outside of Lima, Peru, a network of women's groups and neighborhood associations planted half a million trees, trained hundreds of door-to-door health workers, and built 300 community kitchens, 130 day-care centers, and 26 schools. Through their own efforts, the people now have homes with electricity, over half have water and sewers, and trees and gardens flourish in what was once desert. In this town of 300,000 people, illiteracy has fallen to 3%—one of the lowest rates in Latin America—and infant mortality is 40% below the national average.[11]

I. _____

    A. Rio de Janeiro's Santa Marta slum

    B. Lima, Peru's Villa El Salvador settlement

Selection 3

Malaria once infected nine out of ten people in North Borneo, now known as Brunei. In 1955, the World Health Organization (WHO) began spraying dieldrin (a pesticide similar to DDT) to kill malaria-carrying mosquitoes. The program was so successful that the dreaded disease was almost eliminated from the island.

Other, unexpected things happened however. The dieldrin killed other insects, including flies and cockroaches, living in houses. The islanders applauded, but then small lizards that also lived in the houses died after gorging themselves on dead insects. Then cats began dying after feeding on dead lizards. Without cats, rats flourished and overran the villages. Now people were threatened by sylvatic plague carried by the fleas on the rats. The situation was brought under control when WHO parachuted healthy cats onto the island.

Then roofs began to fall in. The dieldrin had killed wasps and other insects that fed on a type of caterpillar that either avoided or was not affected by the insecticide. With most of its predators eliminated, the caterpillar population exploded. The larvae munched their way through one of their favorite foods, the leaves used in thatching roofs.[12]

I. _____

   A. Dieldrin killed other insects living in houses.

   B. Lizards died after eating dead insects.

   C. Cats died after eating dead lizards.

   D. Rats flourished; their fleas carried sylvatic plague.

   E. Roofs fell in.

Selection 4

A *perpetual resource,* such as solar energy, is virtually inexhaustible on a human time scale. Not wasting energy and living off virtually inexhaustible solar energy in the form of heat, wind, flowing water, and renewable wood and other forms of biomass (tissue from living organisms that can be burned or broken down to provide energy) is a sustainable lifestyle. Depending on indirect solar energy stored in essentially one-time deposits of fossil fuels, or uranium used to fuel nuclear power plants, is sooner or later an unsustainable lifestyle.

A *potentially renewable resource* is one that theoretically can last indefinitely without reducing the available supply because it is replaced more rapidly through natural processes than are nonrenewable resources. Examples are trees in forests, grasses in grasslands, wild animals, fresh surface water in lakes and streams, most groundwater, fresh air, and fertile soil. The planet's most valuable resource is its diversity of potentially renewable forms of life.

Classifying something as a potentially renewable resource does not mean that it can't be depleted and that it will always be renewable. The highest rate at which a potentially renewable resource can be used without reducing its available supply throughout the world, or in a particular area, is called its *sustainable yield*. If this natural replacement rate is exceeded, the available supply of a potentially renewable resource begins to shrink—a process known as *environmental degradation*.[13]

I. Perpetual and potentially renewable resources

   A. _____

   B. _____

       1. _____

       2. _____

Selection 5

Several important, interacting parts play a role in sustaining life on Earth. They are
    The *atmosphere*—a thin, gaseous envelope that surrounds the planet. About 95% of the mass of the planet's air is found in the atmosphere's innermost layer, known as the *troposphere,* extending about 17 kilometers (11 miles) above sea level. The atmosphere's second layer, extending from about 17 to 48 kilometers (11 to 30 miles) above the earth's surface, is called the *stratosphere.*
    The *hydrosphere*—liquid water (oceans, lakes, and other bodies of surface water, and underground water), frozen water (polar ice caps, floating ice caps, and ice in soil known as permafrost), and small amounts of water vapor in the atmosphere.
    The *geosphere*—interior core, mantle, and crust (containing soil and rock). Fossil fuels and the minerals we use are found in Earth's crust and upper mantle, known as the *lithosphere.* The lithosphere consists of several gigantic plates that have been moving very slowly over hundreds of millions of years.
    The *biosphere*—the entire realm where life is found. It consists of parts of the atmosphere (the troposphere), the hydrosphere (mostly surface water and groundwater), and lithosphere (mostly soil and surface rocks and sediments on the bottoms of oceans and other bodies of water) where life is found. The biosphere is a relatively thin, 20-kilometer (12-mile) zone of life extending from the deepest ocean floor to the tops of the highest mountains.[14]

I. Several interacting parts help sustain life

   A. _____

       1. _____

       2. _____

   B. _____

       1. _____

       2. _____

       3. _____

C. _____

    1. _____

    2. _____

    3. _____

D. _____

    1. _____

    2. _____

    3. _____

Skill II: Understanding the Point of View, the Argument, and Supporting Details

In persuasive writing the point of view is similar to the main idea, and you identify it in the same way. First, concentrate on the subject: what is the entire paragraph, selection, chapter, or book about? Then ask yourself what main point the author is trying to make about the subject. This is the point of view. Like the main idea, it may appear at the beginning, in the middle, or at the end, and it may be stated or implied.

The author supports his or her point of view with arguments. There may be one or more arguments, but all of them support the point of view.

Support consists of evidence or other types of details the author uses to bolster his or her arguments. As in other writing, the support may consist of testimonials from convincing people, examples, logical reasons, and statistical or historical facts. For this exercise, we have defined a fact as something that can be proved *or* disproved. Therefore, the statement "Most people like Chinese food" is defined as a fact, whereas the statement "Chinese food is better than Italian food" is not. In Unit Two you will be evaluating the supporting details and looking for faulty logic, bias, opinions masquerading as facts, and loaded language.

Read the following article summaries. Then fill in the point of view, the arguments, and the support for the arguments in the space available. Finally, label the type of support: testimony, examples, reasons, or facts.

1. Sports competition is bad for people. The results of several hundred studies show that competition weakens our self-esteem, harms our relationships with others, and prevents us from doing our best.

Point of view: _____

Argument 1: _____

Argument 2: _____

Argument 3: _____

Support: _____

Type of support (testimony, examples, reasons, facts): _____

2. Sports competition can be good for people, depending on how it is handled. Because women athletes lack the male "Super Bull" mentality, they can handle competition in a healthy way. For example, Martina Navratilova and Chris Evert were former rivals who developed a good rapport.

Point of view: _____

Argument: _____

Support: _____

Type of support: _____

Because people already believe that killing is morally acceptable, we should consider euthanasia (mercy killing) as a viable possibility. We kill in war and in self-defense; we also administer the death penalty for capital crimes.

Point of view: _____

Argument: _____

Support 1: _____

Support 2: _____

Support 3: _____

Type of support: _____

4. Euthanasia is wrong because the experience of dying is a preparation for the afterlife. Patients who have had near-death experiences often report valuable encounters with spirit guides and loved ones who are already dead.

Point of view: _____

Argument: _____

Support: _____

Type of support: _____

5. We have overwhelming evidence, in the form of eyewitnesses from all over the world, that UFOs exist.

Point of view: _____

Argument: _____

Support: _____

Type of support: _____

6.   All of the so-called UFO sightings that were not reported by obvious crack-pots have been explained by the air force and other government agencies. Usually, they consist of airplanes, clouds, and reflections.

Point of view (implied): _____

Argument: _____

Support: _____

Type of support: _____

In the following short article, identify the point of view, the arguments, the supporting details, and type of support as you did earlier.

Pesticides

The benefits of pesticides outweigh their harmful effects. Supporters of pesticide use point out the following benefits:

Pesticides save lives. Since World War II, DDT and other chlorinated hydro-carbon and organophosphate insecticides have probably prevented the premature deaths of at least 7 million people from insect-transmitted diseases such as malaria (carried by the Anopheles mosquito), bubonic plague (rat fleas), typhus (body lice and fleas), and sleeping sickness (tsetse fly).

They increase food supplies and lower food costs. Each year, about 55% of the world's potential food supply is lost to pests before (35%) and after (20%) harvest. Without pesticides, those losses would be much higher and food prices would increase.

They increase profits for farmers. In the United States, 42% of the annual potential food supply is destroyed by pests before and after harvest. Pesticide companies estimate that every $1 spent on pesticides leads to an increase in crop yield worth $3 and $5 to farmers.

They work faster and better than other alternatives. Compared with alternative methods of pest control, pesticides can control most pests quickly and at a reasonable cost, have a relatively long shelf life, are easily shipped and applied, and are safe when handled properly. When genetic resistance occurs in pest insects and weeds, farmers can usually keep them under control by using stronger doses or switching to other pesticides.

The health risks of pesticides are insignificant compared with their health and other benefits. According to Elizabeth Whelan, director of the American Council on Science and Health (ACSH), which presents the position of the pesticide industry, "The reality is that pesticides, when used in the approved regulatory manner, pose no risk either to farm workers or consumers." Will Carpenter, president of Monsanto Agricultural Company, claims that "pesticides are safe and the food supply in the United States is safer than it has ever been." ACSH and pesticide industry scientists argue that most consumers do not realize that the health risk studies carried out by the pesticide industry (as required by law) and by independent researchers are highly unlikely worst-case scenarios. They also point out that the EPA sets maximum allowable levels of pesticide residues in food many times below the levels at which harmful health effects in people are likely to occur. They call the pesticide health-scare stories often appearing in the media examples of scientific distortion and irresponsible reporting.

Safer and more effective products are continually being developed. Pesticide company scientists are continually developing pesticides, such as pyrethroids, that are safer to use and that cause less ecological damage. New herbicides are being developed that are effective at very low dosage rates. Genetic engineering also holds promise.[15]

Point of view: _____

Argument 1: _____

Support: _____

Type of support: _____

Argument 2: _____

Support: _____

Type of support: _____

Argument 3: _____

Support: _____

Type of support: _____

Argument 4: _____

Support: _____

Type of support: _____

Argument 5: _____

Support: _____

Type of support: _____

Argument 6: _____

Support: _____

Type of support: _____

This concludes Unit One. Please check your answers with your instructor and correct your work before proceeding to Unit Two. Study your errors and note where you had problems and what the causes were. If you don't understand why another answer was better, ask your instructor to explain.

Unit Two

Critical Reading

C ritical reading means reading between the lines and making value judgments about what the author is saying. Is it true or false, good or bad, effective or ineffective, practical or impractical? As a college student, many of your written and oral assignments and exam questions will require critical reading and thinking. Yet many students coming out of high school are not prepared to do much more than memorize.

Unit Two deals with persuasive nonfiction writing. An author will employ persuasive writing to try to convince his or her readers to support a certain point of view. Persuasive writing is often found in philosophy and political science material, even in articles on the theoretical aspects of sciences like economics and mathematics. For example, the following issues call for persuasive writing:

Are the new tax laws beneficial to the middle class?

How serious is the budget deficit?

Is America's power declining?

When did the universe begin?

Does psychotherapy work?

Persuasive writing can be found in textbooks, in technical or professional writing, and in popular magazines and newspapers. Persuasion can work by fair means or foul. It can use defective reasoning and manipulation just as easily as logic and fairness. To be an informed voter or consumer, and a successful student, you must be able to critically read persuasive writing.

In Unit Two you will practice critical reading using five pairs of articles on controversial subjects: homelessness, women in combat, the war on drugs, nuclear energy, and capital punishment. Each reading in the pair takes an opposing viewpoint. We believe that the goal of critical reading and thinking is to come as close as possible to the truth, and the best way of figuring out the truth on any subject is to become familiar with the arguments supporting as many points of view as possible. Although everyone is entitled to an opinion on any subject, it is not defensible to hold an opinion while remaining ignorant of opposing points of view.

As an intellectually responsible person, you should analyze arguments with an open mind, allowing yourself to be influenced. You should even be open to opinions that appear highly unconventional, because history has shown that majority approval often shifts. For example, at one time "loyal" Americans supported the Vietnam war; later on, those who opposed the war appeared to be morally correct. Similarly, at one time only heretics believed the earth moved around the sun.

If you can develop an open mind, you will earn higher grades and be more successful in life. You will have better friendships and family relations because you will consider the other person's point of view. You will make better consumer and investment decisions because you will investigate for yourself rather than believe what you are told. You will be a better citizen because you will learn about the issues rather than follow the party line. You will have the sense of confidence that comes from taking charge of your own life. Finally, an active critical thinker is rarely bored *or* boring.

Critical Thinking Using ACT

Critical thinking involves (1) identifying the author's point of view, (2) pinpointing the underlying arguments or major ideas, (3) identifying the supporting details used to strengthen the arguments, and (4) evaluating the supporting details. ACT provides a system you can use to accomplish these steps.

Step 1 Preread

We begin each pair of articles in this unit by briefly introducing the issue and the authors. Before you begin reading, examine your opinions about the issue. Review the difficult vocabulary that precedes each article so unfamiliar words will not interfere with your comprehension. Then quickly skim the article to get an understanding of the subject and the author's point of view. Compare your opinions about the subject with the author's, and think about how open you are to what you are about to read.

Step 2 Read

Read the article without underlining or making notes. Try to understand the author's arguments and support.

Step 3 Analyze What You Read

Go back to the article and identify the arguments and their support. Then evaluate the supporting details. Support can consist of testimonials from convincing people, logical reasons, statistical or historical facts, or examples. You might want to ask the following questions when evaluating supporting details:

1. Testimony. If the author uses testimonials, are his or her sources in a position to give expert testimony about the subject? Are they objective or biased? Did the author select the most-qualified people or merely the ones who would support his or her arguments?

2. Reasons. If the support consists of logical reasons, are they really logical or is the author using faulty reasoning?

3. Facts. If the author uses facts, are they really factual? Are they provable or unprovable? You have heard about lying with statistics, but even with good intentions, facts are open to interpretation. Often, the author's opinions can masquerade as facts.

4. Examples. If the author uses examples, are the examples representative enough to be used for the generalizations the author wants to make?

Loaded Language

Authors can also use loaded language to influence their readers' thinking. For example, supporters of a politician might refer to him or her as a statesman, diplomat, strategist, or tactician, while opponents might refer to the same politician as a bureaucrat, influence peddler, power broker, or as Machiavellian. These loaded words can subtly influence our thinking. Another example of the tremendous importance of words arose recently when feminists succeeded in changing sexist language like *policeman, fireman, mailman,* and *chairman* to *police officer, firefighter, letter carrier,* and *chairperson.*

Guide for Analysis: Graphic Organizers

As part of this step, you will underline and make notes in the margin to highlight the arguments and supporting details. Then you will take the most important ideas and organize them in a visual format that you can easily understand and remember. These formats are called *graphic organizers.* Outlines and study maps are just two examples.

Outlining is one way of organizing ideas in visual form so you can easily see the relationships between them. An outline makes the ideas easier to remember. Here is an example to help you remember the steps in ACT.

I. Steps in ACT

    A. Preread

    B. Read

    C. Analyze what you read

    D. Remember what is important

    E. Make use of what you read

    F. Evaluate your active critical thinking skills

Study maps cover exactly the same material as an outline, but they are even more visual. While one outline looks much like another, no two maps look alike, especially if you use different shapes and different colored pencils. For this reason, many people find the material on maps easier to remember. The drawback is that they generally take up more space. Compare the following example with the outline.

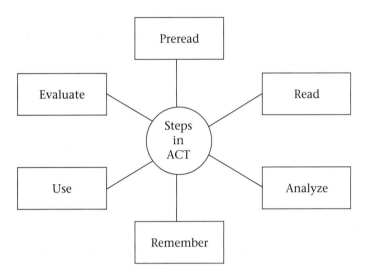

Other graphic organizers might include flow charts to show the steps in a sequence, time lines to show when events occurred, diagrams, charts, tables, and graphs. The type of graphic organizer you pick depends on the type of material. The question you should ask yourself is "Which form will help me learn the material best?"

 ## Step 4   *Remember What's Important*

Review your underlining, marginal notes, and graphic organizers until you feel confident that you understand and remember the information.

 ## Step 5   *Make Use of What You Read*

In college, your instructor will usually guide your use of the information you have prepared: class discussion, a writing assignment, an oral presentation, or a test. At the end of each pair of articles, we provide questions for writing and discussion that you can use to evaluate your understanding of the issue.

Step 6   *Evaluate Your Active Critical Thinking Skills*

When you receive feedback about your performance in the form of a grade, a critique, or other type of evaluation, use the information to improve your weaknesses. In the appendix you will find a form to help with your evaluation.

Issue 1

The Homeless

In this section you will read two articles on homelessness in the United States. Article 1, "Homeless Rights, Community Wrongs," was written by John Leo, who has written for *Reader's Digest, New York,* and *U.S. News & World Report.* Article 2, "The Worthy and Unworthy Homeless," was written by James D. Wright, the Charles and Leo Favrot Professor of Human Relations at Tulane University in New Orleans, Louisiana. In 1987 he coauthored *Homelessness and Health.*

Self-Questioning

It is important to be aware of your beliefs and biases when you read. Responding to the following questions will help you determine your views. Write the number from the rating scale that best expresses your opinion. You will take the same survey to reevaluate your views after you have read articles 1 and 2.

Rating Scale:

1 No

2 Perhaps not

3 No opinion

4 Perhaps

5 Yes

Rate each question from 1 to 5.

_____ 1. Do you think it is the government's responsibility to make sure no one goes hungry or homeless?

2. Rate the extent to which you believe the following people deserve help.

_____ a. An abandoned child

_____ b. An alcoholic or drug addict

_____ c. An elderly person

_____ d. A mentally ill person

_____ e. An army veteran

_____ f. A homeless family

_____ g. A healthy man who doesn't speak much English

_____ h. A mother with young children

_____ i. A teenage runaway

_____ j. A physically handicapped adult

_____ 3. Do you think communities are hurt by homeless street people?

Reading 1

Homeless Rights, Community Wrongs

Vocabulary Preview

Achilles' heel (ə kil′ēz hēl′) weak or vulnerable spot

reflexive (ri flek′siv) automatic, involuntary

beleaguered (bi lē′gʉrd) harassed

disoriented (dis ôr′ē en tid) mentally confused; not sure of one's bearings

demoralization (di môr ə lī zā′shən) weakening of the spirit or morale

destabilize (de stā′bə līz) upset the stability of; unbalance

constraints (kən strānts′) restrictions or confinements

obsessed (əb sest′) preoccupied greatly

gentrify (jen′trə fī) to upgrade a neighborhood, especially from lower class to middle or upper-middle class)

derelict (der′ə likt′) a destitute person, without a home or regular job and rejected by society

brothel (brôth′əl) a house of prostitution

berserk (bər sʉrk′) in a state of violent or destructive rage or frenzy

deride (di rīd′) to laugh at in contempt; ridicule

regimented (rej′ə men′tid) organized in a rigid system under strict discipline and control

intimidated (in tim′ə dāt′id) made timid or afraid

fat, āpe, cär; ten, ēven; is, bīte; gō, hôrn, to͞ol, look; oil, out; up, fʉr; chin, she; thin, *then*; zh, leisure; ŋ, ring; ə for *a* in *ago;* ' as in *able* (ā′b'l)

Step 1 **Preread**

Read the title, the first paragraph, the headings, and the last paragraph.

1. What is the subject of the article? _____

2. What is John Leo's point of view (the main point he is trying to make)?

   _____

3. Now take a moment to compare your beliefs about homelessness with Leo's. On a scale of 1 (no way) to 5 (absolutely), how open is your mind to the author's point of view? _____

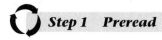 *Step 2* **Read**

Read the article without underlining. Just try to comprehend the author's arguments.

Homeless Rights, Community Wrongs

John Leo

Read a few reports or books on the problem of the homeless, and chances are that in the index, under the letter C, you will find "compassion" and "causes, root," but not "community, rights of."

The reason for this is that the left, which is producing almost all the programs dealing with the growing army of street people, has no tradition at all of thinking about community, towns and neighborhoods. As always, the Achilles' heel of liberalism is its reflexive tendency to convert every social or moral or political problem into a dramatic confrontation between a beleaguered individual and the all-powerful, menacing state. The community is nowhere to be found.

Destabilizing Communities

Each winter, when winos and addicts sleep over the hot-air grates on streets and subways, and apartment dwellers have to step over bodies to get out the door, there is (and should be) much compassion for the disoriented street people. This will lead to discussion of the presumed "right" to sleep wherever one collapses, and the argument that this behavior "does not harm anyone." But there will be no discussion about the demoralization of the neighbors or the connection between the loss of social controls and the destabilization of entire communities. If anyone brings up the point, he will be portrayed as a heartless "have" intent on abusing the "have-nots."

Each spring, the army migrates to the parks, where the destabilization process often seems to work even faster. Sandboxes become urinals. Swings are broken. Every park bench seems to be owned by a permanently curled-up dozing alcoholic or perhaps a street schizophrenic. When the cycle is complete, the community withdraws, serious druggies and criminals move in, and you have what Los Angeles and Washington, D.C., are now calling "dead parks." This cycle can occur without the homeless—the criminals can move directly into a live park and kill it—but only in neighborhoods already softened up by the destabilization process. And today that destabilization is very likely to be spearheaded by the homeless street people.

Napping Campers

New York City is trying to halt the process of deterioration in the parks, within the constraints of a political culture notably blind to community and obsessed by individual rights. This is like wrestling a greased pig blindfolded, but at least the effort is being made. In 1988, the city's parks commissioner proposed regulations against panhandling ("soliciting money"), annoying other people and lying down on park benches for more than 2 hours. "What about Girl Scouts soliciting money for their cookies?" someone asked, so that provision was dropped. "What about a Wall Street broker napping for 2 hours and 1 minute on a park bench?" someone else asked, so the provision was relaxed to allow longer sleeping periods, but not camping without a permit. "Isn't it a mean-spirited attempt to exclude the homeless?" yet another concerned citizen asked, so the parks department apologized for "the insensitivity" of its language, and the parks commissioner insisted, with a straight face, that the rules were not aimed at the homeless at all.

Downtown, in Tompkins Square Park on the Lower East Side, the parks department showed more spine, but then more is at stake. The street people, egged on by an assortment of ax grinders, from dreamy revolutionaries to skinheads, set up what appeared to be a permanent shantytown in the park. Inhabitants included poor people gentrified out of nearby apartments, as well as derelicts, assorted hustlers, drug dealers and the mentally ill. This little community featured the predictable sanitation problems, frequent theft and one full-time brothel.

On order from the parks department, police tore down the shacks and tents. The squatters put them up again. Both sides have promised nonviolence (during the summer of 1988, police went berserk and cracked heads at random), so the police will politely keep tearing down the tents, and the squatters will politely keep putting them back up. This silly arrangement, which could have come from a Chaplin comedy, makes the city's paralysis painfully obvious. The administration won't back down, but it won't clear the park, either.

A Conventionally Liberal Clash

The "heartlessness" refrain is obscuring the very sensible principle that the parks department is trying to uphold, which is that parks are for recreation, not human habitation. The city maintains a huge system of shelters for the homeless and spends more on this safety net than all other large American cities combined, offering food, clothing, social services and medical care.

Leaders of the homeless deride the shelters as unsafe and unclean (i.e., they are filled with homeless people, who bring their habits and problems with them). But instead of pushing for even more guards—security costs at the shelters are already up to $57 million a year—these leaders have reframed the issue as a conventionally liberal clash between a heartless government and beleaguered victims rightly refusing to be regimented. Posing the problem in that manner is a sure-fire way of making it insoluble.

The homeless deserve food and shelter. Certainly, a country as rich as this can afford it. But the homeless should not be allowed to destabilize the live communities still left in our cities. James Q. Wilson's book *Thinking About Crime* has the best discussion of how disordered street life eats away at the informal controls that hold a community together, even before a single street crime has been committed. Muggers and robbers flourish on streets where potential victims are already intimidated by prevailing conditions. The first step to reclaiming a street, or a park, is to change those prevailing conditions.

 ## Step 3   Analyze What You Read

A. Identify Arguments and Supporting Details

John Leo makes two major arguments:

1. The homeless destabilize communities.

2. Liberals prevent us from solving the problem.

In the margin of the article, write *POV* next to the place Leo presents his point of view. Then write *Arg. 1* and *Arg. 2* next to every spot where these arguments are made. We believe argument 1 appears four times and argument 2 appears six times. Next, underline each time Leo offers support for the arguments.

B. Evaluate Supporting Details

Type of Support. What is the primary type of support Leo uses (testimony, reasons, facts, examples)? _____

Provable Versus Unprovable. The following statements are supporting ideas from the article. Evaluate whether each one can or cannot be proved. If the support is provable, write *P* in the space. If it is unprovable, write *U* in the space, as in the following example:

____U____ The left has no tradition of thinking about community, towns, and neighborhoods.

_____ 1. Liberals always convert social, moral, and political problems into confrontations between the individual and the state.

_____ 2. Each winter there will be discussion about the rights of the homeless, but there will be no discussion about the demoralization of neighbors or destabilization of the community.

_____ 3. Anyone who brings up the community will be portrayed as heartless.

_____ 4. Los Angeles and Washington, D.C., have what they call "dead parks."

_____ 5. Criminals can only kill parks in neighborhoods already softened up by the destabilization process.

_____ 6. New York City's proposed regulations against panhandling, annoying other people, and lying down on park benches were relaxed or dropped.

_____ 7. The police will politely keep tearing down the tents, and the squatters will politely keep putting them back up.

_____ 8. New York City spends more on shelters for the homeless than all other American cities combined.

_____ 9. The homeless deserve food and shelter.

_____ 10. Muggers and robbers flourish on streets where potential victims are already intimidated by prevailing conditions.

Loaded Language. John Leo uses language that paints a visual picture supporting his point of view. Examples include the "growing army" of street people, liberalism's "reflexive tendency" to convert issues into confrontations between the individual and the state, "winos and addicts," "disoriented street people."

List five more examples of loaded language from the article.

1. _____

2. _____

3. _____

4. _____

5. _____

C. Make Graphic Organizers

For each of the following arguments, fill in five pieces of support. For the first argument, use an outline form, and for the second argument, use a study map format.

1. The homeless destabilize communities.

   a. _____

   b. _____

c. _____

d. _____

e. _____

2. Liberals prevent us from solving the problem.

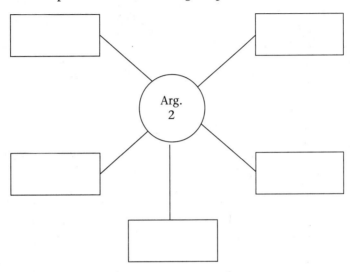

Step 4   *Remember What's Important*

Review your marginal notes that identified the arguments and your underlining of the supporting details. Review your graphic organizers. Continue your review until you feel confident that you understand and remember the information.

Step 5   *Make Use of What You Read*

Your instructor will give you a comprehension check for this article.

Step 6   *Evaluate Your Active Critical Thinking Skills*

After your comprehension check is graded, use the checklist in the appendix to evaluate your skills.

Reading 2

The Worthy and Unworthy Homeless

Vocabulary Preview

concurrent (kən kʉr′rənt) occurring at the same time; simultaneous

mosaic (mō sā′ik) different fragments that, when pieced together, become a whole design, picture, or vision; patchwork

triage (trē äzh′) a system of assigning priorities; prioritizing (esp. in emergency situations)

hypothetical (hī′pə thet′i k′l) supposed; theoretical

degradation (deg′rə dā′shən) a lowering of quality, moral character, dignity, etc.; belittlement

strata (strāt′ə) levels of society

pulmonary (pul′mə ner′ē) of or having to do with the lungs

sporadic (spō rad′ik) happening at intervals; irregular

posttraumatic stress syndrome (post trou mat′ik stres′sin′drōm) delayed reaction to traumatic event; psychological symptoms such as guilt, anger, and alienation from one's own feelings

plight (plīt) sad or dangerous situation

---

fat, āpe, cär; ten, ēven; is, bīte; gō, hôrn, to͞ol, look; oil, out; up, fʉr; chin, she; thin, *then*; zh, leisure; ŋ, ring; ə for *a* in *ago;* ′ as in *able* (ā′b′l)

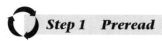 **Step 1   Preread**

Read the title, the headings, the first sentence of each paragraph, and the last paragraph.

1. What is the subject of the article? _____

2. What is the author's point of view? _____

3. Now take a moment to compare your beliefs about the homeless with author James Wright's. On a scale of 1 (no way) to 5 (absolutely), how likely are you to agree with his point of view? _____

Step 2   Read

Read the article without underlining. Just try to comprehend Wright's arguments and support.

The Worthy and Unworthy Homeless

James D. Wright

Americans have always found it necessary to distinguish between the "deserving" and "undeserving" poor—the former, victims of circumstances beyond their control who merit compassion; the latter, lazy, shiftless bums who could do better for themselves "if they wanted to" and who therefore merit contempt . . .

A Heartless Response

So far, the homeless seem to be included among the "deserving poor," at least by the general public. A national survey by the Roper Organization reported by *Newsweek* on September 21, 1987, asked what problems we should be spending more money on. "Caring for the homeless" was the top priority item, favored by 68 percent. (In contrast, foreign aid was mentioned by only 5 percent, and "military, armaments, and defense" by only 17 percent.) Thus, most people seem to feel that the homeless deserve our help, if not our compassion. But an opposite, more mean-spirited view has also begun to surface. On December 1, 1986, Stuart Bykofsky wrote a "My Turn" column for *Newsweek* magazine entitled "No Heart for the Homeless." The analysis turned on the division of the homeless into three groups: "(1) the economically distressed, who would work if they could find work; (2) the mentally ill, who can't work; (3) the alcoholic, the drug-addicted, and others who won't work." His solution to the problem was workfare for the first group, mental institutions for the second, and indifference to (or outright hostility toward) the third.

Bykofsky's simplistic categorization was unburdened by numbers or percentages, and so we are not told how many of the homeless fit his various types. Concurrent with the increased media and political attention being given to the problem, there has also been an outpouring of research studies that provide reliable guides to the relative proportions of "worthy" and "unworthy" homeless. My aim here is to review the findings of some of these studies, to see if we cannot be more precise about how many homeless deserve our sympathies and how many do not . . .

For convenience, it is useful to begin by imagining a sample of 1,000 homeless people, drawn at random, let us say, from the half million or so homeless people to be found in America on any given evening. Based on the research I have sketched, we can then begin to cut up this sample in various ways, so as to portray as graphically as possible the mosaic of homelessness in this country. Our strategy is to work from "more deserving" to "less deserving" subgroups, ending with the absolutely least deserving—the lazy, shiftless bums. Along the way, I call attention to various characteristics of and problems encountered by each of the subgroups we consider.

Among the many tragedies of homelessness, there is none sadder than the homeless family—often an intact family unit consisting of a wife, her husband, and one or more dependent children, victims of unemployment and other economic misfortune, struggling in the face of long odds to maintain themselves as a unit and get back on their feet again. How many members of homeless families can we expect to find among our sample of 1,000 homeless people? . . .

Members of homeless families constitute a significantly large fraction of the homeless population; my guess is that we would find 220 of them in a sample of a thousand homeless people, nearly half of them homeless children. Not only would most people look on homeless families as most deserving of help, there is also reason to believe that they need the least help (in that they appear to have the fewest disabling problems and tend generally to be the most intact), and that even relatively modest assistance would make a substantial difference in their life chances and circumstances. If the available resources are such as to require triage, then homeless families should be the top priority.

Lone Women and Children

By these calculations, there remain in our hypothetical sample of 1,000 some 780 lone homeless persons—single individuals on the streets by themselves. Based on the HCH (National Health Care for the Homeless Program) study, some 6 percent of these 780 are children or adolescents age nineteen or less (which amounts to 47 additional children in the sample of 1,000), 20 percent are adult women (156 additional women), and 74 percent are adult men (which leaves, from the original sample of 1,000, only 580 adult males not members of homeless family groups). Adding these to the earlier results, we get two significant conclusions: First, among the total of a thousand homeless persons, $99 + 47 = 146$ will be children or youths aged nineteen or less, approximately one in seven. Second, among the remaining 854 adults, $156 + 83 = 229$ will be women, which amounts to 229/854 or 27 percent of all adults. Combining all figures, homeless children and homeless adult women themselves comprise $146 + 229 = 375$ of the original 1,000—three of every eight. Adult men comprise the majority of the homeless, but not the overwhelming majority; a very sizable majority—nearly 40 percent of the total—are women and children. . . .

Although precise numbers are hard to come by, there is little doubt that many of these homeless teenagers are runaway or throwaway children fleeing abusive family situations. Among the girls, the rate of pregnancy is astonishing: 9 percent of the girls ages thirteen to fifteen, and 24 percent of the girls ages sixteen to nineteen, were pregnant at or since their first contact with the HCH clinic system; the rate for sixteen-to-nineteen-year-olds is the highest observed in any age-group. There is impressionistic evidence, but no hard evidence, to suggest that many of these young girls are reduced to prostitution in order to survive; many will thus come to possess lengthy jail records as well. Drug and alcohol abuse are also common problems. Indeed, the rate of known drug abuse among the sixteen-to-nineteen-year-old boys—some 16 percent—is the highest rate recorded for any age-group in our data.

Unending Worries

I am discussing a time in life when the average adolescent's biggest worries are acne, or whom to invite to the high school prom, or where to go to college—a time of uncertainty, but also a time of hope and anticipation for the future. In contrast, homeless adolescents must worry about where to sleep tonight, or where the next meal is coming from, or who is going to assault them next. What hope for the future can be nourished under these conditions? Many of these kids—tough kids on mean streets, but kids nonetheless—face an unending downward spiral of booze, drugs, crime, and troubles with the law. They too must surely be counted among the "deserving" homeless; indeed, anything that can be done should be done to break the spiral and set them back on a path to an independent and productive adult existence. . . .

Most people would feel comfortable counting the adult women among the "deserving" homeless as well. Just as women and children are the first to be evacuated from a sinking ship, so too should women and children be the first to be rescued from the degradations of street life or a shelter existence. If we add to the group of "deserving" homeless the relatively small number of adult men in homeless family groups, then our initial cut leaves but 580 persons from the original 1,000 yet to account for.

Lone Adult Men

What is to be said about those who remain—the 580 lone adult males, not members of homeless families? A small percentage of them, much smaller than people would anticipate, are elderly men, over age sixty-five; in the HCH data, the over-sixty-fives comprise about 3 percent of the group in question, which gives us 17 elderly men among the remaining 580. . . .

Those over sixty-five surely are to be included within the "deserving" group. As it happens, only about half of them receive Social Security benefits. Many of those who do receive Social Security payments find that no housing can be purchased or rented within their means. Well over half have chronic physical health problems that further contribute to their hardships. Certainly, no one will object if we include the elderly homeless among those deserving our sympathies.

Lone Veterans

We are now left with, let us say, 563 nonelderly lone adult men. If we inquire further among this group, we will discover another surprising fact: at least a third of them are veterans of the United States Armed Forces. . . .

Most homeless veterans are drawn from the lower socioeconomic strata, having enlisted to obtain, as M. Robertson has put it, "long term economic advantages through job training as well as postmilitary college benefits and preferential treatment in civil service employment," only to find that their economic and employment opportunities remain limited after they have mustered out.

Many of the homeless veterans are alcoholic or drug abusive, and many are also mentally ill; the same could be said for other subgroups that we have considered. Whatever their current problems and disabilities, these men were there when the nation needed them. Do they not also deserve a return of the favor?

The lure of military service proves to have been a false promise for many of these men: "Despite recruitment campaigns that promote military service as an opportunity for maturation and occupational mobility, veterans continue to struggle with postmilitary unemployment and mental and physical disability without adequate assistance from the federal government." One of the Vietnam veterans in Robertson's study summed up the stakes involved: "If they expect the youth of America to fight another war, they have to take care of the vets."

Lone Disabled Men

Sticking with the admittedly conservative one-third estimate, among the 563 adult men with whom we are left, 188 will be veterans; 375 nonelderly, nonveteran adult men are all that remain of the initial 1,000. Sorting out this subgroup in the HCH data, we find that a third are assessed by their care providers as having moderate to severe psychiatric impairments—not including alcohol or drug abuse. Many among this group have fallen through the cracks of the community mental health system. In the vast majority of cases, they pose no immediate danger to themselves or to others, and thus they are generally immune to involuntary commitment for psychiatric treatment; at the same time, their ability to care for themselves, especially in a street or shelter environment, is at best marginal. Compassion dictates that they too be included among the "deserving" group. . . .

Subtracting the 125 or so mentally disabled men from the remaining group of 375 leaves 250 of the original 1,000. Among these 250 will be some 28 or so men who are physically disabled and incapable of working. This includes the blind and the deaf, those confined to wheelchairs, the paraplegic, those with amputated limbs, and those with disabling chronic physical illnesses such as heart disease, AIDS, obstructive pulmonary disease, and others. Like the mentally disabled, these too can only be counted among the "deserving" group. Subtracting them leaves a mere 222 remaining—nonelderly, nonveteran adult males with no mental or physical disability.

Of these 222, a bit more than half—112 men—will be found to have some sort of job: my data suggest that 7 will have full-time jobs, 27 will have part-time jobs, and 78 will be employed on a sporadic basis (seasonal work, day labor, odd jobs, and the like). Peter Rossi's Chicago data show largely the same pattern. The remainder—110 men—are unemployed, and among these some 61 will be looking for work. All told, then, among the 222 will be 173 who are at least making the effort: looking for work, but so far with no success, or having a job but not one paying well enough to allow them to afford stable housing. This then leaves us with 49 people from the initial 1,000 who are not members of homeless families, not women, not children, not elderly, not veterans, not mentally disabled, not physically disabled, not currently working, and not looking for work. Call these the "undeserving homeless," or, if you wish, lazy shiftless bums. They account for about 5 percent of the total—a mere one in every twenty. . . .

Avoiding Indifference

In puzzling through the complex array of factors that cause homelessness, in the hopes of finding some solutions, cold-heartedness is not the proper sentiment. Should we, as Bykofsky suggests, have "no heart" for a disabled thirty-three-year-old Vietnam veteran suffering from posttraumatic stress syndrome, or for a fifteen-year-old runaway girl whose father has raped and beaten her once too often, or for a feverish infant in the arms of her homeless mother, or for an entire family that has been turned out because the factory where the father worked was shut down, or for an arthritic old gentleman who has lost his room in the "welfare hotel" because he was beaten savagely and relieved of his Social Security check? These are very much a part—a large part—of today's homeless population, no less than the occasional "shiftless bum." Indifference to the plight of "shiftless bums" comes all to easily to an illiberal era; but indifference to the plight of homeless families, women, children, old people, veterans, and the disabled comes easily only to the cruel.

 Step 3   *Analyze What You Read*

A. Identify Arguments and Supporting Details

James Wright argues that Stuart Bykofsky's article, "No Heart for the Homeless," gives a faulty impression of the number of homeless who fall into the three categories of economically distressed, mentally ill, or addicted. As support, Wright gives his own breakdown, which he claims is based on reliable research.

Go back to the article and write *POV* next to the place Wright presents his point of view. Then write *Arg.* next to his argument. Next, underline each piece of support he gives for his argument.

B. Evaluate Supporting Details

Type of Support. What is the primary type of support Wright uses (testimony, reasons, facts, examples)? _____

Provable Versus Unprovable. The following statements are supporting details from the article. Evaluate whether each one can or cannot be proved and whether Wright has given proof. In the first column, write *P* or *U* for provable or unprovable. In the second column, write *Y* if the support has been provided, *N* if it has not.

_____ _____ 1. There are research studies that provide reliable guides to the relative proportions of "worthy" and "unworthy" homeless.

_____ _____ 2. Of 1,000 homeless people, 220 would be family members, nearly half of them children.

_____ _____ 3. If the available resources are such that triage is required, then homeless families should be the top priority.

_____ _____ 4. Many homeless teenagers are runaway or throwaway children fleeing abusive family situations.

_____ _____ 5. Anything that can be done should be done to break the spiral and set them back on a path to an independent and productive adult existence.

_____ _____ 6. Just as women and children are the first to be rescued from a sinking ship, so too should women and children be the first to be rescued from the degradations of street life or a shelter existence.

_____ _____ 7. Only about half of those over 65 receive Social Security payments.

Loaded Language. In this article the language is slanted in the opposite direction from article 1. We could summarize the picture John Leo paints of the homeless as an invading army of dysfunctional people who destroy neighborhoods.

Look at the last paragraph of this article, subtitled "Avoiding Indifference." Summarize the picture of the homeless that Wright's choice of words creates in your mind. _____

_____

_____

C. Make Graphic Organizers

The homeless population is made up of different subgroups. Look at the following pie graph. Refer to the article and fill in the names of the subgroups. (Note that the numbers in the article add up to 1,003 rather than 1,000.)

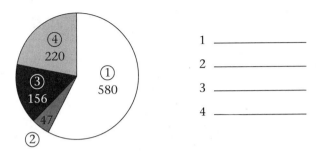

1 _____

2 _____

3 _____

4 _____

Step 4   Remember What's Important

Review your marginal notes that identified the argument and your underlining of the supporting details. Review your graphic organizer. Continue your review until you feel confident that you understand and remember the information.

Step 5   Make Use of What You Read

Your instructor will give you a comprehension check for this article.

Step 6   Evaluate Your Active Critical Thinking Skills

After your comprehension check is graded, use the checklist in the appendix to evaluate your skills.

Comparing Views on Homelessness

Use the following activities to evaluate your understanding of the issue of homelessness.

1. Summarize each article. To summarize means to present the general idea in a brief form. Like all writing, summarizing is easy and efficient only when you use a graphic organizer; you can use your underlining and marginal notes as a graphic organizer. First, write the author's point of view in your own words. Then, in brief form, write each argument and its major support.

2. Evaluate the support for each article.
   a. What type is it?
   b. To what degree is it provable?
   c. To what degree has it been proved?
   d. To what degree is the language loaded?

3. Compare the articles. Do you believe that one author's arguments are stronger than the other's? Why?

4. Go back to the self-questioning survey on pages 25–26. Would you change any of your responses after reading the articles? Summarize your opinion on the issue, noting any ways in which your opinion has been affected by your reading.

Issue 2

Women in Combat

In this section you will read two perspectives on the subject of women in combat. Article 3, "Female Troops Desert Feminist Ranks," was taken from *Human Events,* a weekly newspaper of conservative political and social opinion. Article 4, "Women in Combat: The New Reality," was written by Jeanne M. Holm, a retired Air Force major general and the author of *Women in the Military: An Unfinished Revolution.*

Since these articles were written, about 80,000 new positions have opened up for women in the military. All combat positions are now open except ground combat positions in infantry, armor, and special forces. As of this writing there are only two exceptions: positions that co-locate with infantry, armor, and special forces, and positions in which the cost of berthing and privacy would be prohibitive. An example of a berthing and privacy problem would occur on submarines, where bulkheads cannot easily be moved; however, new procurement will take into account this issue, and it is anticipated that it is only a matter of time before these positions will be gender-neutral.

Self-Questioning

Answering the following questions will help you understand your current views on this issue. You will take the same survey to reevaluate your views after you have read articles 3 and 4.

Rating Scale

1 Absolutely not

2 Perhaps not

3 No opinion

4 Perhaps

5 Yes

Rate each question from 1 to 5.

———— 1. Do you believe that women in the military should be given the same assignments as men as long as they meet the physical requirements?

2. Rate the extent to which you think each of the following women should be assigned to combat duty.

   ———— A single woman

   ———— A married mother of young children

   ———— A single parent

   ———— Any woman who volunteers for combat

   ———— A woman who doesn't want combat duty

———— 3. Do you think the presence of women in the armed forces is good for our country?

Reading 3

Female Troops Desert Feminist Ranks

Vocabulary Preview

deployment (dē ploi'ment) stationing or placement (forces, equipment, etc.) in accordance with a plan

tenet (ten'it) a principle, doctrine, or belief held as a truth, as by some group

dogmatic (dôg ma'tik) stating opinion in a positive or arrogant manner

ideology (ī dē äl'ə jē) the doctrines, opinions, or way of thinking of an individual, class, etc.; specif., the body of ideas on which a particular political, economic, or social system is based

fraternization (frat'er ni zā'shən) association on friendly terms

fat, āpe, cär; ten, ēven; is, bīte; gō, hôrn, tōol, look; oil, out; up, fʉr; chin, she; thin, *then*; zh, leisure; ŋ, ring; ə for *a* in *ago;* ' as in *able* (ā'b'l)

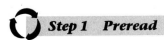 **Step 1 Preread**

Read the title, the first sentence of each paragraph, and the headings.

1. What is the subject of the article? _____

2. What is the author's point of view? _____

3. Now take a moment to compare your beliefs about women in combat with the author's. On a scale of 1 (no way) to 5 (absolutely), how

likely are you to agree with the author's point of view?_____

_____

 Step 2   Read

Read the article without underlining. Just try to comprehend the arguments.

Female Troops Desert Feminist Ranks

Human Events

The U.S. military deployment to the Persian Gulf has dealt a body blow to a key tenet of the radical feminist agenda: that male and female soldiers should be treated exactly alike, with the same expectations and demands applied to each indiscriminately.

Perhaps the last thing dogmatic feminists anticipated was widespread opposition to their propaganda from female soldiers themselves.

Nevertheless, a cascade of news articles and television broadcasts has recently made clear that women in the gulf, especially those who are mothers, think the idea of sending them to a potential war zone is a terrible one.

Perhaps the most impressive of these recent articles was written by *New York Times* reporter Jane Gross. Gross quotes one discharged female soldier, former Sgt. Lori Moore of Ft. Benning, Ga., as saying, "I hate to say it [that women belong at home with their children], because it doesn't fit with the whole scheme of the women's movement, but I think we have to reconsider what we're doing." Although Moore, whose husband is stationed at Ft. Benning, described herself as a "gung-ho careerist," she accepted a slightly tainted general discharge rather than deploy with her unit to the Persian Gulf and leave behind her three children, aged 3, 2, and nine months. "We're [The Army] mission-oriented," explained Moore, "and our mission is combat. Sending my kids [to relatives] was just part of the job—until they left. Then I was overwhelmed with guilt.

"I asked the good Lord, what is going on? Why am I feeling this way? What did I do to my family?

"And what I came up with is [that] a mother should be with her children. I had to pursue that, because if I didn't I couldn't be at peace. . . .

"I produced these kids, and I needed to take responsibility for them. I'm afraid the children are the unsung victims of Operation Desert Shield. There is no question that women can do this [deploy to a potential war zone]. The question is whether we should."

Similarly, Sgt. Twila Erickson-Schamer, about to be deployed to the gulf, now wonders how she could ever have believed that she could be "a soldier and a mother at the same time."

"There are so many feelings," she told Gross. "How can I possibly sort them out? I have tried to convince myself that it's going to be okay and displayed that attitude to other people.

"If I didn't, I'd be in a constant state of emotional breakdown. I'd be crying all the time."

Many reports have also come from female soldiers already deployed to the Persian Gulf that suggest mothers in combat zones have a more difficult time performing their military duties.

Spec. 4 Robin Williams told the Colorado Springs *Gazette-Telegraph,* "It's like this: I'm a woman and a mother before I'm a soldier. . . . Out here I think more about my family than my job. And, yes, that could affect my performance if things got intense here."

At long last, a few within the armed forces have begun to stand up to the powerful feminist lobby. Maj. Brady Lawrence, chief of human resources at San Francisco's Presidio Army base, says the "dismay among mothers proves the wisdom of barring women from combat."

"Do we really want to open up the field," Lawrence asked Gross, "if we're having the problems we're having now?"

Human Events contacted Elaine Donnelly, a former member of the Defense Advisory Committee on Women in the Services (DACOWITS, increasingly a feminist enclave) and asked her about the fast-changing attitudes of female soldiers about serving in war zones while separated from their children.

Donnelly said that it was mainly enlisted women who were paying the price for this social experiment and she cautioned, "Army officials will declare Operation Desert Shield a success if their numerical objectives are reached—regardless of the long-term effects on children, families or society at large.

"But no one knows how far-reaching the real damage could be. Imagine the trauma to a young child whose mother comes back mangled or killed."

Donnelly questioned the continued existence of DACOWITS, "unless they use this new information to reassess their policy of pushing for more women in more roles in the service, even in the combat arms. . . . But feminists never admit mistakes and feminist ideology is in the driver's seat at DACOWITS."

Donnelly predicts that because of publicity about the hardships, both physical and psychological, endured by women in the gulf, future enlistments in the all volunteer armed forces will drop. She also fears the possibility of women being drafted—even for combat units—some day.

"If we have to reinstitute the draft," reasons Donnelly, "and if women are already in the combat zone, then there will be no legal basis to exclude them from the draft."

Even if we should avoid that worst-case scenario, however, Donnelly believes that our present policies regarding women in the military will continue to create problems for our society.

"The more numbers of women in the military you have," Donnelly explains, "the more you're going to multiply the horror stories you've already got. It's a natural progression: When you have a higher percentage of women, you have more fraternization between the soldiers. Then you have more marriages, then you have joint spouse assignment problems, then you have pregnancy problems, then you have child care problems.

"All of these things kind of grow geometrically. We need to decide if this is the kind of military we want.

"We used to have essentially a bachelor army; now we have a family force. Are we going to end up with child care centers in Saudi Arabia?"

No Sympathy for Feminists

Brian Mitchell, author of *Weak Link: The Feminization of the American Military,* shared many of Donnelly's concerns with us.

"We should have known," said Mitchell, "that young mothers sent to the other side of the world where they may die in the desert were going to react this way.

"I have sympathy for the ones who have come to their senses, but not for the radical feminists and military leaders who presented them with a pollyanna vision of simply doing a different, non-traditional kind of job. Nobody pointed out to them the kinds of physical dangers and psychological pressures they might someday find themselves facing."

Mitchell has concluded that we should have a military in which women are not expected to deploy at all, serving instead in garrison units here in the U.S., perhaps in non-deployable finance and personnel units.

"This means women will be limited to very few jobs in the military," Mitchell continued. "We need a much-reduced female presence in the military because you cannot really solve the problems of deployability."

Mitchell hit hard again and again at the military leaders who have, by his lights, ignored the welfare of children in military families.

"How can any of this be good for them?" asked Mitchell. Referring to the problem of so-called joint assignments in which both a husband and a wife are sent overseas, Mitchell warned, "You could have children orphaned because of a political imperative to use women in the military in the same way that you use men."

Mitchell predicted that six months to a year after everyone is home from the Persian Gulf, and after the hurrahs and congratulations, studies will be prepared for arguments against heavy reliance on women in the military.

"The military has not been able, politically, to do this until now. Now at least they have an operation, an experience they can point to and say, 'This is not good.'"

From sources within the Pentagon itself, as well as some in the Persian Gulf, Mitchell reports that he has heard that at least three female soldiers have been sent home for being charged with prostitution. Pregnancy rates are said to be even higher than the 10 percent of military females that are normally pregnant at any given time.

"All sorts of problems are cropping up," Mitchell said. "Women are not as effective, partially because they require more medical attention."

Pro-Family Forces

Problems such as those pointed to by critics like Donnelly and Mitchell provide a ready storehouse of ammunition for pro-family forces in the Congress. Reform is clearly needed if we are to avoid a tragedy.

Some no doubt will resist all evidence, all common sense. Rep. Patricia Schroeder (D.-Colo.), a long-time proponent of women in the combat arms, scolded, "We have to be careful we don't start talking about 'Mommy Tracking.'"

In truth, what we really need to be careful of is "Mommy Burying."

Step 3   *Analyze What You Read*

A. Identify Arguments and Supporting Details

The following are the author's major arguments. Write the name of the person or people quoted in support of each argument. Some people are quoted in support of more than one argument.

1. Women in the gulf, especially those who are mothers, think the idea of sending them to a potential war zone is a terrible one.

    a. _____

    b. _____

    c. _____

2. Mothers in combat zones may have trouble performing their duties.

    _____

3. There may be effects on children, families, or society at large.

    a. _____

    b. _____

4. Future enlistment in the all-volunteer armed forces may drop.

    _____

5. Women may be drafted. _____

6. More women cause more fraternization, marriages, joint spouse assignment problems, pregnancy problems, and child care problems.

    _____

7. We need fewer women because we cannot solve the problem of deployability. _____

8. Some women soldiers become prostitutes. _____

9. Some get pregnant. _____

10. Women require more medical attention. _____

In the margin of the article, write *POV* next to the place the author presents the point of view. Then write *Arg. 1* through *Arg. 10* next to the place the argument appears. Next, underline the support for each argument.

B. Evaluate Supporting Details

Type of Support. What is the primary type of support the author uses (testimony, reasons, facts, examples)? _____

Credibility of Sources. When testimony is used, the sources need to be evaluated. The following criteria may be used in the evaluation:

1. Is this source representative of all the people in a position to testify on this issue?
2. Do you have any reason to believe that the source is biased?
3. Does this source have access to the relevant information?

Find the argument that each of the following people is supporting and write its number (1–10) in the space provided. Using a scale from 1 (poor) to 5 (excellent), rate each of the following sources in terms of how convincing he or she is. Give your reason for the rating.

1. Sgt. Twila Erickson-Schamer

    a. Argument _____

    b. Rating _____

    c. Reason _____

2. Elaine Donnelly

    a. Arguments _____

    b. Rating _____

    c. Reason _____

3. Brian Mitchell

    a. Arguments _____

    b. Rating _____

    c. Reason _____

Do you think the author is selecting people who support this point of view? Why? _____

Loaded Language. The author uses such phrases as "radical feminist agenda," "dogmatic feminists," "propaganda," "powerful feminist lobby," "a feminist enclave," "feminists never admit mistakes," "feminist ideology," "the ones who have come to their senses" versus "radical feminists," "a pollyanna vision of simply doing a different, non-traditional kind of job," and "resist all evidence, all common sense." In your own words, summarize the picture the author paints of those who oppose this point of view. _____

_____

_____

C. Make Graphic Organizers

Information is easier to remember when it is grouped into categories. We have grouped the ten arguments into two categories. Fill in the arguments under each category.

1. Concerns that women in the military have:

a. _____

b. _____

c. _____

2. Concerns the military has:

a. _____

b. _____

c. _____

d. _____

e. _____

f. _____

g. _____

 Step 4   Remember What's Important

Review your marginal notes identifying the arguments and your underlining of the supporting details. Review your graphic organizer. Continue your review until you feel confident that you understand and remember the information.

Step 5   Make Use of What You Read

Your instructor will give you a comprehension check for this article.

 Step 6   Evaluate Your Active Critical Thinking Skills

After your comprehension check is graded, use the checklist in the appendix to evaluate your skills.

Vocabulary Preview

lucrative (lōō′krə tiv) profitable

logistics (lō jis′tiks) the branch of military science having to do with procuring, maintaining, and transporting materiel, personnel, and facilities

vindication (vin′də kā′shən) a clearing from criticism, blame, etc.

detractors (di trak′tôrz) those who belittle

discernable (di sʉrn′ə b′l) recognizable

per se (pʉr′sē′, sā′) by (or in) itself; intrinsically

guise (gīz) a false or deceiving appearance; pretense

insidious (in sid′ē əs) sly; treacherous

profoundly (prə found′lē) deeply; thoroughly

espousing (e spous′iŋ) advocating or supporting (some cause, idea, etc.)

specious (spē′shəs) seeming to be good, sound, correct, etc., without really being so

adversely (ad vʉrs′lē) unfavorably

expedient (ek spē′dē ənt) based on or offering what is of use or advantage rather than what is right or just; politic

volatile (väl′ə t′l) unstable; explosive

equity (ek′wə tē) fairness; impartiality; justice

---

fat, āpe, cär; ten, ēven; is, bīte; gō, hôrn, tōōl, look; oil, out; up, fʉr; chin, she; thin, *then*; zh, leisure; ŋ, ring; ə for *a* in *ago;* ′ as in *able* (ā′b′l)

Step 1   Preread

Read the title, the headings, and the first and last paragraphs.

1. What is the subject of the article? _____

2. What is Jeanne Holm's point of view? _____

_____

3. Now take a moment to compare your beliefs about women in combat with Holm's. On a scale of 1 (no way) to 5 (absolutely), how likely are you to agree with her point of view? _____

Step 2   Read

Read the article without underlining. Just try to comprehend the author's arguments.

Women in Combat: The New Reality

Jeanne M. Holm

Of all the new realities brought home to Americans by the nightly news from Saudi Arabia, none was more startling than seeing a U.S. soldier in full battle gear, M-16 slung over the shoulder, and discovering that "he" was a "she." For most people, this was the first full realization that wives, sisters, daughters and mothers would actually be sent off to a combat theater to serve side-by-side with men in the tough, dirty, risky jobs of war. That some became casualties and prisoners of war was perhaps the biggest surprise of all.

Even more than events a year earlier in Panama, the Persian Gulf War spotlighted the new roles women have assumed in the armed forces and refueled the simmering debate over women in combat.

Operation Desert Storm was the first large-scale test of the all-volunteer force and the troops performed superbly. This war was also the first true test of what former Chairman of the Joint Chiefs of Staff John Vessey has called the "coeducational military." It too succeeded far beyond most expectations.

"Women have made a major contribution to this [war] effort," said Defense Secretary Dick Cheney. "We could not have won without them." Commanders in the field echoed similar sentiments.

More than 33,000 women served in the gulf, 6 percent of the U.S. forces—the largest wartime deployment of American military women in history. They did just about everything on land, at sea, and in the air except engage in the actual fighting, and even there the line was often a fuzzy one.

They piloted and crewed planes and helicopters over the battle area, serviced combat jets and loaded laser-guided bombs on F-117 Stealths for raids on targets in Baghdad. They directed Patriot missiles, drove trucks, ran prisoner-of-war facilities, refueled M-1 tanks on the side of the road and guarded bases. They served on naval replenishment and repair ships, fleet oilers, and hospital ships off shore.

The women shared the same risks as the men with whom they served and 21 paid the ultimate price.

According to their commander, General Norman Schwarzkopf, his American women had performed "magnificently."

But all the praise of women's performance could not mask the conflicts and confusion generated by the rules governing women's roles in combat. The confusion surfaced in all the services but was most apparent in the Army where the policies on women's assignments are so complicated as to be almost incomprehensible to the people in the field.

For years politicians and military leaders have claimed that military women are excluded from combat by law and service policies. Anyone following news out of the gulf could easily see it wasn't so. In the real world theory and reality parted company.

Women are not supposed to be frontline troops or assigned to direct combat units. But in modern war there are no fixed positions or clear lines in the sand, and rear areas are as vulnerable to attack as are forward positions. Moreover, distinctions between support and combat units have blurred to a point that the illusion of "safe havens" has all but disappeared.

Female soldiers are concentrated in combat support units located in rear areas on the theory that they will be less vulnerable to direct enemy fire. But support troops in the rear areas are prime targets for long-range artillery and surface-to-surface missiles. Soldiers watching an incoming Iraqi Scud must have thought they were in combat no matter what the military calls it.

Being in the rear area in a noncombat unit provided little protection to the soldiers of the 14th Quartermaster Detachment when a Scud missile slammed into their barracks near Dhahran, Saudi Arabia, killing 28 of them. Specialist Adrienne L. Mitchell was one of three women to die in the attack—the first U.S. enlisted woman ever killed in action. . . .

Army women are banned from the direct combat branches, namely infantry, armor, and cannon artillery. Patriot missile units are not classified as combat but the soldiers, male and female, who shot down incoming Scuds thought it was a distinction without a difference.

Women are not permitted to fly the Army's Apache attack helicopters—but female pilots of the 101st Airborne Division's Screaming Eagles flew Black Hawk and Chinook helicopters loaded with supplies and troops 50 miles into Iraq as part of the largest helicopter assault in military history.

Air Force women are not permitted to fly F-15 or F-16 fighters but they were at the controls of the KC-135 jet tankers that refueled the fighters in mid-air during attack missions. Women were directing the massive air traffic over the battlefield aboard Airborne Warning and Control Systems (AWACS) aircraft. They also flew giant transports delivering troops and supplies. All of these combat operations were lucrative targets.

Navy women are banned from permanent assignment to combat ships such as destroyers, battleships, and aircraft carriers. But female sailors were aboard combat logistics support ships that provided essential supplies, repair and ammunition to the American fleet during gulf combat operations. Support ships were no less vulnerable to Exocet and Silkworm missiles or floating mines than the combat ships.

By Marine Corps policy, female leathernecks are banned from all combat jobs and units. But more than 170 of them were assigned to the 2nd Forward Marine Support Group dug into the desert near the Kuwait border when the ground attack kicked off. Neither they nor most of their male comrades had ever faced combat before but they were all prepared to do what they had been trained for. According to the Corps' Commandant, General Alfred M. Gray, Jr., they were all superb marines.

Today's Volunteer Military

The superb performance of America's armed forces during Operation Desert Shield/ Storm is a total vindication of the all-volunteer force which many had predicted would not be up to the challenges of war. One reason for uneasiness was the heavy reliance on women. They have been described by some detractors as the military's "weak-link" and by others as a "social experiment."

If there is a weak link in today's armed forces, it was not discernable during the gulf war. They are being described as the finest, most professional forces in our nation's history. More than 11 percent are women, by far the largest female representation in military history, up from one percent just twenty years ago.

The growing use of women in defense was not an experiment but a military manpower necessity—the need to achieve a quality force of volunteers and the inability to do it without women.

When the draft ended the numbers of women expanded from a token 45,000 to 230,000 with an additional 150,000 more women in the reserve components. The Coast Guard, under the Department of Transportation, has another 1,300 women on active duty and in its reserve units.

Once confined to a few selected shore bases and traditional jobs, women now serve at nearly every U.S. military installation in the world and aboard Navy and Coast Guard vessels deployed afloat. They can be found in nearly every noncombat job on land, at sea, and in the air. They are so integrated into the units and ships' crews that the U.S. could not have gone to war without them and their involvement in combat was inevitable and unavoidable.

Contrary to popular mythology (perpetuated by the military itself) there has never been a blanket law excluding women from combat. There are two statutes which prohibit women from serving permanently aboard combat ships of the Navy and from flying in aircraft of the Navy and Air Force when "engaged in combat missions." They neither state the underlying objectives nor define "combat missions." They do not apply to the Army nor do they directly address the subject of combat, per se.

In the absence of any other statutory guidelines, Army and Defense Department leaders have devised a set of policies to comply with what they have perceived to be the law's "intent." At best, this process has been imprecise, since the original laws, passed in 1948, were designed for a set of assumptions entirely different than exist today about the military and women's roles in it. No one at that time contemplated that women would ever constitute more than 2 percent of the armed forces (as in

World War II) or that they would be involved in any roles even remotely involving combat operations. The matter was not even debated by lawmakers.

At that time it was common, accepted employment practice to bar women from risky jobs for their own protection; e.g., police officers and fire fighters. Such policies have since been discarded or overturned by the courts. Only in the armed forces are they still tolerated under the guise of women's best interest and military necessity.

A Risky Profession

The very concept of protection within the military is a contradiction. The military is, by definition, a risky profession. No matter how recruiters may try to mask its true nature, waging war can be dangerous to your health. Taking the military oath is like taking marriage vows—it's for better or for worse. It is the obligation of the services to make this clear to every potential recruit before taking the oath. Any man or woman who volunteers must be prepared to accept that reality or find another line of work.

What little protection the rules provide for women is at the expense of their opportunities for challenging jobs and experiences that enhance career advancement, particularly to the senior officer and enlisted grades. It is also at the expense of military personnel flexibility and efficiency. They waste precious talents and reduce women's ability to contribute to the military mission.

A recent Navy study has identified the most insidious effect of the combat exclusion:

> In the view of all Navy members . . . the law profoundly influences both the acceptance and the quality of treatment accorded to women since they are perceived to be distanced from the heart of the organization and its primary mission-achieving units.

There is hardly a woman who has ever served in the armed forces who does not identify with that observation. Most military men today would also acknowledge its validity, while not necessarily espousing the cure.

Repeal Exclusion

The only cure is repeal of the combat exclusion laws. The only serious attempt to do so was proposed by the Carter Administration in 1979. During Congressional hearings the proposal was abruptly scuttled by the opposition of Navy and Marine Corps leaders.

Many arguments raised against repeal were defused in Panama and the gulf war. But the most frequent one that still survives is that repealing the laws would remove all legal constraints resulting in women being assigned to direct combat positions for which they lack the necessary qualifications. The argument is usually couched in ground combat terms, the infantry especially. The example is chosen for maximum emotional impact because it evokes images of hand-to-hand combat—an idea which offends most people.

It is a specious argument on several counts: first, the law does not apply here, the rules are set by the Army; second, the overwhelming majority of women (and most men) would not volunteer to be "grunts" even if they could; and third, the physical requirements would exclude all but a handful of women.

The bottom line in military personnel utilization is that *no* individual, male or female, should be allowed or required to fill any job he or she cannot perform satisfactorily in war for whatever reason. All the services have aptitude tests and physical standards to prevent just that.

Moreover, Desert Storm demonstrated how dramatically technology has altered the personnel requirements of the military in the forty years since the exclusion laws were enacted. Today's military depends much less on brawn in favor of smart, educated, technically trainable people. As a lieutenant colonel in Saudi Arabia observed: "You can't have space-age technology without space-age personnel." This technological shift clearly accommodates the use of women.

In any case, the fact that the vast majority of women could not qualify for most ground combat duties even if they wanted to, does not justify continuing laws which exclude qualified women from assignments to combat aircraft or ships.

When it comes to flying in combat or serving on combat ships, physical capability is not the issue—the law is. The Air Force's chief of personnel, Lt. General Thomas A. Hickey laid it out during Congressional testimony in March 1990. He acknowledged that there is probably not a combat job in the Air Force that women cannot do. "They can fly fighters, they can pull Gs, they can do all those things," he said. "They are physically [and] emotionally capable," adding that "the issue is if you [Congress] want us to put them there, just change the law and the Air Force will do that."

When Air Force women pilots were surveyed on the subject, overwhelmingly they responded that they are capable and willing to go into combat. "I can fly that F-15 just as well as a man," said Lt. Stephanie Shaw, who controlled missions for a tactical air wing in Saudi Arabia.

As for the element of risk, women pilots call it a "red herring" used to keep them out of high-performance aircraft. Capt. Debra Dubbe, who flew as a navigator on a refueling tanker during the Grenada invasion, believes there is no difference in women or men taking risks—or dying. A graduate of the Air Force Academy, Dubbe says: "I signed up to be an officer, and if it means having to die, that's what I agreed to do."

Effect on Readiness

A fear often expressed is that assigning women to combat units and ships would adversely affect efficiency and readiness. One version of this argument is that the presence of women would distract the men and destroy the "male bonding" that is essential to an effective fighting team. Yet in Panama and the gulf war, combat support units, ships and aircraft with women assigned performed their missions well and team bonding did occur.

The argument raises obvious questions: If a destroyer tender can do its job with women in her crew, why not a destroyer? And, if a tactical air base ashore can perform its combat mission of launching aircraft with women in a wide variety of jobs, why not an aircraft carrier with the same mission and many of the same jobs to be done?

The last defense of the combat exclusion policies is that they reflect the will of the American people. While that was undoubtedly true when the statutes were written, social attitudes and laws on women's employment are light-years from the 1940s. A poll conducted by CBS and *The New York Times* following events in Panama showed that 72 percent of the American people favor women in combat. The media coverage of the deployments to the Persian Gulf has further heightened public awareness of women's ability to perform in a combat environment.

Very probably, the public is far more sophisticated on these matters than the Pentagon and Congress are willing to acknowledge. . . .

To date, five NATO [North Atlantic Treaty Organization] nations have faced the issue and made the decision to allow women in combat: Canada, Denmark, Norway, Greece, and the Netherlands. Also, Great Britain has opened positions on combat ships of the Royal Navy.

Whatever conclusions are drawn from the gulf war, women's place in the U.S. armed forces has been permanently altered and universally recognized. It is time for the leaders in the Pentagon and Congress to bite the bullet and get rid of old laws and policies that both the military and women have outgrown.

The Pentagon still prefers to pass the buck to Congress on questions of repeal saying if you want to open combat assignments to women then you repeal the law and we'll do it. That may be the politically expedient posture to assume considering the volatile nature of the issue both within and outside military circles.

There is evidence on Capitol Hill and within the Pentagon of growing interest in reviewing the exclusion statutes in the light of the Persian Gulf experience. If they are not soon repealed, the courts may act as they have on other laws and practices aimed at "protecting" women from risk in employment.

Without the legal constraints the Secretaries of Defense and the services would be able to set the ground rules on the utilization of all military personnel based on legitimate service requirements and individual capabilities.

In the final analysis, it is a matter of tapping the best talents available from a shrinking pool of young potential recruits to do the jobs required by the military . . . a military that grows technologically more demanding each day.

It is also a matter of equity, or reverse equity, if you will. Sooner or later the question boils down to this: Is it right to expect military men to face the risks of combat while attempting to protect the women who take the same oath, draw the same pay, get the same training, and wear the same uniform?

Today, an increasing number of women are saying: NO. So are growing numbers of men. A young female enlisted paratrooper who had landed in Panama with the 82nd Airborne laid it out in simple terms: "If they are going to let us wear the uniform then they ought to let us defend it. Otherwise, don't let us wear it."

The spirit of many of the women on duty in the gulf was expressed by Captain Ginny Thomas, a reserve pilot flying a C-141 transport in the theater. "I'll be glad when it's over," she said. "But I'd be disappointed if I was not over here doing something for my country."

Military Women

Military women have proven that they are ready, willing and able to accept the risks and responsibilities that go with the oath they have freely taken. They have earned the right to be treated like members of the first team rather than as a protected subclass on the fringes of their profession. As citizens, they deserve the opportunity to be all they can be.

Step 3   Analyze What You Read

A. Identify Arguments and Supporting Details

For each of the following arguments, write the type of support used (testimony, reasons, facts, or examples). If no support is given, write "none."

1. Operation Desert Storm proved that the coeducational military can succeed. _____

2. The idea of "safe havens" has all but disappeared. _____

3. The military needs women to meet its manpower requirements.

   _____

4. The policies about women in the military are outdated.

   _____

5. Anyone who volunteers is agreeing to the risks. _____

6. Barring women from combat reduces their opportunities for challenging jobs and career advancement. _____

7. It also reduces military personnel efficiency and flexibility.

   _____

8. It influences the acceptance and treatment of women.

   _____

9. The issue is the law, rather than physical capability.

   _____

10. Women do not destroy team bonding. _____

11. Social attitudes have changed. _____

12. Five NATO nations allow women in combat. _____

13. It is time to get rid of outgrown laws and policies. _____

14. It's a matter of equity. _____

15. Women have earned the right to full membership.

   _____

   In the margin of the article, write *POV* next to the place Holm presents her point of view. Then write *Arg. 1* through *Arg. 15* next to the place each argument appears. Next, underline the support for each argument.

B. Evaluate Supporting Details

   Type of Support. What is the *primary* type of support the author uses (testimony, reasons, facts, examples)? _____

   Credibility of Sources. When testimony is used, the sources need to be evaluated. You may use the following criteria in your evaluation:

   1. Is this source representative of all the people in a position to testify on this issue?
   2. Do you have any reason to believe this source is biased?
   3. Does this source have access to the relevant information?

   Find the argument that each of the following people is supporting, and write its number (1–15) in the appropriate space. Using a scale from 1 (poor) to 5 (excellent), rate each source in terms of how convincing he or she is. Give your reason for the rating.

   1. Gen. Norman Schwarzkopf

      a. Argument _____

      b. Rating _____

      c. Reason _____

2. Lt. Gen. Thomas A. Hickey

    a. Argument _____

    b. Rating _____

    c. Reason _____

3. Lt. Stephanie Shaw

    a. Argument _____

    b. Rating _____

    c. Reason _____

Logical Reasoning. Several of the arguments are supported with reasons. Give the reason, and rate it on a scale from 1 (not very logical) to 3 (quite logical). State why you rated it as you did.

1. The military needs women to meet its manpower requirements (argument 3).

    a. Reason _____

    b. Rating _____

    c. Explanation _____

2. Combat exclusion influences the acceptance and treatment of women (argument 8).

    a. Reason _____

    b. Rating _____

    c. Explanation _____

3. The issue is the law, rather than physical capability (argument 9).

    a. Reason _____

    b. Rating _____

    c. Explanation _____

4. It is time to get rid of outgrown laws and policies (argument 13).

    a. Reason _____

    b. Rating _____

    c. Explanation _____

5. It's a matter of equity (argument 14).

    a. Reason _____

    b. Rating _____

    c. Explanation _____

C. Make Graphic Organizers

Jeanne Holm's arguments are based on both practical (what works) and moral (what is right) grounds. Sort the fifteen arguments into these two categories.

Practical

1. _____

2. _____

3. _____

4. _____

5. _____

6. _____

7. _____

8. _____

9. _____

Moral

1. _____

2. _____

3. _____

4. _____

5. _____

6. _____

Step 4 **Remember What's Important**

Review your underlining, marginal notes, and graphic organizers. Continue your review until you feel confident that you understand and remember the information.

 Step 5 **Make Use of What You Read**

Your instructor will give you a comprehension check for this article.

 Step 6 **Evaluate Your Active Critical Thinking Skills**

After your comprehension check is graded, use the checklist in the appendix to evaluate your skills.

Comparing Views on Women in Combat

Use the following activities to evaluate your understanding of the issue of women in combat.

1. Summarize each article. Using your underlining, marginal notes, and graphic organizers, make sure to include the point of view, the arguments, and the major supporting details.

2. Evaluate the support for each article.
   a. What type is it?
   b. To what degree are the sources credible?
   c. To what degree is the language loaded?
   d. To what degree is the reasoning logical?

3. Compare the articles. Do you believe that one author's arguments are stronger than the other's? Why?

4. Go back to the self-questioning survey on pages 45–46. Would you change any of your responses after reading the articles? Summarize your opinion on the issue, noting any ways in which your opinion has been affected by your reading.

The War on Drugs

In this section you will read two perspectives on the subject of legalizing drugs. Article 5, "How Best to Solve the Drug Problem: Legalize," was written by Raul Tovares, a drug and alcohol therapist and, at the time of this article, the program director for Catholic Television in San Antonio, Texas. Article 6, "Should Drugs Be Legalized?" was written by William Bennett, also known as "the drug czar" because he headed the war on drugs under President Bush. Bennett was also the Secretary of Education in the Reagan administration.

Self-Questioning

Responding to the following questions will help you understand your current views. You will take the same survey to reevaluate your views after you have read articles 5 and 6.

Rating Scale

1 Absolutely not

2 Perhaps not

3 No opinion

4 Perhaps

5 Yes

Rate each question from 1 to 5.

_____ 1. Should marijuana be legalized?

_____ 2. Should cocaine be legalized?

_____ 3. Should all drugs be legalized?

_____ 4. Should drug users be prosecuted?

_____ 5. Should drug dealers be prosecuted?

_____ 6. Do you think drug use is immoral?

Reading 5

How Best to Solve the Drug Problem: Legalize

Vocabulary Preview

curtailed (kər tāld′) cut short; reduced

condone (kən dōn′) to forgive, pardon, or overlook (an offense)

incarceration (in kär′sə rā′shən) imprisonment

futility (fyo͞o til′ə tē) uselessness

interdiction (in ter dik′shən) prohibition or restraint

incentive (in sen′tiv) motive or stimulus to action

mortify (môr′tə fī) shame; anger

potency (pô′tən sē) powerfulness; effectiveness

mediating (mē′dē āt iŋ) trying to settle differences between two parties

alleviating (ə lē′vē ā tiŋ) relieving; easing

stereotypical (ster′ē ə tip′ə kəl) of or produced by a fixed or conventional notion or conception, as of a person, group, idea, etc., held by a number of people, and allowing for no individuality, critical judgment, etc.

venture capitalists (ven′chər kap′ə tə lists) people who use money or property in a risky business undertaking

entrepreneur (än trə prə nʉr′) one who organizes and operates a business

abstains (ab stānz′) holds oneself back or voluntarily does without; refrains (from)

advent (ad′vent) a coming or arrival

---

fat, āpe, cär; ten, ēven; is, bīte; gō, hôrn, to͞ol, look; oil, out; up, fʉr; chin, she; thin, *then*; zh, leisure; ŋ, ring; ə for *a* in *ago;* ′ as in *able* (ā′b'l)

Step 1   Preread

Read the title, the first paragraph, the headings, and the last paragraph.

1. What is the subject of the article? _____

2. What is the author's point of view? _____

3. Now take a moment to compare your beliefs about drug legalization with Raul Tovares's view. On a scale of 1 (no way) to 5 (absolutely), how likely are you to agree with his point of view? _____

 Step 2   Read

Read the article without underlining. Just try to comprehend the arguments.

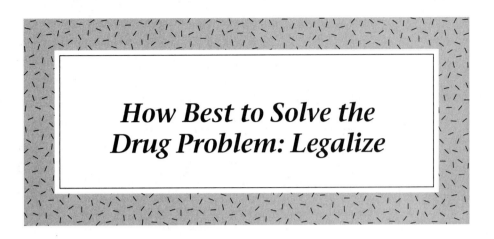

How Best to Solve the Drug Problem: Legalize

Raul Tovares

The present hysteria over controlled substances, such as cocaine and marijuana, has clouded our thinking and caused us to support policies based more on emotion than reason. This trend, if not curtailed by calm reflection and subsequent action to implement a more sane strategy, could result in the waste of billions of dollars and the persecution of some of our community's most ambitious and intelligent young people.

The legalization of the use of cocaine and marijuana is the first step toward developing a more humane drug policy. All other attempts to curtail drug use will fail.

It should be made clear at the outset: In no way do I condone drug abuse. I support all efforts that educate persons about the dangers of drug abuse and that encourage them to refrain from using drugs. What I am against is the arrest, prosecution, and incarceration of drug users.

Attempts to stop the flow of drugs into this country will not solve the problem of drug abuse. Research by Mark A. R. Kleiman of the John F. Kennedy School of Government highlights the futility of trying to suppress drug use. Kleiman found that imports of marijuana, thanks to an intensive policy of border interdictions, were reduced from approximately 4,200 tons in 1982 to 3,900 tons in 1986.

A Rise in Drug Prices

The impact of the "crackdown" was twofold: The price of marijuana went up as the risk factor for suppliers increased, and domestic production increased 10 percent within the same period. The result is that, today, one quarter of the marijuana sold in the United States is homegrown. As supply decreased, profits increased. Time and again, the increased profits have proved to be powerful incentives for dealers. For this reason, production of drugs is never eliminated; it merely moves to another state or country.

Media hype about drug busts creates a dangerous illusion. Every time we read about a major drug bust we can be sure of one thing, the profits for the dealers will go up. Major drug busts cut supply, which in turn increases demand. While the media, state and citizenry engage in victory dances in front of the television set, drug dealers are calculating their increased earnings.

Legalization of cocaine and marijuana, although the idea mortifies some, would immediately give the government more control over these substances, thus allowing it to regulate both the potency and the purity of these drugs.

Those now involved in the distribution of these drugs must work outside the law. Grievances between buyers and sellers can only be settled by violence because there is no mediating body to whom either can go for assistance. If a dealer is selling less than the quantity he actually promised to deliver, he cannot be dragged into court or reported to the Better Business Bureau. Violence is the only way to settle the matter.

Legalization would open the door to a more civilized way to resolve conflicts. The issuing of licenses to sell these products would attract merchants without prior arrest records. Their primary interest would be the management of a legitimate business.

Clearly, the most unjust proposal for dealing with the drug problem is the incarceration of the "user." Currently, U.S. prisons house about one million people, many of them held or convicted on drug-related charges. Each cell built costs the taxpayers about $50,000. Alleviating current overcrowding would cost the state $80 billion.

The fact is, we could never afford to arrest, prosecute and incarcerate the 23 million Americans who use drugs. New York City, for example, has six judges assigned to hear 20,000 narcotics cases a year. That translates into 19,400 plea bargains and an average jail term of seven days.

In Connecticut, prisoners are being released in order to make room for incoming inmates. Those released are chosen from among the least violent. The least violent often turn out to be those imprisoned on drug charges. This pattern is repeated across the nation.

Even if state legislatures did decide to raise revenues for more prisons, such a plan could never be justified when so many of our communities are being faced with the problems of unemployment, underemployment, infant mortality, malnutrition, illiteracy and homelessness—problems that many social scientists tell us lead to drug abuse. Capital is in too short supply to be squandered on a formula we know does not work: Drug user + arrest + prosecution + prison terms = productive citizen.

Drugs are not the cause, but a symptom, of a more profound and complex set of problems we don't want to face, simply because we haven't learned to solve them: unjust economic conditions and our own addiction to consumption masquerading as "the good life."

Development of a healthy and reasonable attitude toward the drug problem begins with the acceptance of the drug user as a human being—not as a "fiend," "junkie" or "enemy." In reality, drug users are our sons and daughters, our friends and neighbors.

Politicians such as Mayor Ed Koch, who want pushers shot on the spot, and bureaucrats such as William Bennett, who have no moral problem with beheading drug dealers, appeal to our society's sense of frustration rather than offering solutions that create a sense of hope. This kind of grandstanding is the scenario for war, and wars are the result of injustice. The drug war is no exception.

Although 75 percent of the users of drugs are white, a majority of those incarcerated for drug use are either black or Hispanic.

The Real Criminals

The stereotypical drug pusher is black or Hispanic. Little is mentioned about the white bankers and investors who supply the capital for major drug deals. Between 1970 and 1976, the currency surplus (the amount of money received minus the amount lent) reported by the Federal Reserve in the state of Florida almost tripled from $576 million to $1.5 billion, according to Jefferson Morely in an article published in the Oct. 2, 1989, issue of *The Nation.* But when was the last time you heard President George Bush call for the immediate execution of bankers who take drug money or William Bennett call for the beheading of venture capitalists who fund major drug deals?

In fact, the typical drug pusher is not a strung-out gang member who lights his cigars with one-hundred dollar bills. A successful drug dealer, like any entrepreneur, is often a hard worker who likely abstains from drug use.

The explanation for this phenomenon is simple. As industry abandoned the inner city and urban areas in general, many blue-collar entry level jobs that had been available to minorities and poor whites were lost. They were replaced by white-collar jobs that require higher levels of education. Inner-city school systems simply could not deliver students prepared to compete for these jobs.

With the advent of crack, a new product that could be sold for as little as five dollars, intelligent, ambitious and aggressive young people who had bought into the culture of consumerism went to work in the only service industry that didn't make them wear funny hats, and it paid 20 times more.

The rise in drug use among our nation's poor and economically disadvantaged is a direct result of our unwillingness as a community to deal with the problems of inadequate school systems, lack of good jobs and the gap that currently exists between our addiction to having it all and our ability to actually pay for it all.

It is simply not fair to incarcerate those who want to live out the dream of consumption when it is our economic system that has both whetted their appetite for such a life-style and simultaneously failed to deliver the opportunities needed to live out that dream. Besides jail terms and prison sentences, we are giving those young people prison records that will follow them for the rest of their lives. These criminal records will hinder them in their future endeavors to live as productive and fully participating members of our society. How many future attorneys, doctors, teachers and such are being cut off at an early age from ever realizing their full potential?

There is a drug problem. But it will not be solved by incarcerating young, poor blacks, Hispanics and whites. It will be brought under control only when the product they are selling is legalized and regulated just like other drugs people use today without a second thought: alcohol, caffeine, nicotine.

Next time we pick up a six-pack at the grocery store, raise our glass of champagne for a toast or fix ourselves a drink to help us relax after a trying day, we should remember that, only a few years ago, in our own nation, it was chic for politicians and bureaucrats to call for the immediate execution of users of alcohol. [Indeed, in the 17th century, the prince of the petty state of Waldeck was paying 10 thalers to anyone who turned in the drug abusers in his kingdom: coffee drinkers. During the same century, Czar Michael Federovitch executed anyone caught in possession of tobacco.]

A Sane Policy

Drugs have always been a part of human culture. Their use, within the context of a healthy and sane community, has never hurt the culture. It is only when the social system begins to break down because of economic and social factors that drugs become a point of focus for the projection of our social ills.

But a reasoned and calm analysis can forge a path through the hysteria and lead us to a sane policy for the control and distribution of cocaine and marijuana.

Step 3   Analyze What You Read

A. Identify Arguments and Supporting Details

For each of the following arguments, fill in the supporting details that Tovares provides.

1. Attempts to stop the flow of drugs into the country will not solve the problem. _____

2. Legalization would improve the situation by giving the government more control.

   a. _____

   b. _____

   c. _____

3. It is wrong to incarcerate the user.

   a. _____

   b. _____

   c. _____

   d. _____

   e. _____

4. It is wrong to incarcerate dealers.

   a. _____

   b. _____

   c. _____

5. Attitudes toward drugs change.

   a. _____

   b. _____

   c. _____

6. Drug use is not the real problem. _____

    In the margin of the article, write *POV* next to where Tovares presents his point of view. Write *Arg. 1* through *Arg. 6* next to each argument, and then underline the supporting details.

B. Evaluate Supporting Details

   Type of Support. What is the primary type of support the author uses (testimony, reasons, facts, examples)? _____

   Credibility of Research. Research evidence, like everything else, must be evaluated critically. If there is anything wrong with the research, then the conclusions drawn from it will also be faulty. The research by Mark A. R. Kleiman is given as support for the argument that attempts to stop the flow of drugs into the country will not solve the drug problem. Kleiman presents three findings: write them in the following spaces and then describe what further information you would need to have confidence that the findings are correct.

   1. Finding _____

      Information needed _____

   2. Finding _____

      Information needed _____

   3. Finding _____

      Information needed _____

Inferences: Some information is implied rather than stated. If you believe that the following statement can be validly inferred, write "yes." If the following statement is not a valid inference, write "no." You should be able to locate a valid inference within the article.

_____ 1. This society places too much emphasis on drugs.

_____ 2. The government has a way of knowing how much marijuana is imported each year.

_____ 3. Each time a dealer is busted, the incentive to become a dealer increases.

_____ 4. Our present drug policy is inhumane.

_____ 5. Cocaine is more profitable than marijuana.

_____ 6. Harsh prison terms deter people from using drugs.

_____ 7. We live in a racist society.

_____ 8. Alcohol is more dangerous than marijuana.

_____ 9. Our society encourages drug dealing.

_____ 10. Politicians and bureaucrats are not addressing the real issues.

C. Make Graphic Organizers

Fill in the following study map for this article. Write the point of view in the center circle, the six arguments in the six rectangles, and the support for the arguments in the triangles.

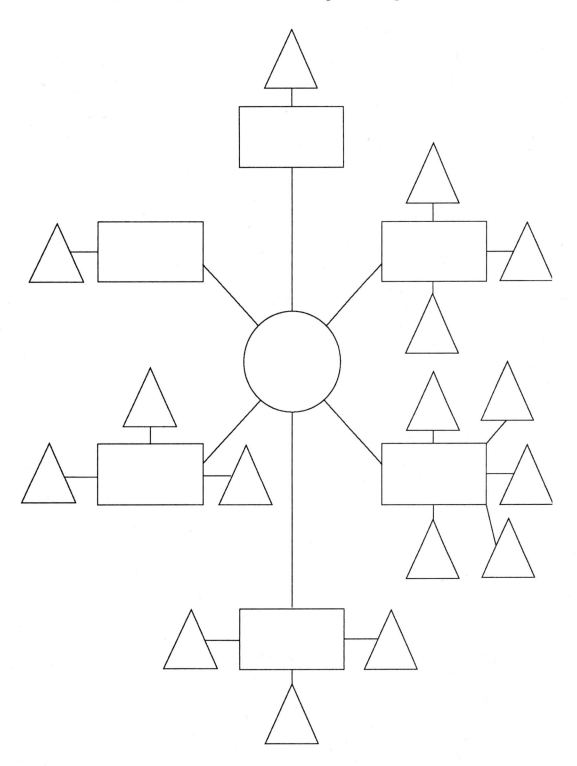

Step 4   Remember What's Important

Review your underlining, marginal notes, and graphic organizer. Continue your review until you feel confident that you understand and remember the information.

 Step 5   Make Use of What You Read

Your instructor will give you a comprehension check for this article.

 Step 6   Evaluate Your Active Critical Thinking Skills

After your comprehension check is graded, use the checklist in the appendix to evaluate your skills.

Reading 6

Should Drugs Be Legalized?

Vocabulary Preview

fatalistic (fā′t′l is′tik) believing that it is impossible to change events

syndicated (sin′də kāt′id) one whose columns are sold to many newspapers or periodicals by an organization

euphoria (yo͞o fôr′ē ə) a feeling of well-being or high spirits

proliferation (prō lif′ ər ā′ shən) rapid growth or increase

intrinsically (in trin′sik lē) inherently; naturally belonging

laureate (lôr′ē it) the most honored

proponent (prə pō′nənt) one who supports a cause

illicit (i lis′it) unlawful

furtive (fʉr′tiv) sneaky

egalitarian (i gal′ə ter′ē ən) advocating equality

garnered (gär′nərd) gathered up and stored

libertarian (lib′ər ter′ē ən) one who believes in full individual freedom of thought, expression, and action

indulgence (in dul′jens) gratification of a craving

clandestine (klan des′tən) secret or hidden

psychopathic (sīk′ə path′ik) criminal, amoral behavior

ramparts (ram′pärtz) defenses or bulwarks

ravages (rav′ij iz) devastating damages

devastated (dev′ə stāt′id) destroyed; overwhelmed

Vocabulary Preview continued

sanctioning (saŋk'shən iŋ) giving approval or permission

revulsion (ri vul'shən) disgust; loathing

---

fat, āpe, cär; ten, ēven; is, bīte; gō, hôrn, tool, look; oil, out; up, fʉr; chin, she; thin, *then*;
zh, leisure; ŋ, ring; ə for *a* in *ago;* ' as in *able* (ā'b'l)

Step 1   *Preread*

Read the title, the first two paragraphs, the italics, and the last paragraph.

1. What is the subject of the article? _____

2. What is the author William Bennett's point of view? _____

   _____

3. Now take a moment to compare your beliefs about drug legalization
   with the author's. On a scale of 1 (no way) to 5 (absolutely), how
   likely are you to agree with his point of view? _____

Step 2   *Read*

Read the article without underlining. Just try to comprehend the arguments.

Should Drugs Be Legalized?

William Bennett

Since I took command of the war on drugs, I have learned from former Secretary of State George Shultz that our concept of fighting drugs is "flawed." The only thing to do, he says, is to "make it possible for addicts to buy drugs at some regulated place." Conservative commentator William F. Buckley, Jr., suggests I should be "fatalistic" about the flood of cocaine from South America and simply "let it in." Syndicated columnist Mike Royko contends it would be easier to sweep junkies out of the gutters "than to fight a hopeless war" against the narcotics that send them there. Labeling our efforts "bankrupt," federal judge Robert W. Sweet opts for legalization, saying, "If our society can learn to stop using butter, it should be able to cut down on cocaine."

Flawed, fatalistic, hopeless, bankrupt! I never realized surrender was so fashionable until I assumed this post.

Though most Americans are overwhelmingly determined to go toe-to-toe with the foreign drug lords and neighborhood pushers, a small minority believe that enforcing drug laws imposes greater costs on society than do drugs themselves. Like addicts seeking immediate euphoria, the legalizers want peace at any price, even though it means the inevitable proliferation of a practice that degrades, impoverishes and kills.

I am acutely aware of the burdens drug enforcement places upon us. It consumes economic resources we would like to use elsewhere. It is sometimes frustrating, thankless and often dangerous. But the consequences of *not* enforcing drug laws would be far more costly. Those consequences involve the intrinsically destructive nature of drugs and the toll they exact from our society in hundreds of thousands of lost and broken lives . . . human potential never realized . . . time stolen from families and jobs . . . precious spiritual and economic resources squandered.

That is precisely why virtually every civilized society has found it necessary to exert some form of control over mind-altering substances and why this war is so important. Americans feel up to their hips in drugs now. They would be up to their necks under legalization.

Even limited experiments in drug legalization have shown that when drugs are more widely available, addiction skyrockets. In 1975 Italy liberalized its drug law and now has one of the highest heroin-related death rates in Western Europe. In Alaska, where marijuana was decriminalized in 1975, the easy atmosphere has increased usage of the drug, particularly among children. Nor does it stop there. Some Alaskan schoolchildren now tout "coca puffs," marijuana cigarettes laced with cocaine.

Many legalizers concede that drug legalization might increase use, but they shrug off the matter. "It may well be that there would be more addicts, and I would regret that result," says Nobel laureate economist Milton Friedman. The late Harvard Medical School psychiatry professor Norman Zinberg, a longtime proponent of "responsible" drug use, admitted that "use of now illicit drugs would certainly increase. Also, casualties probably would increase."

In fact, Dr. Herbert D. Kleber of Yale University, my deputy in charge of demand reduction, predicts legalization might cause "a five-to-sixfold increase" in cocaine use. But legalizers regard this as a necessary price for the "benefits" of legalization. What benefits?

1. *Legalization will take the profit out of drugs.* The result supposedly will be the end of criminal drug pushers and the big foreign drug wholesalers, who will turn to other enterprises because nobody will need to make furtive and dangerous trips to his local pusher.

But what, exactly, would the brave new world of legalized drugs look like? Buckley stresses that "adults get to buy the stuff at carefully regulated stores." (Would you want one in *your* neighborhood?) Others, like Friedman, suggest we sell the drugs at "ordinary retail outlets."

Former City University of New York sociologist Georgette Bennett assures us that "brand-name competition will be prohibited" and that strict quality control and proper labeling will be overseen by the Food and Drug Administration. In a touching egalitarian note, she adds that "free drugs will be provided at government clinics" for addicts too poor to buy them.

Almost all the legalizers point out that the price of drugs will fall, even though the drugs will be heavily taxed. Buckley, for example, argues that somehow federal drugstores will keep the price "low enough to discourage a black market but high enough to accumulate a surplus to be used for drug education."

Supposedly, drug sales will generate huge amounts of revenue, which will then be used to tell the public not to use drugs and to treat those who don't listen.

In reality, this tax would only allow government to *share* the drug profits now garnered by criminals. Legalizers would have to tax drugs heavily in order to pay for drug education and treatment programs. Criminals could undercut the official price and still make huge profits. What alternative would the government have? Cut the price until it was within the lunch-money budget of the average sixth-grade student?

2. *Legalization will eliminate the black market.* Wrong. And not just because the regulated prices could be undercut. Many legalizers admit that drugs such as crack or PCP are simply too dangerous to allow the shelter of the law. Thus criminals will provide what the government will not. "As long as drugs that people very much want remain illegal, a black market will exist," says legalization advocate David Boaz of the libertarian Cato Institute.

Look at crack. In powdered form, cocaine was an expensive indulgence. But street chemists found that a better and far less expensive—and far more danger-ous—high could be achieved by mixing cocaine with baking soda and heating it. Crack was born, and "cheap" coke invaded low-income communities with furious speed.

An ounce of powdered cocaine might sell on the street for $1200. That same ounce can produce 370 vials of crack at $10 each. Ten bucks seems like a cheap hit, but crack's intense ten- to 15-minute high is followed by an unbearable depression. The user wants more crack, thus starting a rapid and costly descent into addiction.

If government drugstores do not stock crack, addicts will find it in the clandes-tine market or simply bake it themselves from their legally purchased cocaine.

Currently crack is being laced with insecticides and animal tranquilizers to heighten its effect. Emergency rooms are now warned to expect victims of "sand-wiches" and "moon rocks," life-threatening smokable mixtures of heroin or crack. Unless the government is prepared to sell these deadly variations of dangerous drugs, it will perpetuate a criminal black market by default.

And what about children and teen-agers? They would obviously be barred from drug purchases, just as they are prohibited from buying beer and liquor. But pushers will continue to cater to these young customers with the old, favorite come-ons—a couple of free fixes to get them hooked. And what good will anti-drug education be when these youngsters observe their older brothers and sisters, parents and friends lighting up and shooting up with government permission?

Legalization will give us the worst of both worlds: millions of *new* drug users *and* a thriving black market.

3. *Legalization will dramatically reduce crime.* "It is the high price of drugs that leads addicts to robbery, murder and other crimes," says Ira Glasser, executive direc-tor of the American Civil Liberties Union. A study by the Cato Institute concludes: "Most, if not all, 'drug-related murders' are the result of drug prohibition."

But researchers tell us that many drug-related felonies are committed by people involved in crime *before* they started taking drugs. The drugs, so routinely available in criminal circles, make the criminals more violent and unpredictable.

Certainly there are some kill-for-a-fix crimes, but does any rational person believe that a cut-rate price for drugs at a government outlet will stop such psychopathic behavior? The fact is that under the influence of drugs, normal people do not act normally, and abnormal people behave in chilling and horrible ways. DEA agents told me about a teen-age addict in Manhattan who was smoking crack when he sexually abused and caused permanent internal injuries to his one-month-old daughter.

Children are among the most frequent victims of violent, drug-related crimes that have nothing to do with the cost of acquiring the drugs. In Philadelphia in 1987 more than half the child-abuse fatalities involved at least one parent who was a heavy drug user. Seventy-three percent of the child-abuse deaths in New York City in 1987 involved parental drug use.

In my travels to the ramparts of the drug war, I have seen nothing to support the legalizers' argument that lower drug prices would reduce crime. Virtually everywhere I have gone, police and DEA agents have told me that crime rates are highest where crack is cheapest.

4. *Drug use should be legal since users only harm themselves.* Those who believe this should stand beside the medical examiner as he counts the 36 bullet wounds in the shattered corpse of a three-year-old who happened to get in the way of his mother's drug-crazed boyfriend. They should visit babies abandoned by cocaine-addicted mothers—infants who already carry the ravages of addiction in their own tiny bodies. They should console the devastated relatives of the nun who worked in a homeless shelter and was stabbed to death by a crack addict enraged that she would not stake him to a fix.

Do drug addicts only harm themselves? Here is a former cocaine addict describing the compulsion that quickly draws even the most "responsible" user into irresponsible behavior: "Everything is about getting high, and any means necessary to get there becomes rational. If it means stealing something from somebody close to you, lying to your family, borrowing from people you know you can't pay back, writing checks you know you can't cover, you do all those things—things that are totally against everything you have ever believed in."

Society pays for this behavior, and not just in bigger insurance premiums, losses from accidents and poor job performance. We pay in the loss of a priceless social currency as families are destroyed, trust between friends is betrayed and promising careers are never fulfilled. I cannot imagine sanctioning behavior that would increase that toll.

I find no merit in the legalizers' case. The simple fact is that drug use is wrong. And the moral argument, in the end, is the most compelling argument. A citizen in a drug-induced haze, whether on his back-yard deck or on a mattress in a ghetto crack house, is not what the founding fathers meant by the "pursuit of happiness." Despite the legalizers' claim that drug use is a matter of "personal freedom," our nation's notion of liberty is rooted in the ideal of self-reliant citizenry. Helpless wrecks in treatment centers, men chained by their noses to cocaine—these people are slaves.

Imagine if, in the darkest days of 1940, Winston Churchill had rallied the West by saying, "This war looks hopeless, and besides, it will cost too much. Hitler can't be *that* bad. Let's surrender and see what happens." That is essentially what we hear from the legalizers.

This war *can* be won. I am heartened by indications that education and public revulsion are having an effect on drug use. The National Institute on Drug Abuse's latest survey of current users shows a 37-percent *decrease* in drug consumption since 1985. Cocaine is down 50 percent; marijuana use among young people is at its lowest rate since 1972. In my travels I've been encouraged by signs that Americans are fighting back.

I am under no illusion that such developments, however hopeful, mean the war is over. We need to involve more citizens in the fight, increase pressure on drug criminals and build on anti-drug programs that have proved to work. This will not be easy. But the moral and social costs of surrender are simply too great to contemplate.

 Step 3   *Analyze What You Read*

A. Identify Arguments and Supporting Details

For each piece of support, fill in the argument.

1. _____

    a. Lost and broken lives

    b. Human potential never realized

    c. Time stolen from families and jobs

    d. Precious spiritual and economic resources squandered

2. _____

    a. Experiments in Italy and Alaska

    b. Testimony from Milton Friedman, Norman Zinberg, and Dr. Herbert D. Kleber

3. _____

    a. Legalizers would have to tax drugs heavily

4. _____

    a. Testimony from David Boaz

    b. Some drugs will be too dangerous to legalize

    c. Pushers cater to those too young to purchase drugs legally

5. _____

    a. Research findings that many drug-related felonies are committed by people already involved in crime before they started taking drugs

b. Drugs make people behave abnormally

c. Police and DEA agents say crime is highest where crack is cheapest

6. _____

a. Bigger insurance premiums

b. Losses from accidents

c. Poor job performance

d. Loss of priceless social currency

7. _____

a. Drug addicts are slaves

8. _____

a. National Institute on Drug Abuse survey

In the margin of the article, write *POV* next to where Bennett presents his point of view. Write *Arg. 1* through *Arg. 8* next to the arguments and then underline the supporting details.

B. Evaluate Supporting Details

Type of Support. What is the primary type of support Bennett uses (testimony, reasons, facts, examples)? _____

Credibility of Research. Research evidence must be critically evaluated to judge whether the conclusions drawn from it are justified. On the basis of its research, the National Institute of Drug Abuse has drawn conclusions that are contrary to the research conclusions found in article 5. Here, the research supports the argument that the war against drugs can be won. Bennett presents three findings in this article. List these findings and then describe further information you would need to have confidence that the findings are accurate.

1. Finding _____

    Information needed _____

2. Finding _____

    Information needed _____

3. Finding _____

    Information needed _____

Inferences. Read the following sentences. If you believe that the statement can be validly inferred, write "yes." If the statement is not a valid inference, write "no." You should be able to locate a valid inference within the article.

_____ 1. The tactics currently being used to fight drugs are effective.

_____ 2. The war against drugs is worth the money.

_____ 3. The people in favor of legalization are liberals.

_____ 4. The war against drugs is more humane than legalization.

_____ 5. Those in favor of legalization agree that drug use would increase.

_____ 6. The government has accurate statistics on the use of illegal drugs.

_____ 7. Legalization would increase the black market.

_____ 8. Drug use is caused by problems in the society.

_____ 9. We should have sympathy for drug addicts.

_____ 10. Marijuana should be treated differently from "hard" drugs.

C. Make Graphic Organizers

Fill in the following study map for this article. Write the point of view in the circle, the eight arguments in the eight rectangles, and the supporting details in the triangles.

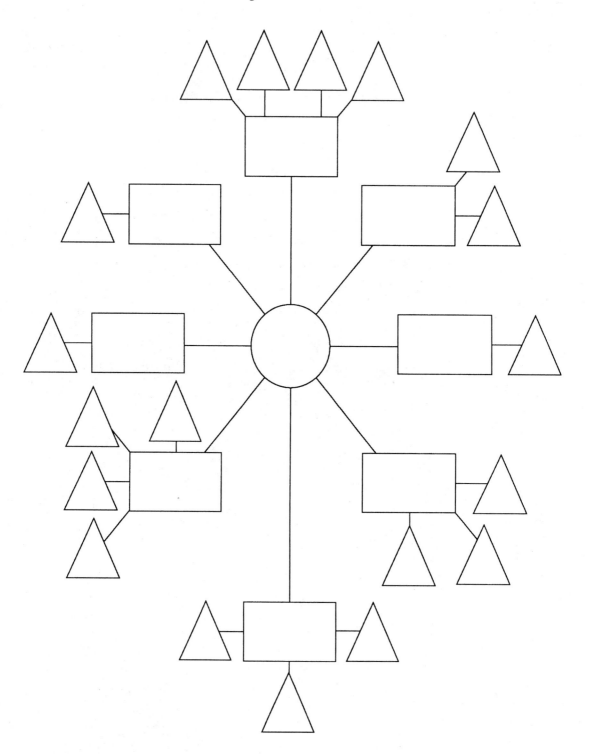

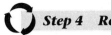

Step 4   *Remember What's Important*

Review your underlining, marginal notes, and graphic organizer. Continue your review until you feel confident that you understand and remember the information.

Step 5   *Make Use of What You Read*

Your instructor will give you a comprehension check for this article.

Step 6   *Evaluate Your Active Critical Thinking Skills*

After your comprehension check is graded, use the checklist in the appendix to evaluate your skills.

Comparing Views on the War on Drugs

Use the following activities to evaluate your understanding of the war on drugs.

1. Summarize each article. Using your underlining, marginal notes, and graphic organizer, make sure to include the point of view, the arguments, and the major supporting details.

2. Evaluate the support for each article.
   a. What type is it?
   b. What degree of confidence can you have in the research findings?

3. Look at each argument (there are six in article 5 and eight in article 6). Does each author address the other author's arguments?

4. Compare the articles. Do you believe that one author's arguments are stronger than the other's? Why?

5. Go back to the self-questioning survey on pages 71–72. Would you change any of your responses after reading the articles? Summarize your opinion on legalizing drugs, noting any ways in which your opinion has been affected by your reading.

Nuclear Power

In this section you will read two perspectives on the subject of nuclear power. Article 7, "The Greenest Form of Power," was written by Fleming Meeks and James Drummond, who are senior editors of *Forbes,* a financial magazine. Article 8, "Nuclear Power: Past and Future," was written by the Union of Concerned Scientists, a nonprofit organization of nearly 100,000 scientists and others interested in the impact of advanced technology on society and the environment.

Self-Questioning

Answering the following questions will help you understand your current views. You will take the same survey to reevaluate your views after you have read the articles.

Rating Scale

1 Absolutely not

2 Perhaps not

3 No opinion

4 Perhaps

5 Yes

Rate each question from 1 to 5.

1. Should nuclear power plants be built

_____ a. wherever they are needed?

_____ b. only in unpopulated areas?

2. Should we spend more money

_____ a. trying to solve the problems of fossil fuels, such as acid rain and the shrinking ozone layer?

_____ b. trying to develop more cost-effective ways of using "clean" power, such as solar and wind power?

_____ c. trying to solve the problems of nuclear power, such as safety and fuel disposal?

3. To help solve the energy crisis, would you be willing to reduce your consumption of gas and electricity by

_____ a. 10 percent?

_____ b. 25 percent?

_____ c. 50 percent?

Reading 7

The Greenest Form of Power

Vocabulary Preview

rhetoric (re′tər ik) artificial eloquence; language that is showy and elaborate but largely empty of clear ideas or sincere emotion

discordant (dis kôr′dənt) not in harmony; clashing

renaissance (ren′ə säns′) rebirth, revival

sacrosanct (sak′rō saŋkt′) sacred, holy, or inviolable

formidable (for′mə də bəl) hard to handle or overcome

---

fat, āpe, cär; ten, ēven; is, bīte; gō, hôrn, tōol, look; oil, out; up, fʉr; chin, she; thin, *then*; zh, leisure; ŋ, ring; ə for *a* in *ago;* ′ as in *able* (ā′b′l)

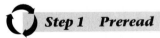 **Step 1   Preread**

Read the title, the first paragraph, the headings, and the last paragraph.

1. What is the subject of the article? _____

2. What is the authors' point of view? _____

3. Now take a moment to compare your beliefs about nuclear power with the authors'. On a scale of 1 (no way) to 5 (absolutely), how likely are you to agree with their point of view? _____

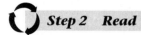 **Step 2   Read**

Read the article without underlining. Just try to comprehend the arguments.

The Greenest Form of Power

Fleming Meeks and
James Drummond

In the fight against nuclear power during the 1970s and 1980s, the U.S. antinuclear groups won. They picketed, they lobbied, they fed the media a steady diet of exaggerated horror stories. They so tied up nuclear plants in the courts and in the regulatory agencies that delays lengthened and costs piled higher and higher. Then the antinukes blamed the nuclear plant owners for their cost overruns. They effectively killed nuclear power as an alternative energy source in the U.S.

Over 100 nuclear plants have been canceled since the mid-1970s. Public Service Co. of New Hampshire was forced into bankruptcy after antinukers delayed operation of its Seabrook plant, upping the plant's cost by $2 billion. (Seabrook, issued a construction permit in 1976, was completed in 1986 but did not receive a full power license until 1990.) And Long Island's Shoreham plant has been mothballed at a cost of $5.5 billion, nearly half of which will be paid by the area's ratepayers for many years to come. All this while, from the San Onofre nuclear plant in southern California to the Indian Point facility in New York, nuclear has proved that it can coexist peacefully with the environment.

Today nuclear accounts for just 20% of electricity in the U.S. Compare this to Sweden, where the figure is 47%, and Belgium, where it is 65%. In France, 74% of electricity is generated in nuclear plants, up from under 4% in 1970.

Not that the nuclear industry didn't make its share of mistakes. The industry oversold the public on the simplicity of nuclear technology, and embarked on projects without sufficient in-house experience to monitor them. They refused to standardize reactor designs. When public relations problems multiplied, the industry did a horrendous job of handling them.

Meanwhile, U.S. oil imports to feed conventional power plants climbed higher and higher.

But as the greens, flush from their nuclear victory, move on to new scares—global warming, acid rain, the ozone hole, the whales and dolphins—their old anti-nuclear rhetoric sounds discordant.

Some of the groups are beginning to concede as much. Testifying before Congress in May 1990, Jan Beyea, National Audubon Society staff scientist, recommended government funding for a new generation of nuclear reactors. Why? "As a sort of global warming insurance policy, in case the transition to renewable energy systems fails to materialize."

There are other signs that, without fanfare, nuclear is in the early stages of a comeback. Nuclear reactor vendors are once again making sales calls on the electric utilities. The U.S. Nuclear Regulatory Commission streamlined the licensing process for new plants. Smelling opportunity, the Europeans, their own nuclear markets near saturation, are buying up American reactor makers.

Environmentalists who object to a nuclear renaissance find themselves in a difficult position. If they argue too loudly that economic growth is bad—that everyone must give up cars and disposable diapers and go back to riding bicycles and manning (or womanning) scrub boards—they will antagonize a public that is sympathetic to their calls for clean air and pure water. But if they support fossil-fuel-fired economic growth, they must accept the likelihood of more oil spills, more acid rain, more disruption of sacrosanct, oil-laden places as the Santa Barbara Channel and Alaska's Arctic National Wildlife Refuge.

Unless the greens are prepared to argue for fewer jobs and a lower standard of living, and thus lose support, they will have to accept some kind of power generation. Solar power and wind power and the like are pie-in-the-sky. Clean, safe nuclear power is a reality. Listen to liberal Senator Timothy Wirth (D-Colo.), who has become increasingly pronuclear: "We have an obligation to try to look toward the future. One of those future technologies is solar, one is conservation, and one is nuclear."

Power Crunch

The U.S. is facing a power crunch in the 1990s. Already the power shortages are beginning to crop up. When the big freeze hit Florida in the winter of 1989/90, utilities had to resort to rolling blackouts—cutting power to particular neighborhoods intermittently for up to two hours. During the sweltering summer of 1988, residents of New England experienced brownouts. And projections show demand for electricity continuing to grow faster than capacity—over twice as fast in New England over the next decade, and nearly twice as fast in Florida.

Even factoring in plants on the drawing board that, if built, will produce 168,000 megawatts by the year 2010, the U.S. will need another 186,000 megawatts of electrical capacity. Filling the gap will require new generating capacity equivalent to a quarter of the current generating capacity in the U.S.—or almost 200 large coal or nuclear plants. This conservative estimate comes from the U.S. Energy Information Administration, an independent forecasting unit within the Department of Energy.

Will they be coal plants? Fifty-six percent of the country's electricity now comes from plants fired by coal, of which plentiful reserves still exist. But it's hard to be for coal and against acid rain. Each 1,000-megawatt coal plant annually spews out 70,000 tons of sulfur oxides—the chief culprit in acid rain.

What of oil- and gas-fired generators? The more oil is shipped, the more Valdez-type oil spills are possible. Moreover, the U.S. is already setting up the world for another round of OPEC-led [Organization of Petroleum Exporting Countries] financial instability: Oil imports are today near their 1977 high of 46.5%. And while natural gas is inexpensive right now, few experts believe it will remain so.

Solar farms? Windmills? After 20 years of costly experiment, these together contribute 1% of total U.S. electric production.

Energy conservation programs have reduced peak U.S. power requirements by 21,000 megawatts, or 3% of total current capacity. That helps, but it is only a beginning.

Quietly, nuclear is already taking the first steps toward a comeback. One important such step is the Nuclear Regulatory Commission's [NRC] streamlined licensing procedures for new nuclear facilities. Unlike big nuclear users like Sweden and France, the U.S. has required a two-step licensing process before a nuclear plant can go on-line. This regulatory system has proved an effective weapon in the hands of the antinuclear forces. Under it, utilities must face months of public hearings to get a construction permit, then run the gauntlet again when the plant is finished many years later. The two-step licensing process dramatically increases the chances of costly delays because of the public hearings and last-minute changes in design standards. As a result, in this country it can take 12 years to complete and operate a plant that the French can have up and running in 6.

The simplified procedure, issued by the NRC in 1989, provides for approval of the complete design at the beginning of the process. Under the new rules, which antinuclear groups are fiercely fighting, the owner of the new reactor would automatically be allowed to fire up the plant on completion, as long as it meets the agreed-upon design standards.

This licensing change is particularly meaningful in light of a new generation of modular 600-megawatt nuclear plants, now on the drawing boards at Westinghouse and General Electric. In theory, once these standardized designs are completed and licensed—perhaps five years down the road—a utility or independent power producer could get site approval in advance and, in effect, buy the generic plans off the shelf, license and all.

Moreover, since the design would be generic, the cost of building nuclear plants could be substantially reduced.

Westinghouse projects the cost of its new modular plant at $1,370 per kilowatt-hour, or about $825 million (not including interest costs) for a 600-megawatt plant. That cost is in line with the cost of comparable coal-fired plants now. . . .

Why would these plants come in so much cheaper than their predecessors, which cost as much as $2,500 per kilowatt (again excluding interest costs) to build? Unlike in the past, each new reactor would not have to reinvent the nuclear wheel, and many of the new reactors' components could be assembled in factories, where inspection and quality control are easy to maintain, rather than on the plant sites themselves.

Signs of Rebirth

Jerome Goldberg is head of nuclear operations at Florida Power & Light, which currently generates 30% of its energy in four nuclear plants. From December 1989 to June 1990, he says, Westinghouse and Combustion Engineering have made several presentations on the new reactors to his engineers and managers. Goldberg says FP&L's immediate plans call for building six new gas-fired generators to ease Florida's power crunch. Just the same, he's listening carefully to what the nuclear vendors are telling him.

"Eventually, there will be the recognition that shutting out the nuclear option was not a good idea," he says.

Here's a telling indication of how interest in nuclear is building again: In its 19-year history, Greenpeace, the radical activist environmental group, never bothered to take a position on nuclear power. Greenpeace leaders say they thought the battles had already been fought and won.

But now that reports of nuclear's death appear to be exaggerated, Greenpeace is mounting its own antinuclear campaign. Says Eric Fersht, who heads the campaign: "We see a lot of signs that things are at work that need to be responded to in a big way." Judging by past Greenpeace campaigns, its antinuclear campaign will be both emotional and confrontational. Nevertheless, sparing dolphins is one thing; turning down the air conditioner on a sweltering day is something else again.

Sensing that the U.S. is becoming a potentially lucrative market for nuclear plants, in January 1990, Asea Brown Boveri, a $25 billion (sales) Zurich-based power and environmental engineering firm, paid $1.6 billion to acquire Combustion Engineering, the nuclear plant maker that built 16 U.S. plants. And in September of 1989, Framatome Group, the big French nuclear plant construction firm, paid $50 million for a 50% interest in Babcock & Wilcox Co.'s nuclear services division. Framatome is working in partnership with the German giant Siemens to develop new reactors in the U.S.

Says Nuclear Regulatory Commission Chairman Kenneth Carr, "The foreigners recognize that the market today is in the U.S., and they're focusing on this tremendously."

Among domestic reactor makers, GE and Westinghouse have designs in the works aimed at making reactors that are even safer than today's reactors, in theory as well as in practice. The new GE and Westinghouse reactors are known as advanced passive light-water reactors. They are designed around an almost fail-safe technology, which uses gravity and natural convection to cool the reactor's core if it begins to overheat. The idea is to leave as little room for human error as possible; it was human error that led to the partial meltdown at Three Mile Island.

Meanwhile, the industry has focused on training programs to keep the skills of operators at current plants well honed. At Three Mile Island, for instance, operators spend one week in six in training. What's more, there are currently 73 elaborate control room simulators in use around the country (up from just a handful before the 1979 accident at Three Mile Island). These simulators, built specifically for individual plants, can run operators through dozens of emergency situations, from a loss of coolant to loss of power within the plant itself.

With the new passive light-water reactors, if the core begins to overheat, valves automatically open, flooding the core with massive amounts of water stored in tanks above the reactor. This automatic process is designed to protect the reactor from damage for three days before human intervention is necessary.

On another front, a new generation of gas-cooled reactors—preferred by the Audubon Society's Beyea and most other environmentalists who are willing to consider nuclear—is under development. Lawrence Lidsky, professor of nuclear engineering at MIT [Massachusetts Institute of Technology], notes that in theory, these gas-cooled reactors are so fail-safe that a plant could withstand the simultaneous failure of the reactor's control rods, as well as a complete failure of the cooling systems. Gas-cooled reactors are probably ten years away from commercial use, but they are on the way . . .

Obstacles to nuclear power remain—and they are formidable. While the Nuclear Regulatory Commission has simplified the federal regulatory process, state utility commissions must also sign off on new nuclear projects. Key to getting the new plants built will be the cooperation of state utility commissions in setting up cost parameters, in advance, and guaranteeing utilities that they will be able to recover costs, so long as they stay within those parameters.

Nuclear waste, too, remains a problem, though not an insurmountable one.

From Emotion to Reason

Severe as these problems are, the need for power is immense if we are to maintain our standard of living and improve it. It may take the balance of this century, but emotion on nuclear power will give way to economic and social necessities. Realities change; perceptions change more slowly. . . .

 Step 3   *Analyze What You Read*

A. Identify Arguments and Supporting Details

In the margin of the article, write *POV* next to where the authors present the point of view. Depending on how you look at it, there are about twelve arguments in this article in favor of the authors' point of view. Write *Arg. 1* through *Arg. 12* next to the place each argument is presented. Then underline the support the authors use for each argument. Use your underlining and marginal notes to fill in the arguments and support:

1. *Argument:* _____

    Support: _____

2. *Argument:* _____

   Support: _____

3. *Argument:* _____

   Support: _____

4. *Argument:* _____

   Support: _____

5. *Argument:* _____

   Support: _____

6. *Argument:* _____

   Support: _____

7. *Argument:* _____

   Support: _____

8. *Argument:* _____

   Support: _____

9. *Argument:* _____

   Support: _____

10. *Argument:* _____

   Support: _____

11. *Argument:* _____

   Support: _____

12. *Argument:* _____

   Support: _____

B. Evaluate Supporting Details

Type of Support. What is the primary type of support the authors use (testimony, reasons, facts, examples)? _____

Provable Versus Unprovable. The following are supporting details from this article. Evaluate whether each one can or cannot be proved. Write *P* or *U* for provable or unprovable.

_____ 1. Nuclear has proved that it can coexist peacefully with the environment.

_____ 2. Nuclear energy is used more extensively in Sweden, Belgium, and France than in the United States.

_____ 3. Jan Beyea of the Audubon Society is beginning to support nuclear energy.

_____ 4. Europeans are buying up American reactor makers.

_____ 5. Liberal Senator Timothy Wirth has become increasingly pro-nuclear.

_____ 6. Florida had rolling blackouts in the winter of 1989–1990.

_____ 7. Solar power and wind power and the like are pie-in-the-sky.

_____ 8. Training programs for operators have increased.

_____ 9. Passive light-water reactors are safer than their predecessors.

_____ 10. The problem of nuclear waste is not insurmountable.

Inferences. If you believe that the following statements can be validly inferred, write "yes." If the statements are not valid inferences, write "no." If a statement is a valid inference, you should be able to locate the place in the article where it is implied.

_____ 1. The unfair tactics of the antinuclear groups caused the cancellation of nuclear plants since the mid-1970s.

_____ 2. The United States should decrease its dependence on foreign oil.

_____ 3. The National Audubon Society is "green."

_____ 4. Energy conservation should be pushed as a viable solution to the power crunch.

_____ 5. U.S. business is antinuclear.

_____ 6. The United States is moving toward stricter licensing requirements for nuclear plants.

_____ 7. Americans will not be willing to make many sacrifices to reduce energy consumption.

_____ 8. Nuclear power is safer than most people think.

_____ 9. Nuclear power is the most practical solution to the energy crunch.

_____ 10. Opponents of nuclear energy are not thinking logically.

C. Make Graphic Organizers

According to the authors, there are drawbacks to all possible solutions to the energy crunch. Fill in the chart with drawbacks for each.

Solution	Drawback(s)
Coal	
Oil and gas	
Solar and wind	
Energy conservation	
Nuclear power	

Step 4   Remember What's Important

Review your underlining, marginal notes, and graphic organizer. Continue your review until you feel confident that you understand and remember the information.

Step 5   Make Use of What You Read

Your instructor will give you a comprehension check for this article.

Step 6   Evaluate Your Active Critical Thinking Skills

After your comprehension check is graded, use the checklist in the appendix to evaluate your skills.

Reading 8

Nuclear Power:
Past and Future

Vocabulary Preview

panacea (pan ə sē′ ə) a supposed remedy for all ills; cure-all

referendum (ref ə ren′dəm) a direct vote of the people

integrity (in teg′rə tē) the quality or state of being in perfect condition; soundness

feasible (fē′zə b′l) capable of being done; possible

repository (ri päz′ə tôr′ē) a place where things may be put for safekeeping

---

fat, āpe, cär; ten, ēven; is, bīte; gō, hôrn, tōol, look; oil, out; up, fʉr; chin, she; thin, *then*; zh, leisure; ŋ, ring; ə for *a* in *ago;* ' as in *able* (ā′b'l)

 Step 1   Preread

Read the title, the first paragraph, the headings, everything in italics, and the last paragraph.

1. What is the subject of the article? _____

2. What is the author's point of view? _____

3. Take a moment to compare your beliefs about nuclear power with those of the Union of Concerned Scientists. On a scale of 1 (no way) to 5 (absolutely), how likely are you to agree with their point of view? _____

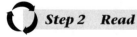

Step 2   Read

Read the article without underlining. Just try to comprehend the arguments.

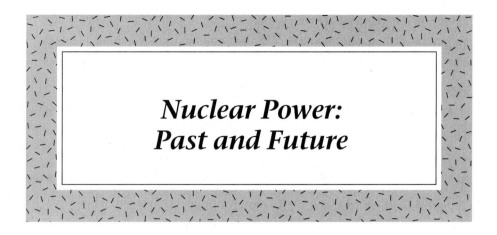

Nuclear Power: Past and Future

Union of Concerned Scientists

Nuclear power is the most controversial of all the energy sources used in the United States. While some people view it as a "clean-fuel" panacea, others consider it a major threat to public health and safety. Some of the key issues in this controversy are discussed below.

There are 110 nuclear power plants licensed to operate in the US, with a combined capacity of 105,000 megawatts. These plants provide about 19% of the nation's electricity. No new nuclear plants have been ordered since 1978, and 118 plants, including all those ordered since 1974, have been canceled or deferred.

Although the cost and performance of nuclear power vary considerably from plant to plant, recent experience suggests that nuclear power has become the least competitive of conventional electricity sources. Costs of $2–$3 billion per plant are now commonplace, with some plants costing upwards of $5 billion. The average output of nuclear plants is only about 60% of designed capacity, because many plants are forced to shut down frequently for repairs and maintenance. (Coal plants run at about 80% of capacity.)

In the 1980s, the time required for construction of a nuclear reactor typically ranged from 8 to 14 years. Although regulatory delays and intervention by citizen groups are often blamed for this poor record, the real roots of the problem lie in faulty and incomplete design work, inadequate quality control during construction, an inability to secure necessary financial backing, poor management, and the nuclear industry's lack of credibility in the eyes of the media and the public. The financial woes of the nuclear industry have continued despite billions of dollars in subsidies from the federal government.

There are a number of major safety issues associated with nuclear power. Some of these include:

Premature Aging. Although nuclear plants are designed and licensed to operate for a period of 40 years, many plants may have to be closed well before their licenses expire. Exposure to levels of humidity, temperature, and radiation more extreme than expected can result in the thinning, cracking, and rupturing of pipes and the malfunctioning of vital instrumentation. Aging increases the probability that safety systems will fail when subjected to the harsh conditions of an accident.

Inadequate Containment Design. In the event of a major accident at a nuclear plant, releases of radioactivity into the environment are supposed to be prevented by a building called a containment structure. One type, called pressure suppression, uses a pool of water or baskets of ice to condense radioactive steam released in an accident that otherwise might rupture the containment structure. Unfortunately, recent assessments by the Nuclear Regulatory Commission (NRC) indicate that this type of containment may not be up to the task. Shortly after the Chernobyl accident in 1986, a top-ranking NRC official concluded that there was a *90%* chance that the thin steel pressure-suppression containment used on 24 General Electric plants would fail during a major accident, jeopardizing the safety and lives of thousands of citizens. Other kinds of containment are not fail-safe either. A 1987 NRC assessment of three so-called dry containments (thick, reinforced-concrete buildings) concluded: "In general these data indicate that early containment failure cannot be ruled out with high confidence for any of the plants" examined.

Problems at Babcock & Wilcox Plants. Eight nuclear plants are based on the same design as the reactor at Three Mile Island (TMI), the site of the nation's worst nuclear accident. Uniquely sensitive to sudden changes in temperature and pressure, these Babcock & Wilcox–built plants have proved to be extraordinarily difficult to control, as evidenced by the meltdown at TMI and near-misses at the Rancho Seco in Sacramento and the Davis-Besse plant in Toledo. This has raised serious questions about their safety during an emergency shutdown. The NRC's own records have clearly shown that these plants are more dangerous than other pressurized-water reactors, yet many of the agency's recommendations for safety upgrades remain unfulfilled. (In response to its poor performance and safety record, the Rancho Seco plant was closed in 1989 by a citizens referendum.)

Generic Safety Issues. Despite the fact that 110 plants have been licensed to operate, a host of so-called generic safety issues common to many plants throughout the country have never been resolved. Acknowledged by the NRC but tabled for further study, the existence of these issues raises serious questions both about the safety of plants now on-line and the NRC's commitment to protect the public. Among the most serious unknowns are: the capability of safety control systems to survive fires, earthquakes, or hydrogen explosions; the capability of reactor systems to respond to an emergency-shutdown command; the integrity of the steel cladding of reactor vessels; and the extent to which human operators will respond correctly to sudden events or abnormal conditions.

Poor Siting. In order to provide "defense in depth," operators of nuclear plants are required to prepare plans for the emergency evacuation of all people living or working within a 10-mile radius. Unfortunately, several plants (e.g., Indian Point and Shoreham in NY and Seabrook in NH) have been sited within or close to densely populated areas where evacuation of large numbers of people is not feasible. Others have been sited in areas prone to earthquakes. Furthermore, when it has become clear that states and communities have been unable to develop an adequate emergency plan for a poorly sited plant, the NRC sometimes has relaxed its rules in order to allow a plant to be licensed.

Overall, the NRC estimates that there is a 45% chance that a meltdown will occur at a US reactor within the next 20 years. Although not every meltdown would lead to a containment failure putting thousands of lives at risk, some would. Beyond the potential loss of lives, the US General Accounting Office has estimated that the financial consequences could range from $67 million at a small plant in a rural area to $15.5 billion at a large plant in an urban environment.

Nuclear Waste

A typical nuclear power plant generates more than 30 metric tons of high-level radioactive waste annually, much of it in the form of spent nuclear fuel consisting of uranium and plutonium isotopes. Some of the waste will remain hazardous to humans for thousands of years and must be disposed of without leakage to the environment. Exposure to even minute amounts can cause death, cancer, or genetic disorders. About 14,000 metric tons of uranium waste are currently stored on-site in spent-fuel pools at reactors throughout the country. By the year 2000, more than half of these pools will be filled to capacity unless they are expanded, the spent fuel rods are reconfigured, or the material is shipped to other, larger sites.

The Department of Energy (DOE) is investigating a site at Yucca Mountain, NV, for a permanent underground nuclear-waste repository. The examination of this site is mired in controversy and has already cost over $500 million. Because of the geologic conditions there, some scientists have questioned whether the proposed deep-underground facility will be safe. DOE recently announced that the facility cannot be opened until 2010—at the earliest. By that time almost all of the spent-fuel pools at US reactors will be full.

Future Reactor Designs

Nuclear power is often offered as a solution to the greenhouse problem, since nuclear reactors do not emit any carbon dioxide, the principal greenhouse gas, into the atmosphere. Several new reactor designs are under investigation, some of which utilize "passive" safety features to minimize the risk of a major accident. In theory, passive safety features would rely on natural forces or physical principles to keep a reactor from going out of control, rather than on mechanical or electronic measures requiring intervention by human operators.

Although some of these reactors may well prove safer than the current generation, a number of important questions remain unanswered:

- Can critical design elements (such as the fuel pellets in the new MHTGR [modular high-temperature gas-cooled reactor]) be manufactured consistently to the exacting specifications that will ensure safety features work as planned?

- Can and will the designs be "proof tested" to demonstrate that safety features are reliable—before any commercial reactors are granted a construction license?
- Will the quality of construction be any better than in the past?
- Given the track record of the last 30 years, how will the cost of advanced reactors compare with conventional power plants and renewable energy sources?
- Where and how will the additional nuclear wastes generated by new plants be disposed of?
- Which states and communities will be willing to accept the siting of additional waste-disposal facilities or the shipment of wastes across their borders?
- How can the diversion of nuclear waste suitable for use in nuclear weapons be prevented?
- Will the nuclear industry be more willing to accept more stringent regulation and enforcement than it has been in the past?

Unless and until these questions are satisfactorily resolved, it is doubtful that the nuclear industry will be able to regain the confidence of the public. In the meantime, the likelihood that an existing reactor will suffer a catastrophic accident remains unacceptably great.

 Step 3   *Analyze What You Read*

A. Identify Arguments and Supporting Details

In the margin of the article, write *POV* next to where the author presents the point of view. Depending on how you look at it, there are four arguments in this article supporting the author's point of view. Write *Arg. 1* through *Arg. 4* next to where each argument is presented. Then underline the support the author uses for each argument. Use your underlining and marginal notes to fill in the arguments and support:

1. *Argument:* _____

    Support: _____

2. *Argument:* _____

    Support: _____

3. *Argument:* _____

    Support: _____

4. *Argument:* _____

    Support: _____

B. Evaluate Supporting Details

Type of Support. What is the primary type of support the author uses (testimony, reasons, facts, examples)? _____

Provable Versus Unprovable. Evaluate whether each of the following ideas can be proved and whether the author has provided proof in the form of testimony, examples, facts, or reasons. In the first space, write *P* or *U* for provable or unprovable. In the second space, write *Y* if the support has been proved, *N* if it has not.

_____ _____ 1. At this time, the risk of a catastrophic nuclear accident is unacceptably great.

_____ _____ 2. Babcock & Wilcox–built plants are more dangerous than others.

_____ _____ 3. Nuclear power could solve the greenhouse problem.

_____ _____ 4. Safety control systems may not survive fires, earthquakes, or hydrogen explosions.

_____ _____ 5. "Passive" safety features may not be reliable.

_____ _____ 6. Nuclear will never be a really safe form of power.

_____ _____ 7. Scientists have not been able to agree on a solution to the problems of nuclear waste disposal.

_____ _____ 8. Early containment failure is possible in all of the existing nuclear plants.

_____ _____ 9. Critical design elements may not be able to be manufactured consistently to exacting specifications.

_____ _____ 10. The steel pressure-suppression containment used on twenty-four General Electric plants is likely to fail during a major accident.

Inferences. If you believe that the following statements can be validly inferred, write "yes." If the statements are not valid inferences, write "no." If a statement is a valid inference, you should be able to locate the place in the article where it is implied.

_____ 1. Long delays in construction of nuclear plants are the result of regulatory delays and intervention by citizen groups.

_____ 2. Coal power plants require more repair and maintenance than nuclear plants.

_____ 3. Nuclear is one of the cheapest forms of power.

_____ 4. There is no type of containment system that is fail-safe.

_____ 5. The siting of nuclear plants in populated areas is dangerous.

_____ 6. The nuclear industry has resisted regulation and enforcement.

_____ 7. It is easy to find communities willing to accept siting of waste-disposal facilities.

_____ 8. The NRC should take more steps to protect the public.

_____ 9. There is a 45 percent chance that a meltdown will occur at a U.S. reactor within the next twenty years.

_____ 10. We should spend more money exploring renewable forms of energy and less on nuclear power.

C. Make Graphic Organizers

Create a study map showing the relationship between the point of view, the four arguments, and their major support. If you need help, refer to the study maps on pages 81 and 92.

Step 4   Remember What's Important

Review your underlining, marginal notes, and graphic organizer. Continue your review until you feel confident that you understand and remember the information.

Step 5   *Make Use of What You Read*

Your instructor will give you a comprehension check for this article.

Step 6   *Evaluate Your Active Critical Thinking Skills*

After your comprehension check is graded, use the checklist in the appendix to evaluate your skills.

Comparing Views on Nuclear Power

Use the following activities to evaluate your understanding of the nuclear power debate.

1. Summarize each article. Use your underlining, marginal notes, and graphic organizer, making sure to include the point of view, the arguments, and the major support.

2. Evaluate the support for each article.
   a. What type is it?
   b. Is the support provable or unprovable? Has the author provided enough proof?

3. Look at each argument (there are twelve in article 7 and four in article 8). Does each author address the other author's arguments? Are there contradictions?

4. Compare the articles. Do you believe that one author's arguments are stronger than the other's? Why?

5. Go back to the self-questioning survey on pages 95–96. Would you change any of your responses after reading the articles? Summarize your opinions on nuclear power, noting any ways in which your opinion has been affected by your reading.

Issue 5

The Death Penalty

In this section you will read two perspectives on capital punishment. "So What If the Death Penalty Deters?" was written by Steven Goldberg, chairman of the sociology department at the City College of New York. The second article, written by Stephen Nathanson, is taken from his book, "An Eye for an Eye? The Morality of Punishing by Death." Nathanson is a professor of philosophy at Northeastern University in Boston, Massachusetts.

Self-Questioning

Responding to the following questions will help you understand your current views on capital punishment. You will take the same survey to reevaluate your views after you have read the two articles.

Rating Scale

1 Absolutely not

2 Perhaps not

3 No opinion

4 Perhaps

5 Yes

Rate each question from 1 to 5.

_____ 1. Does capital punishment deter crime?

_____ 2. Is capital punishment a better deterrent than life imprisonment without parole?

3. Would you approve of capital punishment if

_____ a. it were proved that it deterred crime?

_____ b. the deterrent effect was not proved, but it was proved that capital punishment costs the taxpayers less than life imprisonment?

_____ c. you had evidence that at least 5 percent of those executed were innocent?

_____ d. it were proved that only the poor are executed in the United States?

_____ e. your religion disapproved of capital punishment?

Reading 9

So What If the Death Penalty Deters?

Vocabulary Preview

empirical (em pir'i k'l) based on experiment or experience

a priori (ā pri ôr'ē) based on theory instead of experience or experimentation

dissuasive (di swā'siv) trying or meant to turn (a person) aside (from a course, etc.) by persuasion or advice

a fortiori (ā fôr'shē ôr'ē) the greater reason; sued in arguing, to introduce a point still stronger than the one already accepted

ad hoc (ad'häk') for this case only

invoke (in vōk') to call on or put to use

pacifist (pas'ə fist) a person who opposes the use of force under any circumstances

viz. (viz) namely

alacrity (ə lak'rə tē) quick willingness; readiness

altruism (al'troo iz'm) unselfish concern for the welfare of others

---

fat, āpe, cär; ten, ēven; is, bīte; gō, hôrn, tool, look; oil, out; up, fʉr; chin, she; thin, then; zh, leisure; ŋ, ring; ə for *a* in *ago;* ' as in *able* (ā'b'l)

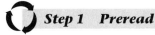 **Step 1   Preread**

Read the title and the first and last paragraphs.

1. What is the subject of the article? _____

2. What is author Steven Goldberg's point of view? _____

3. Take a moment to compare your views about capital punishment with the author's. On a scale of 1 (no way) to 5 (absolutely), how likely are you to agree with Goldberg's point of view? _____

 Step 2   Read

Read the article without underlining. Just try to comprehend the arguments.

So What If the Death Penalty Deters?

Steven Goldberg

D oes the threat of the death penalty deter people from murderous behavior more than the threat of imprisonment for life? We do not yet know with anything even approaching certainty whether the death penalty does or does not deter. The question is clearly empirical; and it is likely that sophisticated statistical techniques will eventually permit us an answer.

Professor Isaac Ehrlich and his colleagues, utilizing his statistical techniques, argue that there can be little doubt about the ability of the death penalty to deter. Ehrlich concludes that each additional execution prevents about seven or eight people from committing murder. All statistical arguments on the death penalty are, however, excruciatingly complex. Some critics, for example, have argued that increased likelihood of execution leads juries to convict fewer people, thereby offsetting the deterrent effect. If anything, the empirical evidence is that the death penalty *does* deter. But this is inevitably open to dispute. As a result, firm conclusions that the death penalty either does or does not deter are unwarranted and usually determined by one's psychological and moral leanings.

In academic and media circles, psychological and moral resistance to the idea of the death penalty usually leads to the assertion that it does not deter. These people's conclusion may or may not be correct, but it does not follow from the arguments they deploy:

1. *Since many murders result from emotional impulse (e.g., the angry husband who kills his wife), the death penalty could have, at best, only the slightest deterrent effect.* If the death penalty deters, it is likely that it does so through society's saying that certain acts are so unacceptable that society will kill someone who commits them. The individual internalizes the association of the act and the penalty throughout his life, constantly increasing his resistance to committing the act. Note that there is no implication here that the potential murderer consciously weighs the alternatives and decides that the crime is worth life in prison, but not death. No serious theory of deterrence claims that such rational calculation of punishment (as opposed to no

rational calculation, or calculation only of the probability of getting caught) plays a role.

Potential Murderers

There is no *a priori* reason for assuming that this process is less relevant to emotional acts than rational acts; most husbands, when angry, slam doors, shout, or sulk. Neither the death penalty nor anything else deterred the husband who did murder his wife, *so the question is not what deterred the person who did murder* (*nothing did*), *but what deterred the person who didn't*. If the death penalty deters, it is, in all likelihood, primarily because it instills a psychological resistance to the act, not because it offers a rational argument against committing the act at the time that the decision is being made. In short, it is only *legislators* who calculate (or at least *should* calculate) the deterrent effect of the death penalty. Potential murderers simply act; the deterrent effect of the death penalty, if there is one, acts upon them. If it acts with sufficient strength, it prevents their becoming murderers. The legislator is the physicist studying the forces that move particles; the potential murderers are the moving particles.

2. *There is no evidence that the death penalty deters.* This is simply untrue. Ehrlich's complex statistical techniques establish a real case that the death penalty deters. But here let us assume, for argument's sake, that there was no such evidence. The more important point is that there is crucial difference between there being *no evidence* that two things are correlated and there being evidence that two things are *not* correlated. The latter means that we have good evidence that the two things are not related; the former means simply that we have no evidence on either side of the case.

Now, it is quite true that we must have some sort of evidence in order to even entertain the idea that two things are related. Our reason for not believing that tall Italian men are smarter than short Italian men is not simply because we have no direct evidence, but also because we have no informal evidence suggesting that this is true—and so we do not bother to even investigate the possibility. It is the lack of relevant informal evidence that permits us to ignore the difference between not having evidence that the hypothesis is true and having evidence that the hypothesis is not true.

But, in the case of penalties, we have an enormous amount of both informal and formal evidence—from everyday experience of socializing children and limiting adult behavior and from such "experiments" as increasing the fees for parking violations—that, as a general rule, the greater a punishment, the fewer people will behave in the punished way. Thus, it is perfectly reasonable to expect that the death penalty would have a more dissuasive effect than would life imprisonment.

Imposing Death on the Innocent

Finally, nearly every popular article and a good many academic articles invoke the experience of the British with public hangings of pickpockets as proof that the death penalty does not deter. The argument sees the fact that pickpocketing continued long after the introduction of (public) hanging as demonstrating that the death has no deterrent effect. It demonstrates no such thing, of course; at best, it demonstrates that not *every* pickpocket was dissuaded, a fact no one would doubt. Even if it could be shown that all practicing pickpockets continued to pick pockets at the same rate, this would still not address the more important question of whether some people who had not yet become pickpockets were dissuaded from doing so by the death penalty. I have no idea whether they were, but neither do those who deny the death penalty's effect.

3. *The death penalty will inevitably be imposed on some innocent people.* This is, of course, true. But it also true that, *if* the death penalty deters, the number of innocent people whose lives are saved will, in all likelihood, dwarf the number of people executed—and *a fortiori,* the number wrongfully executed. Moreover, even the opponent of the death penalty who emphasizes wrongful executions is willing to sacrifice thousands of lives each year for the social advantages of motor vehicles. Realizing this, the opponent differentiates between the death penalty and the use of motor vehicles on the grounds that:

4. *In the case of the death penalty, it is the state that takes a life.* This seems to be an argument but is, in fact, merely a restatement of the basic ad-hoc moral objection to the death penalty. Therefore, it is fair to point out that those basing their opposition to the death penalty on the fact that it is the state that takes a life are, *if* the death penalty deters, maintaining their belief by sacrificing the (innocent) people who will be murdered because the death penalty is not invoked.

5. *The death penalty exchanges "real lives" (those of the executed) for "statistical lives" (those of the people who will not, if the death penalty deters and is invoked, be murdered).* This argument is essentially a sentimental shrinking from reality. But even if one grants this dubious distinction, this defense is available only to the pure pacifist. The most justified military action makes exactly this exchange when it sacrifices many of society's young men in order to avoid a greater loss of life.

6. *If we do not know whether the death penalty deters, we should not use it.* As we have seen, *if* the death penalty deters, it deters the murder of people who are, in addition to being innocent, in all likelihood more numerous than the murderers who are executed. Thus, if society *does* invoke the death penalty on the assumption that the death penalty deters and is incorrect in this assumption, it unnecessarily accepts the deaths of a relatively small number of (nearly always guilty) individuals. On the other hand, if society refuses to invoke the death penalty on the assumption that the death penalty does *not* deter and is incorrect in *this* assumption, then it unnecessarily accepts the deaths of a relatively large number of innocent people. Consideration of this casts doubt on the intuitively plausible claim that, for as long as it is not known whether the death penalty deters, it should not be used. Supporters of the death penalty might turn this argument on its head, *viz.,:* if we do not know for certain that the death penalty does *not* deter, then we are obliged to use it to save an unknown number of innocent lives.

7. *The death penalty is "uncivilized."* If the death penalty deters, then, by definition, it results in a society in which there are fewer murders than there would be if the death penalty were not invoked. The opponent of the death penalty can, of

course, render this fact irrelevant and immunize his argument by detaching it from deterrence altogether; he can assert that the death penalty is wrong *even if it deters.* He can, in other words, see the death penalty as analogous to torture for theft: the threat of torture would no doubt deter some people from theft, but would still be unjustified. This is what is implied in the rejection of the death penalty on the grounds that it is "uncivilized" or that it "increases the climate of violence." Ultimately, these defenses of opposition are as invulnerable to refutation as they are incapable of persuading anyone who does not already accept their assumption that the deterrence of murders would not justify the use of the death penalty.

One might ask, however, what, precisely, are the definitions of "civilization" that see as "more civilized" a society in which *more* (innocent) people are murdered than would be the case if the society did not refuse to use the death penalty. Indeed, one might ask the opponent of the death penalty just how many innocent people he is willing to sacrifice to avoid executing the guilty.

8. *It is those who oppose the death penalty who act out of humane motives.* Motivation is irrelevant to the correctness of an empirical claim. However, since nearly every article on the subject accords to the opponent of the death penalty the right to claim a greater humanity (a right the opponent invokes with alacrity), it is worth noting there are alternative views of the opponent's motivation.

One such view is that the opponent's opposition flows not from feelings of humanity, but from the fact that the opponent can picture the murderer being executed, while he cannot picture the statistical group of innocent people who will be murdered if the death penalty deters but is not employed. The picture of the execution is capable, as the murder of the statistically expected victims is not, of eliciting guilt and fear of aggression with which the opponent cannot deal. He rationalizes his avoidance of these with feelings of humanity which bolster self-esteem and avoid awareness of his true motivation.

No Altruism

It is every bit as reasonable to see this as the opponent's motivation as it is to accept that his opposition flows from his self-proclaimed greater humanity. Like opponents of the death penalty, I too hope that the death penalty does not deter. If this proves to be the case, we will avoid the terrible choice that deterrence forces upon us. Unlike the opponents of the death penalty, however, I do not fool myself into thinking that this hope speaks well of one's character. After all, it is a hope that is willing to sacrifice the possibility of saving innocent people in order to avoid personal psychological pain. This doesn't count as altruism where I come from.

 Step 3   Analyze What You Read

A. Identify Arguments and Supporting Details

In the margin of the article, write *POV* next to where Goldberg presents his point of view. He refutes eight arguments allegedly presented by opponents of the death penalty, and then he presents his own arguments. Write *Arg. 1* through *Arg. 8* next to where each of Goldberg's arguments is presented. Using your marginal notes, write each of the arguments presented by opponents of the death penalty, and then Goldberg's refutation.

Opponents' Arguments	Goldberg's Arguments
1. _____	1. _____
2. _____	2. _____
3. _____	3. _____
4. _____	4. _____
5. _____	5. _____
6. _____	6. _____
7. _____	7. _____
8. _____	8. _____

B. Evaluate Supporting Details

Type of Support. What is the primary type of support Goldberg uses (testimony, reasons, facts, examples)? _____

Logical Reasoning. Go back to the list of arguments and circle the number of the argument you find most convincing. For example, if you find Goldberg's reasoning for argument 1 stronger than the opponents', circle 1 on Goldberg's side. Be prepared to defend your reasons.

Inferences. We can make many inferences from what Steven Goldberg implied in this article. In this exercise, each quotation is followed by two statements. If the statement is a valid inference, write "yes." If it cannot be validly inferred from what the author wrote, write "no."

1. ". . . it is likely that sophisticated statistical techniques will eventually permit us an answer."

    _____ a. The techniques that were used in the past are not sophisticated enough to permit an answer.

    _____ b. Someday we will know definitely whether the death penalty deters.

2. "In academic and media circles, psychological and moral resistance to the idea of the death penalty usually leads to the assertion that the death penalty does not deter."

    _____ a. Academic and media types cannot be relied on to be objective about the death penalty.

    _____ b. People who are not in academia or the media are more likely to use logical arguments.

3. "If the death penalty deters, it is, in all likelihood, primarily because it instills a psychological resistance to the act, not because it offers a ratio-

nal argument against committing the act at the time that the decision is being made."

_____ a. Criminals are less rational than the rest of us.

_____ b. Rational arguments are not important when people are in the grip of emotion.

4. ". . . even the opponent of the death penalty who emphasizes wrongful executions is willing to sacrifice thousands of lives each year for the social advantages of motor vehicles."

_____ a. These opponents of the death penalty are hypocrites.

_____ b. Deaths from motor vehicles are morally similar to deaths from execution.

5. ". . . this defense is available only to the pure pacifist. The most justified military action makes exactly this exchange when it sacrifices many of society's young men in order to avoid a greater loss of life."

_____ a. People who believe that some wars are justified cannot logically oppose execution on the grounds that the death penalty exchanges "real lives" for "statistical lives."

_____ b. Society does not sacrifice women in wars.

C. Make Graphic Organizers

You can use the list of arguments on page 125 as a graphic organizer. Simply add the point of view as a caption.

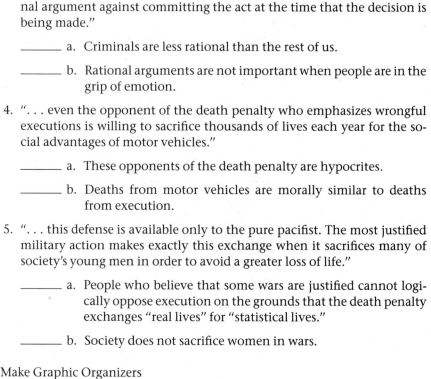

Step 4   Remember What's Important

Review your underlining, marginal notes, and graphic organizer. Continue your review until you feel confident that you understand and remember the information.

Step 5   Make Use of What You Read

Your instructor will give you a comprehension check for this article.

Step 6   Evaluate Your Active Critical Thinking Skills

After your comprehension check is graded, use the checklist in the appendix to evaluate your skills.

Reading 10

An Eye for an Eye: The Morality of Punishing by Death

Vocabulary Preview

advocate (ad'və kit) a person who speaks or writes in support of something

plausibility (plô'zə bil'i tē) credibility

termination (tʉr min ā'shən) the end of something

per capita (pər kap'ə tə) for each person

corroborated (kə räb'ə rāt'id) confirmed

---

fat, āpe, cär; ten, ēven; is, bīte; gō, hôrn, tōōl, look; oil, out; up, fʉr; chin, she; thin, *then*; zh, leisure; ŋ, ring; ə for *a* in *ago;* ' as in *able* (ā'b'l)

Step 1   Preread

Read the title, the first paragraph, the headings, and the last paragraph.

1. What is the subject of the article? _____

2. What is author Stephen Nathanson's point of view? _____

3. Take a moment to compare your beliefs about capital punishment with the Nathanson's. On a scale of 1 (no way) to 5 (absolutely), how likely are you to agree with the author's point of view? _____

Step 2   Read

Read the article without underlining. Just try to comprehend the arguments.

Stephen Nathanson

One of the most powerful arguments made by death penalty supporters is based on the idea that the death penalty is a uniquely effective deterrent against murder. I want to examine the deterrence argument in order to see whether it is consistent with moral principles and whether it is supported by factual evidence.

The Moral Force of Deterrence

We have seen that although killing is generally immoral, there are certain kinds of killings which are justifiable, and one of them is killing in self-defense or in defense of others. Executing a murderer is not itself a case of killing in self-defense, but if death penalty advocates could show that the practice of executing murderers strongly resembles defensive killings in morally relevant ways, that would be an argument for including it on our list of justifiable exceptions. In other words, if there is some property possessed by defensive killings which makes these killings morally right and if executing murderers possesses this same property, then executing murderers would likewise be morally right.

When we compare executions with defensive killings, however, a problem arises immediately. A key factor in our judgment that killing in defense of oneself or others is morally justified is that the victim's life is actually saved by killing the attacker. This crucial factor is missing, however, when the death penalty is inflicted, for the victim is already dead, and the execution of his murderer will not restore him to life. It is hard to imagine that anyone would object to the death penalty if it did restore the victim's life, but we know that it does not have this effect.

Even though the execution of a particular murderer will neither prevent the death of the victim nor restore the victim to life, it might prevent other murders and thus prevent the deaths of other victims. This is the deterrence argument. Though we are powerless to restore life to the dead through executing murderers, we can prevent other murders from occurring by imposing this punishment. The death penalty, on this view, is a kind of social self-defense, an act which, like cases of individual self-defense, results in saving the lives of innocent persons. . . .

The Fear of Death

The common sense argument that death is the best deterrent rests on the belief that people fear death more than they fear anything else. If this is true, then threatening a person with death will have a greater effect on his behavior than any other threat. In particular, the threat of death is more likely to deter a person from committing murder than the threat of long term imprisonment.

Like many of the beliefs expressed in debates about the death penalty, this one has a great deal of surface plausibility, but a bit of reflection shows it to be unfounded. It is simply false that people fear their own deaths more than they fear anything else. This is not to deny that death is a significant evil, for surely it is that. Death is not the loss of one or two things that matter to us. It brings with it the loss of all experience, the termination of all personal plans and hopes, the extinction of all of our potential. Nonetheless, in spite of the genuine loss which typically comes with death, it is not true that death is feared more than anything else. . . .

Indeed, when one begins to think about it, all of us risk our lives on many occasions. Mountain climbers risk their lives for thrill and adventure. Patriots risk their lives for their country. Speeding drivers risk their lives to get to their destinations a bit faster. Airplane passengers risk their lives in order to visit distant parts of the world, see friends, or complete business transactions. Cigarette smokers risk their lives for pleasure, relaxation, or just out of habit. If we all feared death more than anything else, we would engage in none of these activities.

But we don't fear death more than anything else. We are willing to risk death for innumerable reasons, ranging from the lofty and momentous to the vile and trivial. People who commit murder are like the rest of us in this respect. If they very much want to kill someone, they may well be willing to risk their own lives to do so. One might object that when people engage in the activities I have described, they don't expect to die. They may see that there is a risk, but they really don't expect death to result from their actions. If they really expected to die as a result of their actions, they would not engage in them. The lesson to be learned, according to this objection, is that if we could administer the death penalty effectively, then prospective murderers would know that if they choose to kill, their own deaths would result. If the death penalty were properly administered and potential murderers faced the certainty of their own deaths rather than a minimal risk of dying, then they would refrain from killing.

The problem with this objection is that we cannot guarantee that all murderers will be executed. Some will not be found out. Some will be tried but acquitted. Some will be found guilty of lesser charges. Some will have their sentences commuted or reversed on appeal. At best, we can increase the probability that murderers will be executed, but it is mere fantasy to expect that we can make execution certain. The result is that someone who wants to kill will be faced with the *risk* of death and not the certainty of death. There is no way that we can transform this risk into a certainty. Like the rest of us, prospective murderers will often choose to take that risk.

Lesser Punishments

It is worth noting, too, that even if people did fear death more than anything else, that would not establish that death was necessary for deterring people from committing murder. Lesser punishments might be feared enough to have the desired deterrent effect. All of us fear ten years in prison more than one year in prison, but the threat of a one year prison sentence would be quite enough to deter us from parking meter violations. The extra severity is unnecessary for insuring adequate compliance. Likewise, for most of us, the prospect of life imprisonment (or even five or ten years in prison) is so dreadful that increasing the penalty for murder from life imprisonment to death would not provide any additional discouragement. Even if death is more feared than imprisonment, it might be that long-term imprisonment would deter as well as death. The added severity might not save additional lives.

We can see, then, that the deterrence argument based on the "common-sense" belief that people fear death more than anything else fails. It fails because it does not show either that the threat of death is sufficient to deter murders or that it is necessary to deter murders. What is surprising about the argument is that one continues to hear it and that people take it as obvious, in spite of the fact that it is inconsistent with so much of what we know about our own behavior and the behavior of others around us.

Again, none of this should suggest that death is not a great evil for most of us. It is a significant evil, but for a variety of reasons, we frequently do not take seriously the risks involved in our actions, and this results in our not being deterred from acting in ways which make death more likely. . . .

Systematic Studies of Deterrence

In trying to estimate the deterrent force of the death penalty, as compared with other punishments, one might decide to leave behind assumptions about psychological motivation and try to examine instead the actual effects of imposing or not imposing the death penalty. If proponents of the deterrence argument are correct that the death penalty reduces killings and therefore saves lives, then it is reasonable to expect that fewer people will be murdered in areas where the death penalty has been adopted and that more people will be murdered in areas where there is no death penalty. We can test the deterrent argument, then, by seeing whether more murders occur when people face the possibility of life imprisonment as the maximum sentence and whether fewer murders occur when people are threatened with the possibility of execution. . . .

Ehrlich's Analysis

The recent focus of discussion and controversy has been the work of Isaac Ehrlich.

Ehrlich is an economist whose application of techniques of economic analysis to the death penalty problem led him to conclude that each execution might be responsible for the prevention of eight deaths by murder. . . .

Ehrlich's formula represents the homicide rate as a function of several factors: the probability of a murderer being caught, the probability of his being convicted if he is caught, the probability of his being executed if he is convicted, the unemployment rate, the percentage of adults employed, per capita income levels, and the proportion of the population between fourteen and twenty-four years old. Through statistical analysis, Ehrlich thought he could pin down just how much the homicide rate was affected by the probability of execution. He concluded that there was a significant effect—about eight murders were prevented by each execution. . . .

It is clear that if Ehrlich was to succeed in measuring the effect of executions, he needed to identify correctly the main variables that affect the homicide rate and then use statistical techniques to isolate the amount of the effect due to any single variable. His result would not hold if he failed to include variables which significantly affect homicide rates. David Baldus and James Cole argue that Ehrlich did omit important variables, citing such factors as the rate of migration from rural to urban areas, the rate of weapons ownership among the population, and the rate at which violent crimes other than murder were occurring. Since it is plausible to believe that these factors affect the homicide rate and Ehrlich's formula omitted them, his analysis could make it appear that changes in the homicide rate were caused by executions when in fact they resulted from these omitted variables. . . .

In addition, Ehrlich studied the number of executions and homicides for the United States as a whole, rather than focusing on particular states or regions. This means that if there were significant variations among different regions, these would not be revealed by Ehrlich's study. To take an extreme case, if homicide rates had gone down drastically in non–death penalty states and risen sharply in death penalty states, Ehrlich's figures would not reveal this. Both his data and his conclusions deal only with the overall rate for the entire United States. For his results to stand up, they need to be corroborated by studies of smaller units. Peter Passell carried out state-by-state analyses of the relationship between executions and homicide rates, using methods similar to Ehrlich's. Analyzing data on forty-one states in 1950 and forty-four states in 1960, he found no deterrent effects of the sort Ehrlich claimed exists.

A final powerful criticism of Ehrlich's finding is that although his study covers a long period of time, 1932–1970, the apparent deterrent force of the death penalty emerges only as a result of homicide and execution rates after 1962. In other words, if one considers only the period up to 1962, Ehrlich's striking result does not emerge.

One would think that if the death penalty exercised a steady influence on homicides, then there would be no difference if a few years were dropped from the sample, yet this is not so. The omission of the years from 1962 to 1970 has a drastic effect on Ehrlich's result.

Moreover, it is easy to account for the change which occurs after 1962. Starting at that point, the attack on capital punishment in the courts was leading to a radical drop in the number of executions. Likewise, beginning in 1965, there was a tremendous surge in the homicide rate. The result is that murders increased while executions decreased. This set of events in the 1960s is responsible for most of the effect which Ehrlich's analysis purports to find operating through the earlier decades.

Special Deterrence

These criticisms strike me as being quite forceful and, in my judgment, they effectively undermine Ehrlich's alleged vindication of the superior deterrent force of the death penalty. . . .

Before concluding, we should turn briefly to another kind of deterrence argument. The argument we have so far considered involves "general deterrence," the idea that by punishing one person, we discourage others from committing crimes. Some arguments, however, focus on "special deterrence," preventing a person who has already violated the law from committing additional crimes. Sometimes this effect of punishment is called "incapacitation."

According to the special deterrence argument for the death penalty, we ought to execute a person who commits murder because that is the surest way of preventing that person from murdering again.

This argument rests on a proposition that no one would deny: Murderers who have been executed will not commit additional murders. The truth of this statement, however, is not enough to make the argument succeed. As we noted earlier, the analogy with killing in self-defense requires that killing to save lives is justified only if there is no less severe action which would have the same effect. In this case, however, life imprisonment would provide the same protection to society that execution does. It would isolate convicted murderers and thus deprive them of further opportunities to kill innocent citizens. . . .

Conclusions

I believe that there is a basis for a confident rejection of the deterrence thesis, but even the more cautious and limited conclusion that the deterrent effect has not been proved is sufficient for undermining the deterrence argument. The death penalty can be justified as analogous to defensive killing only if it can be shown that it does save lives. Since that has not been shown, one cannot appeal to this protective function as providing a moral basis for executing murderers. Despite the initial moral force of the deterrence argument, its factual presupposition—that the death penalty saves lives—is not sufficiently supported by available evidence. The deterrence argument fails to justify the death penalty.

Step 3   *Analyze What You Read*

A. Identify Arguments and Supporting Details

In the margin of the article, write *POV* next to where Stephen Nathanson presents his point of view. He gives three major arguments supporting his view. Write *Arg. 1* through *Arg. 3* next to where each argument is presented. Then underline the support the author uses for each argument. Use your underlining and marginal notes to fill in the arguments and support:

1. *Argument:* _____

    Support: _____

2. *Argument:* _____

    Support: _____

3. *Argument:* _____

    Support: _____

B. Evaluate Supporting Details

Type of Support. What is the primary type of support Nathanson uses (testimony, reasons, facts, examples)? _____

Logical Reasoning. Examine the reasons given to support the arguments in this article and the previous one by Steven Goldberg. Following each piece of support given by Nathanson, think about whether Goldberg would have an answer. If you can think of an answer, write it on the blank line. If you cannot think of a logical answer, write "no answer."

1. Proponents of the death penalty have failed to show that the threat of death is either sufficient or necessary to deter murders. _____

2. Critics say that Ehrlich's study omitted important variables, that his results were not corroborated by state-by-state analysis, and that the result does not emerge if the years 1962 to 1970 are omitted. _____

3. Life imprisonment would provide the same protection to society as execution does. _____

Inference. Read the following statements. If you can infer the statement from what the author implies, write "yes." If not, write "no." To make the inference, you should be able to find the place in the article where the statement was implied.

_____ 1. If murderers thought they were going to get caught, they would commit fewer murders.

_____ 2. Even if we could prove that the death penalty deterred murder, capital punishment would still be immoral.

_____ 3. There was no significant difference in the number of homicides committed in states that had capital punishment versus states that did not.

_____ 4. The real motive for capital punishment is revenge rather than deterrence.

_____ 5. If we cannot prove a deterrent effect, then capital punishment is immoral.

_____ 6. Nathanson admires people who are willing to risk their lives.

_____ 7. The deterrence argument can never be proved or disproved.

_____ 8. Capital punishment is wrong when there is a lesser punishment that would provide the same deterrence.

_____ 9. Murderers are so desperate that they don't care whether they live or die.

_____ 10. Nathanson believes that most murderers are executed.

C. Make Graphic Organizers

Create a study map showing the relationship between the point of view, the three arguments, and their support.

Step 4   *Remember What's Important*

Review your underlining, marginal notes, and graphic organizer. Continue your review until you feel confident that you understand and remember the information.

Step 5   *Make Use of What You Read*

Your instructor will give you a comprehension check for this article.

Step 6   *Evaluate Your Active Critical Thinking Skills*

After your comprehension check is graded, use the checklist in the appendix to evaluate your skills.

Comparing Views on the Death Penalty

Use the following activities to evaluate your understanding of the capital punishment issue.

1. Summarize each article. Use your underlining, marginal notes, and graphic organizer, making sure to include the point of view, the arguments, and the major supporting details.

2. Evaluate the support for the article.
   a. What type is it?
   b. How logical are the reasons?

3. Look at each argument (there are eight in the first article and three in the second). Does one author address the other author's arguments? Are there contradictions?

4. Compare the articles. Do you believe that one author's arguments are stronger than the other's? Why?

5. Go back to the self-questioning survey on pages 117–118. Would you change any of your responses after reading the articles? Summarize your opinion on the death penalty, noting any ways in which your opinion has been affected by your reading.

Unit Three

Textbook
Reading

An important difference between good students and poor students is the way they study. Poor students use the passive "sponge" method: they read their textbooks, underline, and hope they absorb the significant points. Good students use a study system. A study system helps you actively choose the key ideas that are likely to be on a test and gives you a way to learn these ideas.

Using ACT for Study

Some students have already figured out a study system for themselves, and these students may be earning acceptable or even superior grades. The six-step ACT system offers these students an opportunity to save time and to increase their confidence, because it is a highly efficient study system.[1]

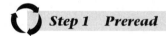 **Step 1   Preread**

Prereading increases your comprehension of what you are about to read because it introduces you to all the major ideas, activates knowledge you already have, and gives you a mental picture, sometimes called a *schema*. Research evidence shows that the mind organizes material by categories, like a library. Knowing the categories in advance increases comprehension and memory, and allows you to read much faster.

Early in the academic term, preview each textbook. First, look at the front matter: the title, author, date of publication, table of contents, and the preface or introduction. Second, look at the back matter: the index, glossary, and appendixes. Then thumb through the book, checking the organization within the chapters. Note whether there are chapter outlines, summaries, review questions, and illustrations. This type of survey gives you an idea of the subjects in the book and the way they are organized. It also lets you know whether there are any study aids.

[1] Based on Francis P. Robinson's SQ3R method in *Effective Study,* 4th ed. (New York: Harper & Row, 1970).

When a chapter is assigned, take a minute or two to preread it. Read the chapter outline, if there is one, the title, and all the headings and subheadings. If there are no subheadings, read the first sentence of each paragraph. Look at the illustrations and try to figure out the main idea of each one. If there is a summary or review questions, read those as well. This prereading will give you a quick overview of all the main ideas and will increase your comprehension, memory, and speed.

Now take a moment to activate your mind. Think about what you already know about the topics you just preread. Think about what you don't know, and what you might find out from your reading. Generate a few questions.

Step 2   Read

If the chapter is long, break it into logical subsections for this step, using the headings or topics as guides. Take the first major section and read *with your pencil down.* Do not underline or highlight. Just try to understand it. If you aren't sure of something, mark it so you can ask your instructor or another student to explain. Instructors do not mind explaining, as long as you are specific about what you don't understand. Another way of comprehending difficult concepts, especially in math or science, is to get another book, or a tape or computer program, that explains the same concept in different words. One way or another, try to understand everything in the section.

Step 3   Analyze What You Read—Create a Study Guide

College testing can be divided into four types: objective, essay, problem solving, and application. Problem-solving tests often occur in mathematics and science courses, and application tests occur when you have to *use* what you've learned, as in foreign languages or music. To be successful, however, there are certain active critical skills you must use regardless of the type of testing.

First, find out whatever you can about the test from the instructor and from other students. The instructor will probably not tell you the questions. However, to guide you through your studying, most instructors will tell you the most important topics that will be covered. They will also tell you the number and type of questions (objective, essay, problem solving, application) and which chapters or other materials the test will cover. You may or may not be able to get other information from students who have already had the class; for example, how hard the tests are and what topics are stressed.

Second, you must predict the questions. This sounds difficult, but it really isn't. Put yourself in the instructor's place. All you (the instructor) really want to know is who knows the material and who doesn't. Most instructors hope the students do well on the test, because that means their teaching was successful.

Review both your text and lecture notes, paying attention to the topics and types of questions stressed by your instructor in the classroom. Let's say the test has fifty objective items (true/false, multiple choice, matching, and completion or short answer) and covers five chapters. The instructor will probably pick the fifty most obvious items. If you (the student) pick the seventy most obvious items, you will very likely get an A. If the test has five essay questions and covers five chapters, and you pick the ten most obvious questions, you should score very well. For problem-solving and application tests, you will need to predict the type of problem or skill that will be required on the test. Like everything else, your skill at predicting questions will improve with practice.

Study Guide for Objective Tests

Look back over the section you just read. Think about what is likely to be on the test, and which of those things you might have trouble remembering. Underline or highlight *only those things*. Do not underline too much. The purpose of underlining is quick review for tests; underlining too much will defeat your purpose.

Marginal Notes. In the margin, next to each thing you have underlined, write a note that you can use to test your memory. Don't write a summary; write something you can use as a question. Look at this example:

	Human cells reproduce in two ways: *mitosis* and *meiosis*. Mitosis is the process by which a cell and its twenty-three pairs of chromosomes splits into two identical cells. Each new cell bears twenty-three iden-
Mitosis	tical pairs of chromosomes. Body cells reproduce this way, so every
vs.	cell in your body has the same genetic structure. Meiosis, however, is
Meiosis	the process by which a cell splits into cells that are not identical. Sex cells reproduce this way, giving rise to cells that do not contain twenty-three *pairs* of chromosomes but instead contain twenty-three *single* chromosomes.

Notice that the marginal notes do not define the terms or discuss the differences between them. They merely let you test your memory.

Flash Cards. Sometimes students don't want to mark in their books, either because the books don't belong to them or because they want to sell them back to the bookstore. In that case, we recommend a variation of the underlining and marginal notes: the use of *flash cards*. On the front of the flash card, write what you *would* have put in the margin (the subject). On the back, write what you would have underlined (the main idea). Here is an example:

Front   Back

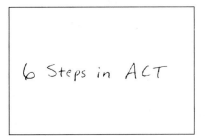

Flash cards have the advantage of being easily carried in a pocket or purse. One secret of successful study is to use small bits of time instead of waiting until you have a few hours free. For example, while you are standing in line at the bank, waiting for a bus, or eating lunch alone, you could be using your flash cards to test yourself on what you believe will be on the test. If you prefer, you could use a loose-leaf notebook with the pages arranged the same way as the flash cards. However, it should be small enough to carry with you.

Study Guide for Essay Tests

Essay questions are broader and more general than objective questions, so you have to look for major ideas rather than details. Remembering for essay tests can be harder than for objective tests, because for most objective questions (true/false, multiple choice, matching), the answer is given and you only have to recognize which one it is. Most essay questions give no clues at all. Researchers find that recognition (for objective tests) is easier than recall (for essay tests).

Graphic Organizers. are used to help you visually organize the materials that you want to remember. You can use either flash cards or paper, depending on the amount of room you need, but if you can carry your graphic organizers with you, you can once again use small bits of time for self-testing. This will leave you relatively free the night before the exam and allow you to keep your mind calm.

Study Guide for Problem-Solving or Application Exams

Try to predict the types of problems or performance that will be tested and make a plan that will provide enough practice so you can reach mastery. For example, if you know that the test will involve square roots, schedule enough time to practice square roots until you are comfortable with them. If the test requires doing the breast stroke, arrange to get enough practice doing the breast stroke.

Some tests require several types of preparation. For example, a Spanish test might require memorization (flash cards) for vocabulary and grammar rules and might also have an application section, as in a test of reading comprehension or of speaking ability. Many classes have both essay and objective questions. Furthermore, some objective questions can contain application or problem-solving items, as in the following examples:

_____ True or False: The product of 7 and 8 is 56.
_____ Write the letter preceding the study map that is correctly organized.

a.   Objective   Problem Solving

Essay

Application   Types of Tests

b.   Types of Tests   Essay

Application

Objective   Problem Solving

c.   Objective   Types of Tests

Problem Solving

Essay   Application

d.   Objective   Essay

Types of Tests

Application   Problem Solving

Learning Style

Throughout your years in school, you probably liked some subjects more than others, and those you liked probably were easier for you. Part of the reason is your learning style, or the way you absorb information. For example, some people understand and appreciate the logic of mathematics and science; others like the creativity of literature or history. Some people find memorization easy, but they hate to write essays. Others enjoy expressing themselves in speech or in writing, but they hate to memorize lists of new terms or mathematical formulas. Some learn best from reading (visual); others from lectures and discussions (auditory).

Just as you have a learning style, each of your instructors has a teaching style. Some prepare well-organized lectures; others come to class without notes and teach through informal class discussion. Some give tests that focus on the facts; others give tests that require you to analyze information and to draw conclusions.

If your learning style matches your instructor's teaching style, you will probably have little problem with the class, as long as you do the work. Problems are more likely to arise when there is a mismatch. One of the best things you can do in that case is to join a study group with students whose learning styles more closely match the instructor's. For example, if you are studying for an exam in history that requires analysis, and you have trouble with analysis, you might join a study group and learn how they predict questions. Then you can make your graphic organizers and memorize. On the other hand, if you have trouble memorizing details, you might try to join a study group that can show you how to predict the questions and memorize them.

The ACT method is systematic and primarily visual, but you can adapt that, too. For example, if you learn from hearing, you can put the topics you want to learn on tapes and listen to them in the car or (with headphones) on the bus.

 Step 4   *Remember What's Important*

This step involves memorizing what is on your study guides for essay and objective tests, or practicing what is on the study guide for problem-solving and application tests.

Remembering

Many students think that remembering involves reading a chapter or at least the underlining over and over, hoping something will stick. A more efficient way to remember is by self-testing. Test yourself the first time immediately after step 3. If you cannot remember the material at this time, you probably won't remember it for the test.

If your study guide consists of underlining and marginal notes, cover the page and use the marginal notes to test your knowledge of what you have underlined. Pay attention to any you miss, and keep self-testing until you get them right.

If you are using flash cards, test yourself on the subject on the front of the card. Put the cards away as you memorize them, so you don't keep retesting what you already know. That way you won't have more than ten or twenty with you at any one time. The night before the exam you should have just a few that still need reviewing. Review them before going to bed, get a good night's sleep, and review them again just before the test.

If you have broken down the chapter into subsections for steps 2, 3, and 4, repeat these steps until you reach the end of the chapter. Then pull the study session together by self-testing on the entire chapter.

When you have finished a chapter, retest yourself on the marginal notes or flash cards for the whole chapter, concentrating on the most difficult, and keep testing until you reach mastery. If you are using graphic organizers, self-test as you would with flash cards. If there are any study questions, answer them. Check your answers by looking back at the chapter. Review again one week later, then review occasionally until the test. The more difficult the chapter, the more frequent the review should be. That way you won't have to cram for the test.

Practicing

If your study guide contains a plan or schedule for practicing for application or problem-solving tests, follow the study guide and keep practicing until you reach mastery.

Step 5   *Make Use of What You Read—Take the Test*

The following suggestions are appropriate for taking all types of tests:

1.   Arrive at the test on time and equipped with pencils, blue books, calculator, or whatever you need.

2.   Look the test over and then look at the clock. Make a schedule designed to maximize your score. For example, if there are fifty multiple-choice questions and you have fifty minutes, make sure you are keeping up. If there are two 25-point essay questions and twenty-five objective questions, make sure you spend half your time on the essays. Allow enough time to review the test before you turn it in.

3.   Answer the easy questions first. Mark those you don't know and come back to them later. Unless there is a penalty for guessing, don't leave anything blank. If there is a penalty, find out what it is and compute when you should guess. If, for example, there are five multiple choices and 25 percent is deducted for wrong answers (as on the SAT), a wild guess has a one-fifth chance of being correct, but one-fourth of a point will be deducted if you are wrong. However, if you can eliminate one of the choices, your chances increase to 25 percent. If you can eliminate two choices, the odds are in your favor.

Essay Tests

In addition to the skills described above, there are some skills that are specific to essay tests:

1. Follow Directions. The topics you learned using your graphic organizers will be converted to actual questions by your instructor. You will have to direct your answers in such a way that they answer the questions that are asked. The following words are frequently used in the directions for essay tests. Review them carefully and be sure you know what they mean so you can do exactly what they say on a test:

List = make a list

Compare = show similarities

Contrast = show differences

Discuss = give an overview

Outline = make an outline

Enumerate = list with numbers

Trace = describe in order

Summarize = write the major ideas in a few words

Diagram = draw an illustration

Criticize = say what's wrong with it

Evaluate = give good and bad points

2. Organize. Before writing an essay, reproduce the outline, map, or other graphic organizer from your study guide. Write the essay from the graphic organizer, and use an introduction, conclusion, and signal words (*first, most important, finally*). If your essay is disorganized, the instructor will think you don't know the answer. If you really don't know the answer, write anything that comes to mind in the hopes that you will pick up a few points.

Application and Problem-Solving Tests

Follow the general directions given earlier. As with essay tests, if you don't know an answer or have not mastered a skill, and if credit is given for partial mastery, do whatever you can in the hopes of picking up a few points.

 Step 6 *Evaluate Your ACT Skills—Analyze Test Results*

When you get your test back, make sure you understand your errors, and then analyze your test-taking skills. Answering the following questions will help you do better next time.

- Did you find out enough about the test? For example, did you study the right chapters, did you prepare for the right number and type of questions (essay, objective)? If not, ask more questions next time.
- Did you predict the right questions? If there were any questions you didn't expect, go back to the book and find out why you didn't anticipate them.

- Did you use appropriate test-taking skills? Did you arrive on time with the right materials? Did you organize your time so you were able to answer all the questions and check them over before turning in the test?
- Did you remember the material you studied? If not, make better use of marginal notes, flash cards, and graphic organizers.
- If there were essay questions, did you follow directions and organize your material before beginning to write?
- If there were problem-solving or application questions, did you practice enough?

At first this system might seem uncomfortable because it is new, but keep trying. By the end of this unit, you will find that your time and effort has been well spent.

Reading 11

Remembering What You Hear

Vocabulary Preview

embed (im bed′) to fix in the mind, memory, etc.

mnemonic (nē män′ik) helping, or meant to help, memory

chronological (krän′ə läj′i kəl) arranged in the order of occurrence

spatial (spā′shəl) happening or existing in space

topical (täp′i k′l) of, using, or arranged under topics, subjects, or headings

---

fat, āpe, cär; ten, ēven; is, bīte; gō, hôrn, tōōl, look; oil, out; up, fur; chin, she; thin, *th*en; zh, leisure; ŋ, ring; ə for *a* in *ago;* ′ as in *able* (ā′b′l)

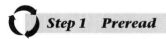 **Step 1   Preread**

Preread the following article by reading all the headings and boldface print. For now, ignore the lines in the margin. Answer the following questions without looking back at the article.

1. What is the subject of the article? (Who or what is the article about?)

    _____

2. What is the main idea of the article? (Note: The main idea is the main thing the author is saying about the subject. If you need to review main idea, go back to Unit I.) _____

    _____

3. Now take a moment to think about what you know about memory, what you don't know, and what you might find out by reading this article. Make up three questions that might be answered by reading it.

a. _____

b. _____

c. _____

Step 2   Read

Read the article without underlining.

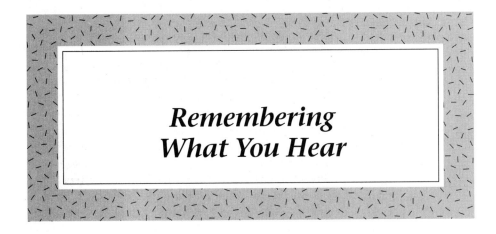

Remembering What You Hear

Rudolph F. Verderber

Too often, people forget almost immediately what they've heard. Have you not found yourself in a situation where you were unable to recall the name of a person to whom you were introduced just moments earlier? On the other hand, ideas and feelings sometimes imprint themselves so deeply in your memory that a lifetime of trying to forget them will not erase the images. For instance, a song may rattle around in your mind for days, or a cutting remark made by a loved one may haunt your mind for years. Remembering requires conscious application of techniques that more firmly embed ideas in your memory. Let's consider four techniques that are likely to work for you: repetition, recognition of patterns, regrouping of material, and note-taking.

1. _____
   _____
   _____

Repetition

Repetition is, of course, the act of saying something more than once. Repeating information two, three, or even four times makes it far more likely that you will remember it at a later date. So, when you are introduced to a stranger named Jack McNeil, if you mentally say, "Jack McNeil, Jack McNeil, Jack McNeil, Jack McNeil," your chances of remembering the name increase dramatically. Likewise, when a person gives you the directions "Go two blocks east, turn left, turn right at the next light, and it's in the next block," your immediate mental repetition, "two blocks east, turn left, turn right at light, next block—that's two blocks east, turn left, turn right at light, next block," increases the likelihood that you will remember.

2. _____
   _____
   _____

Recognition of Patterns

If you can find or create some organizational pattern, you are far more likely to remember the material. One way of organizing information is to use mne-

3. _____
   _____
   _____

4. _____
_____
_____

monic devices to remember lists of items. A **mnemonic device** is any artificial technique used as a memory aid. One of the most common mnemonic devices involves taking the first letters of items you are trying to remember and forming a word. For example, a very easy mnemonic device for remembering the five Great Lakes is HOMES (*Huron, Ontario, Michigan, Erie, Superior*). When you are trying to remember some items in sequence, you can form a sentence that includes the names of the items themselves, or you can assign, in sequence, words that start with the same first letters as the items and form some easy-to-remember statement. For instance, when you first studied music, you may have learned the notes of the scale (EGBDF) by memorizing the saying "*every good boy does fine.*" And for the notes on the treble clef spaces (FACE) you may have memorized the word *face.* A second way of organizing information is to identify a chronological, spatial, or topical relationship among the ideas and then group them accordingly. Directions are best remembered chronologically, descriptions may be remembered spatially, and other kinds of material can be grouped topically.

5. _____
_____
_____

Regrouping of Material

6. _____
_____
_____

If you can regroup long lists of items under two or three headings, you have a better chance of remembering them. Many times, people will express their thoughts as a series of items of equal weight. For instance, when a person is trying to show you what you need to do to complete a wood-working project, the person might tell you to gather the materials, draw a pattern, trace the pattern on wood, cut out the pattern so that the tracing line can still be seen, file to the pattern line, sandpaper edges and surfaces, paint the object, sand lightly, apply a second coat of paint, and varnish. This list includes ten steps of apparently equal weight, and the chances of remembering all ten steps in order are not very good. But if you analyze the ten steps, you will see that you can regroup them under three headings: (1) Plan the job (gather materials, draw a pattern, trace the pattern on wood), (2) cut out the pattern (saw so the tracing line can be seen, file to the pattern line, sand edges and surface), and (3) finish the object (paint, sand lightly, apply a second coat of paint, and varnish). The regrouping appears to add three more steps, but in reality, by turning ten separate steps of apparently equal weight into three steps with three, three, and four subdivisions, respectively, you are much more likely to remember the entire process.

7. _____
_____
_____

8. _____
_____
_____

This technique is effective because it takes into consideration the limitations of most people's abilities to process information. Psychologists who study human memory processes have discovered that most of us can hold a maximum of four to seven bits of information in our active consciousness at one time. Thus, the list of ten steps is too long for us to remember. Instead, we "store" three main points and groups of three to four subpoints, an amount of information that can easily be retained.

Note-Taking

Although note-taking would be inappropriate in most casual interpersonal encounters, it is highly recommended in group discussion and public-speaking settings because it represents a powerful tool for increasing recall of the information you have heard.

What constitutes good notes will vary depending on the situation. Good notes may consist of a brief list of main points and key ideas plus a few of the most significant details. Or good notes may be a short summary of the entire concept (a type of paraphrase) after the message is complete. For lengthy and rather detailed information, however, good notes probably will consist of a brief outline of what the speaker has said, including the overall idea, the main points of the message, and key developmental material. Good notes are not necessarily lengthy; in fact, many excellent lectures can be reduced to a short outline of notes.

Suppose you are listening to a supervisor instruct his or her staff about the importance of clear writing in their reports. In the instructions the supervisor discusses the need to test the readability of the report by computing a fog index. The supervisor might say:

> The brass is really concerned with the quality of the report writing that is coming from the major divisions. The word is that reports just aren't as readable as they should be. In the future every report will be required to include its fog index, including a summary of the figures used for the computation.
>
> A fog index is one of the most common tests of readability. It's an easy one to use and generally reliable. Like most readability tests it is based on computations of sentence length and word length. The theory is that the shorter the sentences and the words, the easier the reading.
>
> Computing a fog index for a report involves six easy steps.
>
> First, select five random sections of at least 100 words each. In a five-page report this would be one passage per page. Begin at the start of a paragraph and count off 100 words, and then continue to count until the end of that sentence. So your passage will have 100 words or more.
>
> Second, compute the average sentence length of each passage. If a 116-word passage has five sentences, then the average sentence length of that passage would be 23.2 words.
>
> Third, compute the number of difficult words per hundred. The beauty of this test is that "difficult" words are easily identified as *any* word of more than two syllables except proper names and verbs that become three syllables by adding *-es, -ed,* or *-ing.* So, if that 116-word passage has 12 difficult words, you would divide 12 by 116. That passage then would have 10.3 difficult words per hundred. For both steps two and three, round off the figures to the nearest whole number.
>
> Fourth, add the average sentence length to the number of difficult words per hundred. In the case of the example you would add 23 and 10.
>
> Fifth, multiply the answer by .4. The result is the fog index. The resulting figure stands for the number of years of schooling required to read the passage *easily.*

9. _____
_____
_____

10. _____
_____
_____

Sixth, because you will have done five passages, you will then compute the average index for the five passages. Write that figure at the end of the report and include computations.

We have been instructed to rewrite reports until we achieve a fog index of between 10 and 13 for each.

This short passage includes a great deal of specific detail, much more than you will find in most instructions. Yet the 397 words of explanation can

11. _____

_____

_____

be outlined in just 134 words (see Figure 1). In good note-taking the number of words used may range from 10 percent of the original material to as high as 30 percent (the amount in our example). The point is not the number of words, however, but the accuracy of the notes in reflecting the sense of what the speaker has said.

Notes

Computing a Fog Index

I. Include a fog Index on future reports
    Fog Index: a readability test based on sentence and word length.
    Short sentences and words, easier reading.

II. Computing involves six steps
    1. Select five random sections, at least 100 words each.
    2. Compute the average sentence length of each.
    3. Compute number of difficult words per hundred.
       Count words three syllables or more.
       Don't count proper names verbs that become three syllables by adding es, ed, or ing.
       Round off
    4. Add two figures
    5. Multiply answer by 4 to get a FI.
       Number of years of schooling required to read the passage easily.
    6. Compute the average for the five passages.
       Write figure at the end of the report with computations.

III. Rewrite reports until FI is between 10 and 13.

Figure 1 *Example of effective note-taking.*

Step 3   *Analyze What You Read—Create a Study Guide*

Objective Questions

Go back to the article and underline what you believe will be on the test and fill in the missing marginal self-test notes. To make this easier, all the self-test notes appear in random order here. Write each note on its correct lines in the article. If you prefer, you may write the self-test note on the front of a flash card, and paraphrase the underlining (the answer) on the back.

How to regroup

When to take notes

2 patterns for organizing info.

4 techniques

% of words in outline

Mnemonic device

Repetition

Reason for effectiveness of grouping

Example of regrouping

What constitutes good notes

Grouping: chronological, spatial, topical

Essay/Application Questions

A. *Predict Essay Questions*

There is only one informational topic that you would need to study for this article, because all other possible questions are part of it. Write the topic here: _____

B. *Predict Application Questions*

The instructor might also ask you to apply some of the techniques in the article to a memorization task. Think of an example of each of the four techniques:

1. Repetition _____

2. Recognition of patterns _____

3. Regrouping of material _____

4. Note-taking _____

C. *Make Graphic Organizers*

1. *Essay:* Prepare for an essay question on the four ways to remember what you hear by filling in the following graphic organizer. Give an example of each method.

Front	Back
4 ways to remember what you hear	1 _____ Ex _____ 2 _____ Ex _____ 3 _____ Ex _____ 4 _____ Ex _____

2. *Application:* Here are the steps for writing a term paper. Regroup them into three groups so you can remember them: (a) think of a topic; (b) go to the library and check the number of books, articles, and reference materials on the topic, noting the number of possible subtopics; (c) decide whether to broaden or narrow the topic; (d) make a final choice of topic; (e) read material and make note cards and bibliography cards; (f) arrange your note cards in order; (g) use the note cards to make an outline; (h) write a rough draft from the outline; (i) edit your rough draft; (j) write a final draft including footnotes and bibliography.

   a. Group 1 _____

   b. Group 2 _____

   c. Group 3 _____

3. *Application:* Make up a sentence that you can use as a mnemonic device for the order of the planets from the sun outward: Mercury, Venus, Earth, Mars, Jupiter, Saturn, Uranus, Neptune, Pluto. _____

_____

Step 4   Remember What's Important

Use the marginal self-test items and the graphic organizers to memorize the material. Keep testing yourself until you know the material. Now look at both the objective and essay/application parts of your study guide. Look for anything you had difficulty memorizing and see whether you can detect a pattern. For example, some people have trouble in classes, such as biology, that often require them to memorize many new terms. Others find it harder to analyze material in order to predict the broader questions that appear on history and English tests.

There are essentially two things you can do to help your memory. First, you can give yourself more repetitions (self-testing sessions) on the items that are hard to remember. Second, you can apply the techniques of regrouping and pattern recognition discussed in article 11 by adapting them to your learning style. Make up a visual or auditory device (i.e., rhymes, mental pictures, word associations, sentences); there are no right or wrong mnemonics. Analyze your memory problems, and try to understand what works for you.

Step 5   *Make Use of What You Read*

Your instructor will give you a mastery test for this article.

Step 6   *Evaluate Your Active Critical Thinking Skills*

After the mastery test is graded, use the checklist in the appendix to evaluate your skills.

Reading 12

Working with Graphs

Vocabulary Preview

functional (funk′shən əl) a mathematical term meaning that changes in one variable are functions of (caused by) changes in the other

variable (ver′ē ə b′l) *Math.* a quantity that may have a number of different values

inverse (in vʉrs′) opposite; as one variable increases the other decreases

ceteris paribus (set′ər is par′ə bəs) all else remaining the same

erratic (i rat′ik) irregular; random; wandering

---

fat, āpe, cär; ten, ēven; is, bīte; gō, hôrn, to͞ol, look; oil, out; up, fʉr; chin, she; thin, *then*; zh, leisure; ŋ, ring; ə for *a* in *ago;* ′ as in *able* (ā′b′l)

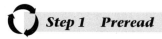 **Step 1   Preread**

Preread the following article by reading all the boldface and italics and examining all the graphs and tables. For now, ignore the lines and notes in the margin. Answer the following questions without looking back at the article.

1. What is the subject of the article? _____

_____

2. What is the main idea of the article? _____

_____

3. Look at table 1 and figures 1 through 7. Without reading the article, explain what an inverse relationship is. _____

_____

4. Look at table 2 and figures 10 and 11. Without reading the article, explain what a time-series graph is. _____

_____

5. Now take a moment to think about graphs. Think about what you know about them, what you don't know, and what you might find out from reading this article. Make up three questions that might be answered by reading the article.

    a. _____

    b. _____

    c. _____

 Step 2   Read

Read the article without underlining.

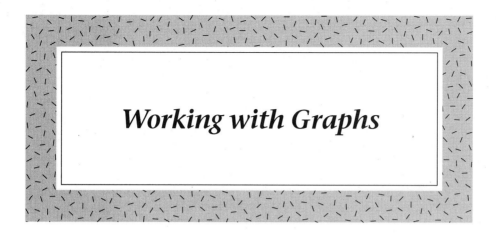

Working with Graphs

Philip C. Starr

Economists often use graphs to illustrate their models. There are many different types of graphs. We will use two of the most common types in this book: functional graphs and time series graphs. Functional graphs show the effect of one variable on another. Sometimes they show opportunity cost; that is, how the decision to buy more of one thing means the loss of something else. Sometimes they show how changes in income or prices cause changes in spending. The term *functional* is taken from the vocabulary of mathematics to convey the idea that changes in one variable are functions of (caused by) changes in the other.

A **functional graph** is a picture of the relationship between two variables. A **variable** is simply a quantity whose numerical value is allowed to change. One variable is shown on the horizontal axis, and the other is shown on the vertical axis (Figure 1).

To take a simple example, suppose you have $20 in your pocket. With it you can buy five $4 movie tickets or ten $2 six-packs of a soft drink. If you buy five movie tickets, you can buy zero six-packs. If you buy four movie tickets ($16), you will have $4 left and can buy two $2 six-packs. We can represent this relationship by a table (Table 1).

Let us graph the relationship by putting the number of movie tickets on the horizontal axis and the number of six-packs on the vertical axis (Figure 2). Note that in each case we start with 0 at the intersection of the horizontal and vertical axes (called the **origin**) and increase the numbers at equal intervals, moving right on the horizontal axis and up on the vertical axis.

Suppose we want to represent the option three movie tickets and four six-packs. We read up from the horizontal axis at 3 to a point opposite 4 on

1. _____
_____
_____

2. _____
_____
_____

3. _____
_____
_____

4. _____
_____
_____

5. _____
_____
_____

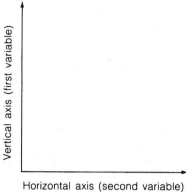

Figure 1 *How economists use graphs to picture relationships between two variables.*

Table 1 *Movie Tickets or Six-Packs?*

No. of $4 Movie Tickets	No. of $2 Six-Packs	Total $ Spent
5	0	$20
4	2	20
3	4	20
2	6	20
1	8	20
0	10	20

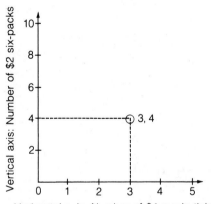

Figure 2 *How to locate a point on a graph.*

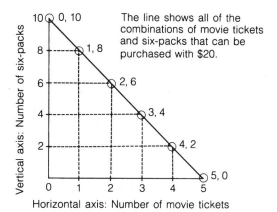

Figure 3 *Example of an inverse relationship.*

the vertical axis, and we find a point that represents the combination of four six-packs and three movie tickets on the graph. If we find all of the points in the table and connect them by a line, we have a graph that slopes downward from the left to the right, as shown in Figure 3. This is called an **inverse relationship** because the more movie tickets we buy the fewer six-packs and vice versa. As one variable increases, the other decreases. (This example also illustrates opportunity cost: Each additional movie ticket costs two six-packs; each additional six-pack costs one-half of a movie ticket.)

Figure 3 shows the combination of six-packs and movie tickets that can be purchased with a fixed amount of money ($20). In this type of graph, the quantities of each item that can be purchased are determined by something that the graph does not show, that is, by a third variable. In this case, that third variable is the amount of money we have to spend. If the amount changes to more or less than $20, the line will shift to the right or left. Consequently, the line as presently shown depends on the *ceteris paribus* assumption: that nothing outside the graph (like the amount of money we have to spend) changes.

To make this point clear, let's show what happens if the amount we can spend increases from $20 to $40. Figure 4 illustrates this increase. (The line shifts to the right. Visualize the line shifting to the left if the amount we can spend becomes less than $20.)

Now let us illustrate a **direct relationship,** one in which as one variable increases so does the other. In this example, the two variables are spending and income. The graph is a functional one because it shows the degree to which spending is a function of changes in income, that is, that changes in income cause changes in spending. Suppose you are taking home $200 a week of your earnings. You spend $180 and save $20. Now

6. _____

_____

_____

7. _____

_____

_____

8. _____

_____

_____

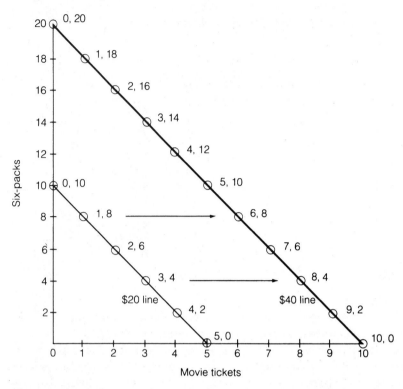

Figure 4 *The combination of six-packs that can be purchased at $20 and $40.*

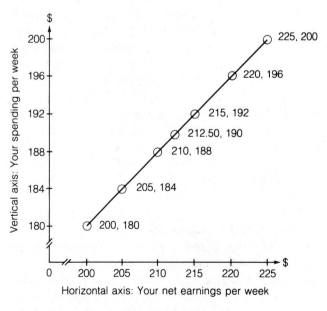

Figure 5 *Example of a direct relationship.*

162

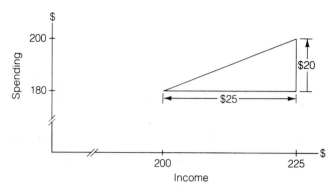

Figure 6 *The slope of the line tells all.*

suppose you get a series of $5 raises—to $205, $210, $215, and so forth. With each $5 raise, you increase your spending $4—to $184, $188, $192, and so on. This time we will cut out the part of the graph from 0 to $200 on the horizontal axis and from 0 to $180 on the vertical axis to save space; the broken lines illustrate this omission. As Figure 5 shows, the line connecting the points now slopes upward from left to right and represents a direct relationship. Graphs are handy to use because with a single line we can represent many points—$200, $180; $205, $184; and so on—and even points in between, $212.50, $190.

Look back at Figure 5 and you'll see how the slope of the line tells what is really going on. The line begins at an income of $200 where spending is $180. As income increases to $225, spending increases to $200. Thus, as income increases by $25, spending increases by $20, another way of saying that with each $5 increase in income, spending increases by $4. Figure 6 will help you see this.

Because the line shows a spending increase of $20 for every income increase of $25, we have a 20/25 = 4/5 = .8 = 80 percent slope. Finally, we can say that for any increase in income, you increase your spending by 80 percent of that increase in income (and save the other 20 percent).

Even when we don't know the exact numbers, a graph can instantly show us what the relationship is between two variables. For example, look at the graph shown in Figure 7.

Functional graphs can also tell us the extent of the effect of one variable   **9.** _____
on another. Let's consider the response of buyers to price changes for boxes   _____
of toothpicks: _____

Price per Box	Quantities an Average Family Will Buy Every 6 Months
10¢	2
15¢	2

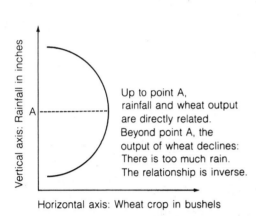

Figure 7 *A changing relationship between two variables.*

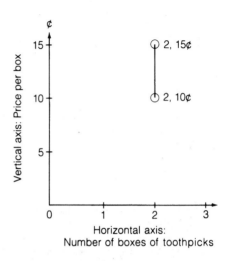

Figure 8 *When the line is straight up and down, changes in the vertical axis variable have no effect on the horizontal axis variable.*

The graph would look like Figure 8.

Suppose, however, we change the quantities as follows:

Price per Box	Quantities Purchased
10¢	5
15¢	2

The graph would then look like Figure 9. In other words, as the line becomes more horizontal, changes on the vertical axis variable cause larger changes on the horizontal axis variable. The slope of the line tells us as much as the direction of the line.

10. _____
_____
_____

   Time series graphs are also two-variable graphs, but one variable is always some measure of time such as weeks, months, or years. These graphs are very useful for displaying historical data to show what has happened in the past and to enable us to guess about the future. Time series information can be shown in various ways. To illustrate, we'll pretend that we own and operate a small company that makes a product called Invigorol. Invigorol is designed to be sold to the ever-growing over-65 population. It comes in 12-ounce bottles, 24 to a case. The contents are highly secret as far as the public is concerned, but *we* know that the major ingredient is water, followed by sugar, caffeine, a massive dose of vitamins, and, most important, 15 percent alcohol. Many people enjoy the tonic effect of Invigorol and begin the day with a refreshing glass of it.

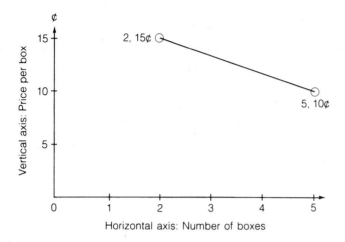

Figure 9 *A small change on the vertical axis produces a large change on the horizontal axis.*

But, in 1987 we notice that sales are erratic. During the months of February through June in our sample city, sales (in 24-bottle cases) are 105 in February, 95 in March, 102 in April, 98 in May, and 110 in June. One way of displaying this information is shown in Table 2. This information can also be displayed in a graph (Figure 10).

As you can see, Figure 10 takes up a great deal of unnecessary space because there are no sales below 95 cases. The customary way to get rid of the unneeded space is shown in Figure 11. Figure 11 presents the same information that Table 2 and Figure 10 do but in a more efficient form. A broken line on the vertical axis solves the problem as it does in Figure 5.

Suppose that we know from other marketing surveys that the average quantity sold for each of these months is 100 cases. We want to show variations from this average. As you can guess, we're using the number 100 to make it easy to show percentage variations. February is 5 percent above the average; March is 5 percent below; April is 2 percent above; May is

Table 2 *Invigorol Sales, February to June, 1987*

Months	Cases Sold
February	105
March	95
April	102
May	98
June	110

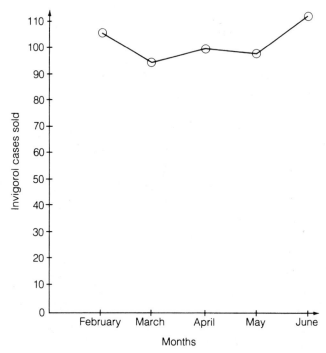

Figure 10 *Invigorol sales during the months February to June.*

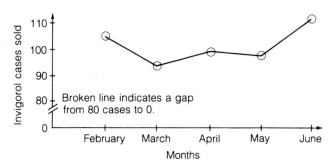

Figure 11 *Invigorol sales during the months February to June.*

2 percent below; and June is 10 percent above. We can easily show these variations, as in Figure 12.

Finally, we can show the percentage increase or decrease of the sales in each month relative to that of the previous month. (We can't do February because we don't have January figures.) Thus, March is 9.5 percent below February (the 10 case drop divided by February sales of 105, $10 \div 105 = 0.5$ percent). The April sales figure is 7/95, or 7.4 percent above March. The May sales figure is 4/102, or 3.9 percent below April. June sales are 12/98, or 12.2 percent above May. Figure 13 illustrates these changes.

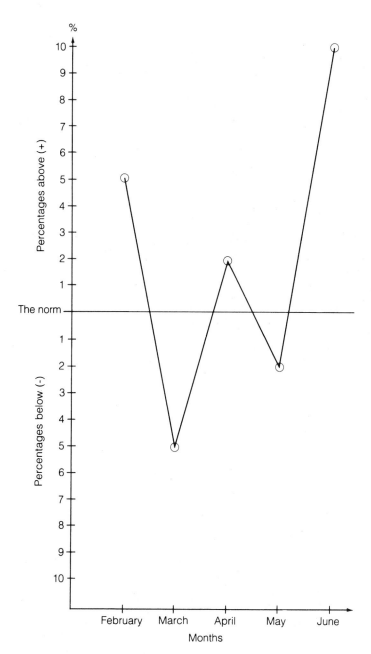

Figure 12 *Invigorol sales during the months February to June, 1987; each month's percentage variation from the norm (average) in 1987.*

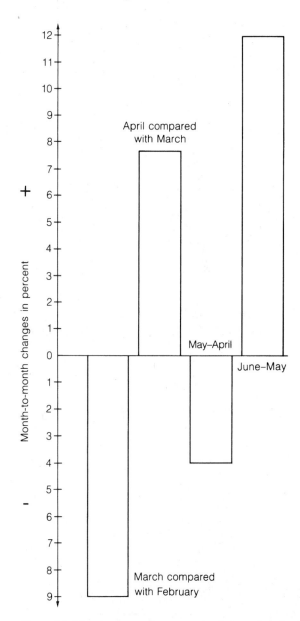

Figure 13 *Month-to-month percentage changes in sales, February to June, 1987.*

11. _____

_____

_____

Figure 13 is a bar chart, a very common type of graph. Typically, cost-of-living changes are shown in bar charts if the purpose is to show how fast prices are rising. Sometimes, bar charts are also used to show year-to-year percentage changes in a nation's total output.

We hope this brief explanation has made you feel more comfortable with graphs. Remember that they are just pictures designed to show the effect of one variable on another—like the effect of caloric intake on weight or the effect of prices on the quantities of things people will buy or sell.

Step 3   *Analyze What You Read—Create a Study Guide*

Objective Questions

Go back and underline what you believe will be asked on a test. Then fill in the missing marginal notes to test your memory of what you have underlined. To make this easier, the self-test notes are written in random order here. Write each note on its correct lines in the article. If you prefer not to mark in your book, you may put the self-test note on the front of a flash card, and the main idea—what you have underlined—on the back.

Variable	Functional graphs
Direct relationship	Inverse relationship
Use for functional graphs	Types of graphs
Opportunity cost	Origin
Ceteris paribus	Time-series graphs
Bar chart	

Essay/Application Questions

A. *Predict Essay Questions*

Two topics would be likely to appear on a test. They are

1. _____

2. _____

B. *Predict Application Questions*

The instructor would probably ask application questions concerning these topics. Think of some variables that would require each of the following graphs.

1. Time-series graph _____

2. Inverse relationship _____

3. Direct relationship _____

4. Bar chart _____

C. *Make a Graphic Organizer*

Prepare for an application question concerning graphs by choosing variables from the following list to answer the four questions. You may use a variable more than once, and you may create your own data.

Variables

The effect of increased earnings on savings
The effect of increased cost-of-living on savings
Monthly changes in the Consumer Price Index

Questions

1. Draw a time-series graph.
2. Graph an inverse relationship.
3. Graph a direct relationship.
4. Draw a bar chart.

Step 4   *Remember What's Important*

Use the marginal notes and your graphs for self-testing. Keep testing yourself until you know the material.

Step 5   *Make Use of What You Read*

Your instructor will give you a mastery test for this article.

Step 6   *Evaluate Your Active Critical Thinking Skills*

After the mastery test is graded, use the checklist in the appendix to evaluate your skills.

Reading 13

The Venusian Greenhouse

Vocabulary Preview

infrared (in'frə red') designating or of those invisible rays just beyond the red end of the visible spectrum; their waves are longer than those of the spectrum colors but shorter than radio waves, and have a penetrating heating effect; used in cooking, photography, etc.

photon (fō'tän) a quantum of electromagnetic energy having both particle and wave behavior; it has no charge or mass but possesses momentum; the energy of light, X-rays, gamma rays, etc., is carried by photons

sediment (sed'ə mənt) matter deposited by water or wind

fossil fuel (fäs''l fyo͞ol) coal, petroleum, and natural gas

inundate (in'ən dāt') to flood

---

fat, āpe, cär; ten, ēven; is, bīte; gō, hôrn, to͞ol, look; oil, out; up, fʉr; chin, she; thin, *then*; zh, leisure; ŋ, ring; ə for *a* in *ago;* ' as in *able* (ā'b'l)

 Step 1   Preread

Preread the following article by reading the title, examining the pictures, and reading their captions and the first sentence of every paragraph. For now, ignore the lines in the margin. Answer the following questions without looking back at the article.

1.   What is the subject of the article? _____

_____

2. What is the main idea of the article? _____

_____

3. Look at figure 1. Without reading the article, explain in your own words the greenhouse effect on Venus. _____

_____

4. Now take a moment to think about the greenhouse effect. Think about what you know about it, what you don't know, and what you might find out from reading this article. Make up three questions that this article might answer.

a. _____

b. _____

c. _____

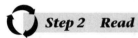 *Step 2   Read*

Read the article without underlining.

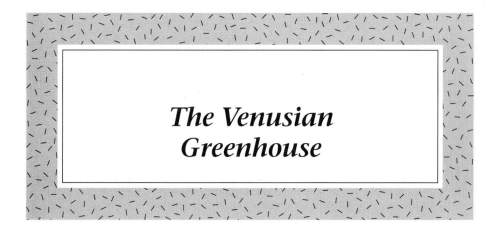

The Venusian Greenhouse

Michael A. Seeds

A carbon dioxide atmosphere can trap heat by a process called the **greenhouse effect.** When sunlight shines through the glass roof of a greenhouse, it heats the benches and plants inside (Figure 1a). The warmed interior radiates heat in the form of infrared radiation, but the infrared photons cannot get out through the glass. Heat is trapped within the greenhouse, and the temperature climbs until the glass itself grows warm enough to radiate heat away as fast as the sunlight enters.* In the case of a planet, carbon dioxide in the atmosphere admits sunlight and the surface grows warm. However, carbon dioxide is not transparent to infrared radiation, so heat is trapped, and the planet's surface temperature rises.

Venus was caught in a runaway greenhouse effect (Figure 1b). The rising temperature baked more carbon dioxide out of the surface, and the atmosphere became even less transparent to infrared, which forced the temperature even higher. The surface is now so hot even chlorine and fluorine have baked out of the rock and formed hydrochloric acid and hydrofluoric acid vapor.

Earth avoided this runaway greenhouse effect because it was farther from the sun and cooler. Thus, it could form and preserve liquid-water oceans to absorb the carbon dioxide, which left a nitrogen atmosphere that was relatively transparent in some parts of the infrared. If all the carbon dioxide in Earth's sediments were put back into the atmosphere, our air would be as dense as that of Venus.

This points out the risk we run by burning fossil fuels and adding carbon dioxide to Earth's air. Since the late 1950s, the Scripps Institution of Ocean-

1. _____
_____
_____

2. _____
_____
_____

3. _____
_____
_____

4. _____
_____
_____

*A greenhouse also grows warm because the walls prevent the warm air from mixing with the cooler air outside.

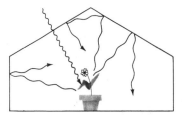

Figure 1a *The greenhouse effect. Short-wavelength light can enter a greenhouse and heat its contents, but the longer-wavelength infrared cannot get out.*

Figure 1b *The same process heats Venus because its atmosphere of CO_2 is not transparent to infrared. Because we are burning fossil fuels, we are increasing the abundance of CO_2 in Earth's atmosphere.*

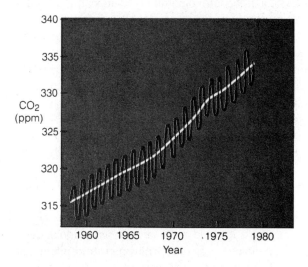

Figure 1c *The wavy line shows the seasonal variation caused by photosynthesis; the smoother line is the averaged trend.*

ography has monitored the abundance of carbon dioxide in Earth's atmosphere at the peak of Mauna Loa in Hawaii and at the South Pole. At both places, the abundance of carbon dioxide has been increasing year after year

(Figure 1c). Our burning coal, oil, and natural gas has added at least 40 gigatons (40 × 10⁹ tons) of carbon to the atmosphere in 20 years.

This rise in carbon dioxide is increasing the greenhouse effect on Earth and is believed to be causing a slight warming of our climate. One study has found a 0.7°C increase in the average temperature since 1861. In addition to the danger of reducing agriculture's ability to feed the 5 billion people on Earth, we should be concerned about melting part of the ice caps. That would raise the sea level and inundate low-lying regions. A rise of only 1 m would be disastrous to many ocean-side cities. Although it is unlikely that we will soon trigger a runaway greenhouse effect on Earth, we may have already added enough carbon dioxide to the atmosphere to change our climate for the next century.

5. _____
_____
_____

6. _____
_____
_____

 Step 3   Analyze What You Read—Create a Study Guide

Objective Questions

When you finish reading, go back and underline what you believe will appear on a test. Then fill in the marginal self-test items. We have not written out the topics for you for this article, but we have left blank lines. You will have to figure out the note for each line. If you prefer, you may use flash cards instead. Write the self-test item (the subject) on the front, and what you have underlined (the main idea) on the back.

Essay/Application Questions

A. *Predict Questions*

One major topic would be likely to appear on an essay or application test.

It is _____

B. *Make Graphic Organizers:*

Prepare for application questions by drawing diagrams to show

1. how a greenhouse traps heat,
2. why Venus is so hot, and
3. how burning fossil fuel adds to the greenhouse effect.

 Step 4   Remember What's Important

Use the self-test items and graphic organizers to memorize the material. Use mnemonic devices as needed. Repeat the self-testing until you know the material.

Step 5   *Make Use of What You Read*

Your instructor will give you a mastery test for this article.

 Step 6   *Evaluate Your Active Critical Thinking Skills*

After the mastery test is graded, use the checklist in the appendix to evaluate your skills.

Reading 14

Early Numeration Systems

Vocabulary Preview

symbolic (sim bäl′ik) of or expressed in a symbol or symbols (a symbol is something that stands for, represents, or suggests something else)

analogous (ə nal′ə gəs) similar or comparable in certain respects

dynasty (dī′nəs tē) 1. a series of rulers who are members of the same family 2. the period during which a certain family reigns

succession (sək sesh′ən) a number of persons or things coming one after another in time or space; series; sequence *succession* of delays

abacus (ab′ə kəs) frame with beads or balls sliding back and forth on wires or in slots, for doing or teaching arithmetic

cuneiform (kyo͞o nē′ə fôrm′) wedge-shaped; esp., designating the characters used in ancient Akkadian, Assyrian, Babylonian, and Persian inscriptions.

algorism (al′gər iz′m) the Arabic system of numerals; decimal system of counting

status quo (stat′əs kwō) the existing state of affairs (at a particular time)

theology (the äl′ə jē) the study of God and the relations between God and the universe; study of religious doctrines and matters of divinity

inherent (in hir′ənt) existing in something as a natural quality or characteristic; basic

fat, āpe, cär; ten, ēven; is, bīte; gō, hôrn, to͞ol, look; oil, out; up, fʉr; chin, she; thin, *then*; zh, leisure; ŋ, ring; ə for *a* in *ago;* ′ as in *able* (ā′b′l)

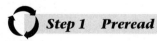

Step 1   *Preread*

Preread the following article by reading the headings, examining the illustrations, and reading the first sentence of each paragraph. Answer the following questions without looking back at the article.

1. What is the subject of the article? _____

    _____

2. What is the main idea of the article? _____

    _____

3. Look at tables 1 and 2. Without reading the article, compare the symbols

    used by the Egyptians and the Babylonians. _____

    _____

4. Take a moment to think about the origin of numbers. Think about what you
    know, what you don't know, and what you might find out from reading this
    article. Make up three questions that might be answered by reading the
    article.

    a. _____

    b. _____

    c. _____

Step 2   *Read*

Read the article without underlining.

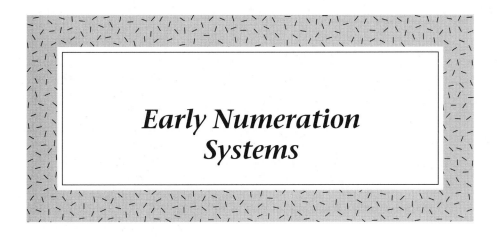

Early Numeration Systems

Karl J. Smith

A numeration system is a set of basic symbols and some rules for making other symbols from them, the purpose of the whole game being the identification of numbers. The invention of a precise and "workable" system is one of the greatest inventions of humanity. It is certainly equal to the invention of the alphabet, which enabled humans to carry the knowledge of one generation to the next. It is simple for us to use the symbol 17 to represent this many objects:

■■■■■ ■■■■■
■■■■■ ■■

However, it took us centuries to arrive at this stage of symbolic representation. It wasn't the first and probably won't be the last numeration system to be developed. Here are some of the ways that 17 has been written:

Tally   卌 卌 卌 ||
Egyptian   ∩||||||
Roman   **XVII**
Mayan   ≡̇
Linguistic   seventeen
            siebzehn
            dix-sept

The concept represented by each of these symbols is the same, but the symbols differ. The concept or idea of "seventeenness" is called a *number;*

the symbol used to represent the concept is called a *numeral.* The difference between *number* and *numeral* is analogous to the difference between a person and his or her name.

Two of the earliest civilizations known to use numerals were the Egyptian and Babylonian. We shall examine these systems for two reasons. First, it will help us more fully to understand our own numeration (decimal) system; second, it will help us to see how the ideas of these other systems have been incorporated into our system.

The Egyptian Numeration System

Perhaps the earliest type of written numeration system developed was that of a *simple grouping system.* The Egyptians used such a system by the time of the first dynasty, around 2850 B.C. The symbols of the Egyptian system were part of their hieroglyphics and are shown in Table 1.

Table 1 *Egyptian Hieroglyphic Numerals*

Our numeral (decimal)	Egyptian numeral	Descriptive name
1			Stroke
10	∩	Heel bone
100	9	Scroll
1,000	ℒ	Lotus flower
10,000	⌒	Pointing finger
100,000	⌐	Polliwog
1,000,000	☒	Astonished man

Any number is expressed by using these symbols additively; each symbol is repeated the required number of times, but with no more than nine repetitions.

$$12,345 = \mathcal{C\,\mathcal{L}\,\mathcal{L}\,}{}^{99\cap\cap}_{9\ \cap\cap}{}_{|||||}$$

The position of the individual symbols is not important. That is,

$$\mathcal{C\,\mathcal{L}\,\mathcal{L}\,}{}^{99\cap\cap}_{9\ \cap\cap}{}_{|||||} = \mathcal{L\,\mathcal{L}\,}{}^{99}_{9}\,\mathcal{C}{}^{\cap\cap}_{\cap\cap}{}_{|||||}$$

$$= |||||\mathcal{C}\,\mathcal{L}\,{}^{99}_{\cap\cap\cap\cap}\mathcal{L}\,9$$

The Egyptians had a simple repetitive-type arithmetic. Addition and subtraction were performed by repeating the symbols and by regrouping:

Examples:

1. 245

+ 457

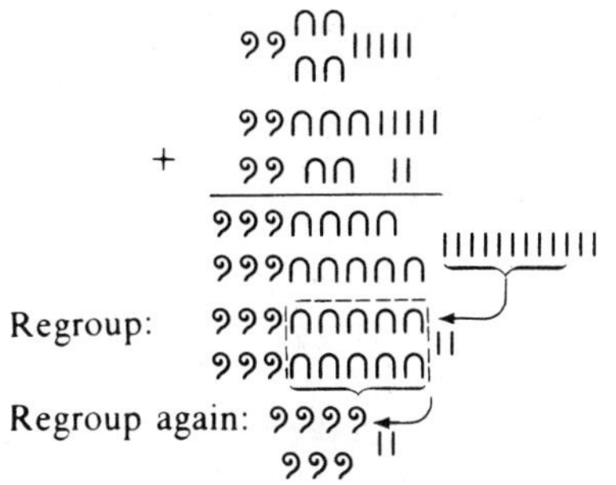

2. 142

− 67

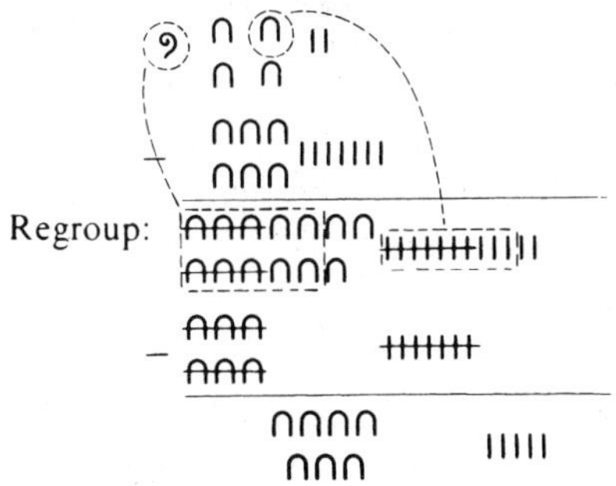

Multiplication and division were performed by successions of additions that did not require the memorization of a multiplication table and could easily be done on an abacus-type device.

The Egyptians also used unit fractions ($1/n$) in their computations. These were indicated by placing the symbol 𓂋 over the numeral for the denominator. Thus,

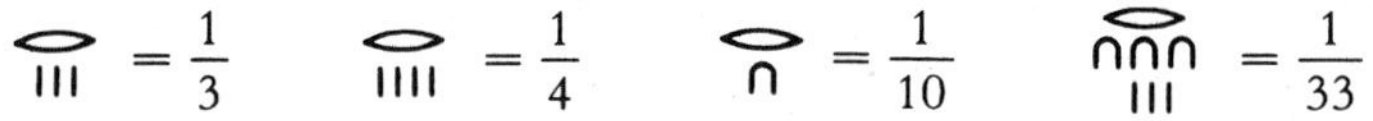

The Babylonian Numeration System

The Babylonian numeration system differed from the Egyptians in several respects. Whereas the Egyptian system was a simple grouping system, the Babylonians employed a much more useful *positional system.* Since they lacked papyrus, they used mostly clay as a writing medium, and thus the Babylonian cuneiform was much less pictorial than the Egyptian system. They employed only two wedge-shaped characters, which date from 2000 B.C. and are shown in Table 2.

Notice from the table that, for numbers 1 through 59, the system is repetitive. However, unlike in the Egyptian system, the position of the symbols was important. The 𒌋 *must* appear to the left of any 𒁹 to represent numbers smaller than 60. For numbers larger than 60, the symbols 𒌋 and 𒁹 are

Table 2 *Babylonian Cuneiform Numerals*

Our numeral (decimal)	Babylonian numeral
1	▼
2	▼▼
9	▼▼▼▼▼▼▼▼▼
10	◁
59	◁◁◁▼▼▼▼▼ ◁◁ ▼▼▼▼

to the left of ◁, and any symbols to the left of the ◁ have a value 60 times their original value. That is,

◁◁▼▼▼ ◁ ▼▼   means $(1 \times 60) + 35$.

1. ▼▼▼◁ ◁◁▼▼▼ ▼▼▼ ◁◁▼▼▼ $= (3 \times 60) + 59 = 239$

2. ▼▼▼ ▼▼ ◁▼ $= (5 \times 60) + 11 = 311$

3. ◁◁▼▼▼◁▼▼▼ $= (23 \times 60) + 16 = 1396$

This system is called a *sexagesimal system* and uses the principle of position. However, the system is not fully positional, since only numbers larger than 60 use the position principle; numbers within each basic 60-group are written by a simple grouping system. A true positional sexagesimal system would require 60 different symbols.

The Babylonians carried their positional system a step further. If any numbers were to the left of the second 60-group, they had the value 60×60 or 60^2. Thus,

▼▼ ◁◁▼▼▼ ◁◁ ▼▼ ◁◁▼▼ $= (2 \times 60^2) + (45 \times 60) + 24$
$= 7200 + 2700 + 24$
$= 9924$

The Babylonians also made use of a subtractive symbol, $\ulcorner$. That is, 38 could be written

◁◁◁▼▼▼▼ ▼▼▼▼   or   ◁◁◁▼▼ ◁

Although this positional numeration system was in many ways superior to the Egyptian system, it suffered from the lack of a zero or placeholder symbol. For example, how is the number 60 represented? Does ▼▼ mean 2 or 61? (Scholars tell us that such ambiguity can be resolved only by a careful study of the context.) However, in later Babylonia, around 300 B.C., records show that there is a zero symbol, ⋞, and this idea was later used by the Hindus.

Arithmetic with the Babylonian numerals is quite simple, since there are only two symbols. A study of the Babylonian arithmetic will be left for the student.

Hindu-Arabic Numeration System

The numeration system in common use today has ten symbols, the digits 0, 1, 2, 3, 4, 5, 6, 7, 8, and 9. The selection of ten digits was no doubt a result of our having ten fingers (digits).

The symbols originated in India in about 300 B.C. However, because the early specimens do not contain a zero or use a positional system, this numeration system offered no advantage over other systems then in use in India.

The date of the invention of the zero symbol is not known. The symbol did not originate in India but probably came from the late Babylonian period via the Greek world.

By the year 750 A.D. the zero symbol and the idea of a positional system had been brought to Baghdad and translated into Arabic. We are not certain how these numerals were introduced into Europe, but they likely came via Spain in the 8th century. Gerbert, who later became Pope Sylvester II, studied in Spain and was the first European scholar known to have taught these numerals. Because of their origins, these numerals are called *Hindu-Arabic numerals.* Since ten basic symbols are used, the Hindu-Arabic numeration system is also called the *decimal numeration system,* from the Latin word *decem,* meaning "ten."

Although we now know that the decimal system is very efficient, its introduction met with considerable controversy. Two opposing factions, the "algorists" and the "abacists," arose. Those favoring the Hindu-Arabic system were called algorists, since the symbols were introduced into Europe in a book called (in Latin) *Liber Algorismi de Numero Indorum,* by the Arab mathematician Al-Khwarizmi. The word *algorismi* is the origin of our word *algorism.* The abacists favored the status quo—using Roman numerals and doing arithmetic on an abacus. The battle between the abacists and the algorists lasted for 400 years. The Roman church exerted great influence in commerce, science, and theology. Roman numerals were easy to write and learn, and addition and subtraction with them were easier than with the "new" Hindu-Arabic "heathen" numerals. It seems incredible that our decimal system has been in general use only since about the year 1500.

Let's examine the Hindu-Arabic or decimal numeration system a little more closely.

1. It uses 10 symbols, called digits: 0, 1, 2, 3, 4, 5, 6, 7, 8, and 9.
2. Larger numbers are expressed in powers of 10.
3. It is positional.
4. It is additive.

Now let's review how we count objects.

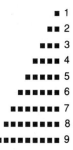

At this point we could invent another symbol, as the Egyptians did, or we could reuse the digit symbols by repeating them or by altering their position. That is, 10 will mean 1 group of ▪▪▪▪▪▪▪▪▪▪. The symbol 0 was invented as a placeholder to show that the 1 here is in a different position from the 1 representing the ▪.

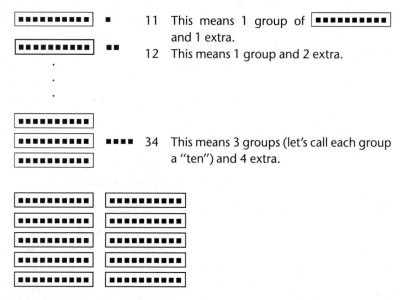

In the last instance we have a group of groups, or ten groups (or ten-tens, if you like). Let's call this group of groups a "10 · 10" or "10^2" or a "hundred." We again use position and repeat the symbol 1 with a still different meaning: 100.

Thus, what does 134 represent? It means we have the following:

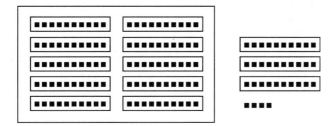

We could denote this more simply by writing:

$$(1 \times 10^2) + (3 \times 10) + 4$$

These represent the name of the group.
These represent the number of groups.

This leads us to the name,

"one hundred, three tens, four ones,

which is read "one hundred thirty-four." A number written in this fashion is in *expanded notation.* As we pointed out earlier, mathematicians often look for patterns; so we notice that the expanded notation for 31,452 suggests a pattern:

$$(3 \times 10^4) + (1 \times 10^3) + (4 \times 10^2) + (5 \times 10) + 2$$

We write $10 = 10^1$ and $1 = 10^0$. Recall that we defined $10^0 = 1$. Then the pattern is complete:

$$(3 \times 10^4) + (1 \times 10^3) + (4 \times 10^2) + (5 \times 10^1) + (2 \times 10^0)$$

A period, called a *decimal point* in the decimal system, is used to separate the fractional parts from the whole parts.

For example,

$1/10 = 10^{-1}$
$1/100 = 10^{-2}$
$1/1000 = 10^{-3}$, since $10^{-3} = 1/10^3 = 1/10 \cdot 10 \cdot 10 = 1/1000$

Recall that 10 is called the *base.* Notice the pattern of the exponents on the base.

We often fail to see all the great ideas that are incorporated into this system, and it is difficult to understand the problems inherent in developing a numeration system.

Step 3   *Analyze What You Read—Create a Study Guide*

Objective Questions

Go back and underline what you believe will be on a test. Then write marginal notes to test yourself on what you have underlined. If you prefer, you may use flash cards instead of underlining. Put the marginal note (subject) on the front and the underlining (main idea) on the back.

Essay/Application Questions

A. *Predict Questions*

There is one broad topic that encompasses three subtopics. Write them below:

1. Major topic _____

    a. Subtopic 1 _____

    b. Subtopic 2 _____

    c. Subtopic 3 _____

B. *Create Graphic Organizers*

1. Following is a time line. Label it with the major milestones in the development of numeration systems.

_____

2850 B.C.   2000 B.C.   300 B.C.   750 A.D.   1500 A.D.

2. Describe and give an example of how a grouping versus a positional system would handle the following operations:

	Grouping	Positional
Addition		
Subtraction		

3. Fill in the following study map with the four main features of the decimal numeration system.

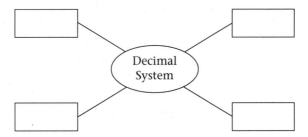

 Step 4 **Remember What's Important**

Use your marginal notes and graphs for self-testing. Use mnemonic devices as needed. Keep testing yourself until you know the material.

Step 5 **Make Use of What You Read**

Your instructor will give you a mastery test for this article.

Step 6 **Evaluate Your Active Critical Thinking Skills**

After the mastery test is graded, use the checklist in the appendix to evaluate your skills.

Reading 15

Human Population Growth

Vocabulary Preview

monumental (män′yə men′təl) very great; colossal

marginal (mär′jənəl) close to a margin or limit, esp. a lower limit

savanna (sə van′ə) a treeless plain or a grassland characterized by scattered trees, esp. in tropical or subtropical regions having seasonal rains

radiate (rā′dē āt′) to spread out in rays from a central point

stratification (strat′ə fi kā′shən) classification or separation (of people) into groups graded according to status as variously determined by birth, income, education, etc.

ominous (äm′ə nəs) of or serving as an omen; esp., having the character of an evil omen; threatening; sinister

demographic (de mə graf′ik) concerned with such characteristics as the distribution, density, vital statistics, etc., of populations

draconian (drə kō′nē ən) extremely severe or cruel

exponential (eks′pō nen′shəl) produced or expressed by multiplying a set of quantities by themselves; extremely rapid increase

magnitude (mag′nə tōōd′, tyood′) greatness; specif., (a) of size, (b) of extent, (c) of importance or influence

---

fat, āpe, cär; ten, ēven; is, bīte; gō, hôrn, tōōl, look; oil, out; up, fʉr; chin, she; thin, *then*; zh, leisure; ŋ, ring; ə for *a* in *ago;* ′ as in *able* (ā′b'l)

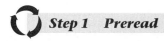

Step 1 Preread

Preread the following article by reading the headings, boldface and italics, and the captions for the illustrations. Answer the following questions without looking back at the article.

1. What is the subject of the article? _____

    _____

2. What is the main idea of the article? _____

    _____

3. What is the subject of figure 1? _____

    _____

4. What is the main idea of figure 1? _____

    _____

5. What is the main idea of figure 2? _____

    _____

6. Take a moment to think about population growth. Think about what you know, what you don't know, and what you might find out from reading the article. Make up three questions that might be answered by reading the article.

    a. _____

    b. _____

    c. _____

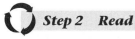

Step 2 Read

Read the article without underlining.

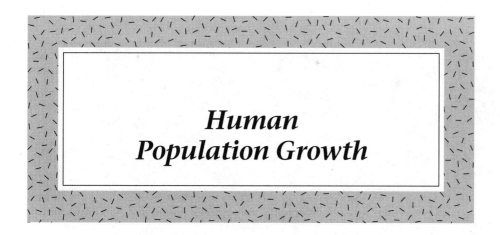

Human Population Growth

Cecie Starr

In 1990, the human population reached 5.3 billion. In 1988 alone, almost 87 million more individuals were added to it. That amounted to an average of 1.7 million more per week, 238,000 per day, or 9,900 per hour. This staggering display of growth is occurring while at least one in six humans already on the planet is malnourished or starving, without clean drinking water, and without adequate shelter. It is occurring while health care delivery and sewage treatment facilities are nonexistent for a third of the population.

Suppose it were possible, by monumental efforts, to double food production to keep pace with growth. We would do little more than maintain marginal living conditions for most of the world, and death from starvation could still reach 10 million to 40 million a year. Even this would come at great cost, for we are introducing serious new pressures on resources into the environment that must sustain us. Salted-out cropland, desertification, deforestation, global pollution—they do not bode well for our future.

For a while, it would be like the Red Queen's garden in Lewis Carroll's *Through the Looking Glass,* where one is forced to run as fast as one can to remain in the same place. But what happens when the human population doubles again? Can you brush this picture aside as being too far in the future to warrant your concern? It is no farther removed from you than your own sons and daughters.

How We Began Sidestepping Controls

How did we get into this predicament? Human population growth has been slow for most of human history, but in the past two centuries, there have

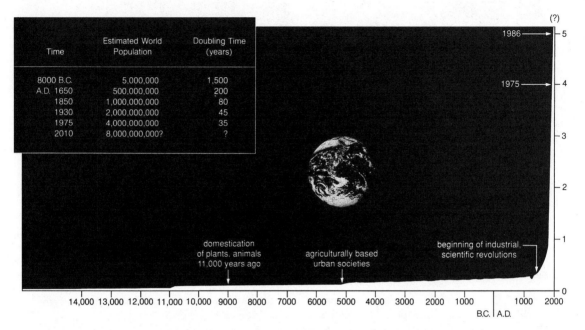

Time	Estimated World Population	Doubling Time (years)
8000 B.C.	5,000,000	1,500
A.D. 1650	500,000,000	200
1850	1,000,000,000	80
1930	2,000,000,000	45
1975	4,000,000,000	35
2010	8,000,000,000?	?

Figure 1 The curve of global human population growth. The vertical axis of the graph represents world population, in billions. (The slight dip between the years 1347 and 1351 shows the time when 5 million people died in Europe as a result of bubonic plague.) The growth pattern over the past two centuries has been exponential, sustained by revolutions in agriculture, industrialization, and improvements in health care.

been astounding increases in the rate of population growth (Figure 1). Why has our growth rate increased so dramatically? There are three possible reasons:

1. We steadily developed the capacity to expand into new habitats and new climate zones.
2. Carrying capacities increased in the environments we already occupied.
3. We removed several limiting factors.

Let's consider the first possibility. Early human populations apparently were restricted to savannas, and they were mainly vegetarians with scavenged bits of meat added opportunistically to the diet. By 150,000 years ago, small bands of hunters and gatherers had emerged; and within another 50,000 years, hunter-gatherers had radiated through much of the world.

For most animal species, such extensive radiations did not occur nearly as rapidly. Humans were able to do so with the application of learning and memory to problems such as how to build fires, assemble shelters, create clothing and tools, and plan a community hunt to exploit the abundance of wild game. Learned experiences were not confined to individuals but spread quickly from one band to another because of language—the ability for cultural communication. (It took less than seven decades from the time we first ventured into the air until we landed on the moon.) Thus, *the human population expanded into new environments, and it did so in an extremely short time span compared with radiations of other organisms.*

What about the second possibility? About 11,000 years ago, people began to shift from the hunting and gathering way of life to agriculture—from risky, demanding moves following the game herds to a settled, more dependable basis for existence in more favorable settings. A milestone was the domestication of wild grasses, including the species ancestral to modern bread wheat and rice. Seeds were harvested, stored, and planted in one place; animals were domesticated and kept close to home for food and for pulling plows. Water was diverted into hand-dug ditches to irrigate crops. These practices increased productivity, and with a larger, more dependable food supply, the rate of human population growth increased. Towns and cities emerged, and so did the social stratification that provided a labor base. Much later, food supplies increased again with the use of fertilizers and pesticides. Thus, *even in its simplest form, management of food supplies through agriculture increased the carrying capacity for the human population.*

What about the third possibility—removing a series of limiting factors? Consider what happened when medical practices and sanitary conditions improved. Until about 300 years ago, malnutrition, contagious diseases, and poor hygiene kept the death rate relatively high (especially among infants), and this more or less balanced the birth rate. Contagious diseases (density-dependent factors) spread rapidly through crowded settlements and cities. Without proper hygiene and sewage disposal methods, and plagued with such disease carriers as fleas and rats, population size increased only slowly at first. Then plumbing and sewage treatment methods developed. Bacteria and viruses were recognized as disease agents. Vaccines, antitoxins, and drugs such as antibiotics were developed.

And consider what happened when humans discovered how to harness the energy stored in fossil fuels, beginning with coal. This discovery occurred in the mid-eighteenth century, and within a few decades, large industrialized cities emerged in Western Europe and North America. After World War I, more efficient technologies developed. Cars, tractors, and other economically affordable goods were now mass-produced in factories; the use of machines reduced the number of farmers needed to produce food. Thus, *by bringing many disease agents under control and by tapping into concentrated, existing stores of energy, humans removed some of the factors that had previously checked their population growth.*

Present and Future Growth

What are the consequences of our farflung radiations and advances in agriculture, industrialization, and health care? It took *2 million years* for the hu-

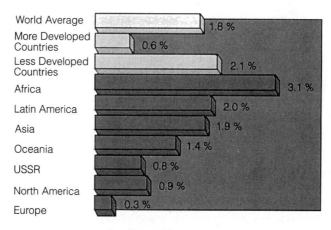

Figure 2 *Average annual population growth rate in various groups of countries in 1990.*

man population to reach the first billion. It only took 130 years to reach the second billion, 30 years to reach the third, 15 years to reach the fourth, *and only 12 years to reach the fifth!*

Figure 2 shows the annual growth for different parts of the world for 1990. If, as projected, the world average growth rate dips to 1.7 percent, we can expect the population to soar past 6 billion within the next decade. It may be very difficult to achieve similar increases in food production, drinkable water, energy reserves, and all the wood, steel, and other materials we use to make the planet habitable for us. There is evidence that harmful by-products of our existence—pollutants—are changing the land, seas, and atmosphere in ominous ways. From what we know of the principles governing population growth, we can realistically expect an imminent crash in our numbers; *although exponential growth continues, it is not sustainable.*

Controlling Population Growth

Today, there is widespread awareness of the links between overpopulation, resource depletion, and increased population. Many governments attempt to control their population size by restricting immigration from other countries; only a few (chiefly the United States, Canada, and Australia) allow large annual increases. Some attempt to reduce population pressures by encouraging emigration to other countries. But most efforts focus on decreasing the birth rate.

Two general approaches to decreasing birth rates are through economic development and family planning. The first involves providing more economic security and educational programs so that there will be less pressure on individuals to have large numbers of children to help them survive.

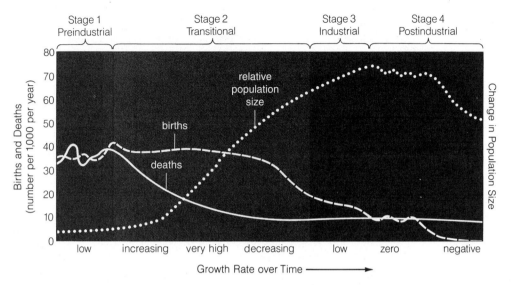

Figure 3 *The demographic transition model of changes in population size as correlated with changes in economic development.*

Family planning involves educating individuals in ways to regulate when and how many children they will have.

Control Through Economics

In the **demographic transition model,** changes in population growth are linked with changes that unfold during four stages of economic development (Figure 3). In the *preindustrial stage,* living conditions are harsh and birth rates are high, but so are death rates; there is little population growth. In the *transitional stage,* industrialization begins, food production rises, and health care improves. Death rates drop, but birth rates remain high, so the population grows. Growth continues at high rates (2.5 to 3 percent, on the average) over a long period, but then starts to level off as living conditions improve. Growth slows in the *industrial stage,* when industrialization is in full swing, mostly because urban couples regulate family size. Many decide that raising children is expensive and having too many puts them at an economic disadvantage. In the *postindustrial stage,* zero population growth is reached. Then the birth rate falls below the death rate, and the population slowly decreases in size.

Today, the United States, Canada, Australia, Japan, the Soviet Union, New Zealand, and most countries of Western Europe are in the industrial stage, and their growth rate is slowly decreasing. Fourteen countries, including Sweden, the United Kingdom, and West Germany, are close to, at, or slightly below zero population growth.

Mexico and other less-developed countries are in the transition stage. At current growth rates, Mexico's population may reach 138 million by the year 2020. Like many countries in this stage, its huge population does not include enough skilled workers to compete effectively in today's technological markets. Fossil fuels and other resources that drive industrialization are being used up—they are not renewable—and fuel costs will become too high for countries at the bottom of the economic ladder. If population growth keeps outpacing economic growth, the death rate may increase. Thus the countries now stuck in the transitional stage won't stay there; they may well return to the harsh conditions of the preceding stage unless birth rates are controlled.

Control Through Family Planning

Family planning programs that are well conceived and carefully administered may bring about a faster decline in birth rates, at less cost, than economic development alone. Such programs vary from country to country, but all provide information on methods of birth control.

Suppose family planning programs were successful beyond our wildest imagination, so that all couples decided to have only two children to replace them. (Actually, the average "replacement level for fertility" is slightly higher, for some female children die before reaching reproductive age. It is about 2.5 children per woman in less-developed countries, and 2.1 in more-developed countries.) Even if the replacement level for fertility were achieved globally, the human population would keep on growing for at least another sixty years! Why? An immense number of already existing children will themselves be reproducing.

Take a look at Figures 4 and 5, which show age structure diagrams for three populations growing at different rates. (In these diagrams, ages 15 to 44 are used as the average range of childbearing years.) The one for Mexico, a rapidly growing population, has a broad base. It is filled not only with reproductive-age men and women but with a large number of children who will move into that category during the next fifteen years. As Figure 6 indicates, *more than one-third of the world population now has an age structure with a broad reproductive base.* This gives us an idea of the magnitude of the effort it will take to control population growth.

One way to slow down the birth rate is to encourage delayed reproduction—childbearing in the early thirties as opposed to the mid-teens or early twenties. This practice slows population growth by lengthening the generation time and by lowering the average number of children in each family.

China, for example, has established the most extensive family planning program in the world. Couples are strongly urged to postpone the age at which they marry. Married couples have ready access to free contraceptives, abortion, and sterilization; paramedics and mobile units ensure access even

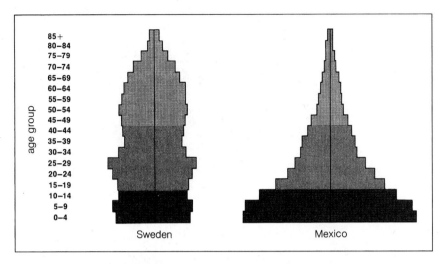

Figure 4 Age structure diagrams for two countries in 1977. Dark gray indicates the pre-reproductive base. Medium gray indicates reproductive years; light gray, the post-reproductive years. The portion of the population to the left of the vertical axis in each diagram represents males; the portion to the right represents females. Mexico has a very rapid rate of increase. In 1980, Sweden showed zero population growth.

in remote rural areas. Couples who pledge not to have more than one child are given extra food, better housing, free medical care, and salary bonuses; their child will be granted free tuition and preferential treatment when he or she enters the job market. Those who break the pledge forgo benefits.

These may seem like draconian measures unless you know that family planning has been China's alternative to mass starvation. (Between 1958 and 1962 alone, an estimated 30 million Chinese died because of famine.) By 1987, the fertility rate had dropped from a previous high of 5.7 to 2.4 children per woman. Even so, the population time bomb has not stopped ticking. China's population now numbers 1.1 billion—and 340 million of its young women are about to move into the reproductive age category.

Questions About Zero Population Growth

For the human population, as for all others, the biological implications of exponential growth are staggering. Yet so are the social implications of achieving and maintaining zero population growth.

For instance, most members of an actively growing population fall in younger age brackets. Under conditions of constant growth, the age distribution means that there is a large work force. A large work force is capable of supporting older, nonproductive individuals with various programs, such as social security, low-cost housing, and health care. With zero population growth, far more people will fall in the older age brackets. How, then, can

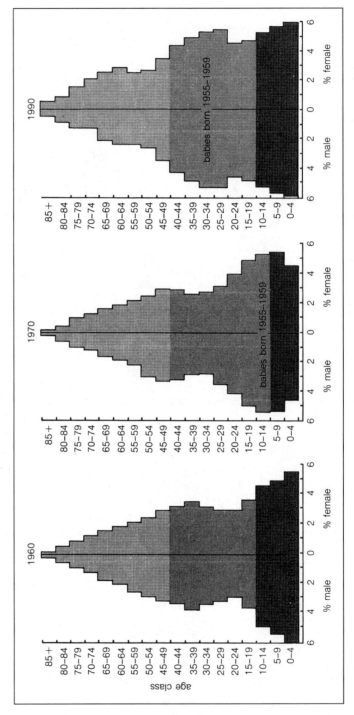

Figure 5 *Age structure of the U.S. population in 1960, 1970, 1990 (projected). The population bulge of babies between 1955 and 1959 will slowly move up.*

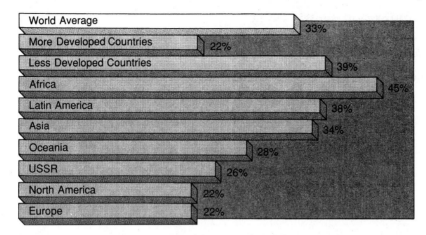

Figure 6 *Percentage of individuals under age 15 in various regions in 1987.*

goods and services be provided for nonproductive members if productive ones are asked to carry a greater and greater share of the burden? These are not abstract questions. Put them to yourself. How much are you willing to bear for the sake of your parents, your grandparents? How much will your children be able to bear for you?

We have arrived at a major turning point, not only in our biological evolution but also in our cultural evolution. The decisions awaiting us are among the most difficult we will ever have to make, yet it is clear that they must be made, and soon.

All species face limits to growth. In one sense, we may think that we are different from the rest, for our unique ability to undergo cultural evolution has allowed us to postpone the action of most of the factors that limit growth. But the key word here is *postpone.* No amount of cultural intervention can hold back the ultimate check of limited resources. We have repealed a number of the smaller laws of nature; in the process, we have become more vulnerable to those laws which cannot be repealed. Today there may be only two options available. Either we make a global effort to limit population growth in accordance with environmental carrying capacity, or we wait until the environment does it for us.

 Step 3   Analyze What You Read—Create a Study Guide

Objective Questions

Go back and underline what you believe will be on a test. Make marginal self-test notes. If you prefer, you may put the marginal note (subject) on the front of the card and the underlining (main idea) in your own words on the back.

Essay/Application Questions

A. *Predict Questions*

We believe that there are about six subtopics in this article important enough to justify essay questions. List them here.

1. _____

2. _____

3. _____

4. _____

5. _____

6. _____

B. *Make Graphic Organizers*

1. In the space provided, fill out the map for the following question: What will be the results of continued population growth?

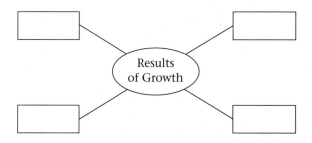

2. Fill out a flash card for the following question: Why did human but not animal populations show exponential growth? Give examples.

Front   **Back**

3. Fill out a flash card for the following question: List the stages of the demographic transition model. Give the population growth characteristic of each stage.

<table>
<tr><td align="center">**Front**</td><td align="center">**Back**</td></tr>
<tr><td>

</td><td> </td></tr>
</table>

Step 4   *Remember What's Important*

Self-test using the marginal notes and graphic organizers. Use mnemonic devices as needed.

Step 5   *Make Use of What You Read*

Your instructor will give you a mastery test for this article.

Step 6   *Evaluate Your Active Critical Thinking Skills*

After the mastery test is graded, use the checklist in the appendix to evaluate your skills.

Reading 16

Interpersonal Influence

 Step 1   Preread

Preread the following article by reading the title and the headings and examining the illustrations. Then answer the following questions without looking back.

1. What is the subject of the article? _____

   _____

2. What is the main idea of the article? _____

   _____

3. Based on information in the illustrations, what was the subject of Solomon Asch's experiment? _____

_____

4. Based on the illustration, what was the subject of the Milgram experiment?

_____

5. Take a moment to think about conformity, compliance, obedience to authority, and diffusion of responsibility. Think about what you know, what you don't know, and what you might find out by reading the article. Make up three questions that might be answered by reading the article.

   a. _____

   b. _____

   c. _____

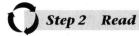

Step 2   Read

Now read the article without underlining.

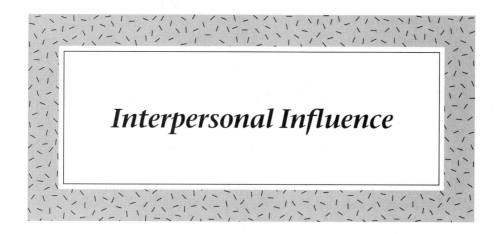

Interpersonal Influence

James W. Kalat

In the spring of 1983, a strange epidemic swept through a Palestinian village in one of the territories occupied by Israel. The hospitals were flooded with people, mostly adolescents, complaining of headaches, dizzy spells, stomach pains, blurred vision, and difficulty breathing. The Palestinians accused the Israelis of poisoning the air or the water, perhaps in an effort to sterilize the young Palestinian women. The Israelis replied with heated denials.

Meanwhile, although physicians conducted extensive tests on all the patients, they could find nothing medically wrong. They studied the food, the air, the water, every possible source of poison or of contagious disease. They found no signs of anything that could cause illness. Finally they concluded that all the symptoms were the result of anxiety, coupled with the power of suggestion. The Palestinians were understandably nervous about the political tensions in the region; as soon as one person reported symptoms of poisoning, other people experienced the same symptoms.

Most people are strongly influenced by what other people say and do. What have social psychologists learned about interpersonal influence?

Conformity

Social psychologists define a group as two or more people who are united by some common characteristic or interest and who act together in some way. A group may be temporary and informal, such as a few people who go to the movies together, or permanent and well organized, such as the Republican party or the United Methodist Church.

Membership in a group can exert strong influence on the behavior of an individual. Conformity means maintaining or changing one's behavior in

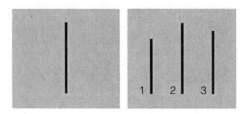

Figure 1 *Choosing conformity: In Asch's conformity studies, subjects asked to match a line with one of three other lines on another card were surrounded by experimental accomplices who gave obviously wrong answers.*

order to be consistent with group standards. Sometimes conformity is good, as when everyone agrees to drive on the right side of the road. Sometimes conformity is neither good nor bad, as when people dress like their friends. Sometimes conformity is dangerous, as when someone uses drugs because "everyone else is doing it."

Do people conform more in some situations than in others? Early research suggested that people conform strongly when they are not confident of their own opinions and look to others for guidance. Do people conform even when they are confident of their own opinions? To answer that question, Solomon Asch carried out a now-famous series of experiments.

Asch showed bars like those in Figure 1 to college students in groups of 8 to 10. He told them he was studying visual perception and that their task was to decide which of the bars on the right was the same length as the one on the left. As you can see, the task is simple, and the correct answer is obvious. Asch asked the students to give their answers aloud. He repeated the procedure with 18 sets of bars.

Only one student in each group was a real subject. All the others were confederates who had been instructed to give incorrect answers on 12 of the 18 trials. Asch arranged for the real subject to be the next-to-the-last person in each group to announce his answer so that he would hear most of the confederates' incorrect responses before giving his own. Would he go along with the crowd?

To Asch's surprise, 37 of the 50 subjects conformed to the majority at least once, and 14 of them conformed on more than 6 of the 12 trials. When faced with a unanimous wrong answer by the other group members, the mean subject conformed on 4 of the 12 trials. Asch was disturbed by these results: "That we have found the tendency to conformity in our society so strong that reasonably intelligent and well-meaning young people are willing to call white black is a matter of concern. It raises questions about our ways of education and about the values that guide our conduct."

Why did the subjects conform so readily? When they were interviewed after the experiment, most of them said that they did not really believe their conforming answers, but had gone along with the group for fear of being ridiculed or thought "peculiar." A few of them said that they really did believe the group's answers were correct.

Asch conducted a revised version of his experiment to find out whether the subjects truly did not believe their incorrect answers. When they were permitted to write down their answers after hearing the answers of others, their level of conformity declined to about one third what it had been in the original experiment.

Apparently, people conform for two main reasons: because they want to be liked by the group and because they believe the group is better informed than they are. Suppose you go to a fancy dinner party and notice to your dismay that there are four forks beside your plate. When the first course arrives, you are not sure which fork to use. If you are like most people, you look around and use the fork everyone else is using. You do this because you want to be accepted by the group and because you assume the others know more about table etiquette than you do.

Asch found that one of the situational factors that influence conformity is the size of the opposing majority. In a series of studies, he varied the number of confederates who gave incorrect answers from 1 to 15. He found that the subjects conformed to a group of 3 or 4 as readily as they did to a larger group (see Figure 2). However, the subjects conformed much less if they had an "ally." In some of his experiments, Asch instructed one of the confederates to give correct answers. In the presence of this nonconformist, the real subjects conformed only one fourth as much as they did in the original experiment. There were several reasons: First, the real subject observed that the majority did not ridicule the dissenter for his answers. Second, the dissenter's answers made the subject more certain that the majority was wrong. Third, the real subject now experienced social pressure from the dissenter as well as the majority. Many of the real subjects later reported that they had liked their nonconformist partner (the similarity principle again). Apparently, it is difficult to be a minority of one but not so difficult to be part of a minority of two.

Compliance

Compliance is the tendency to do what someone asks us to do. For example, you may comply with someone's request to vote for a candidate, to contribute to a nonprofit organization, or to buy a product.

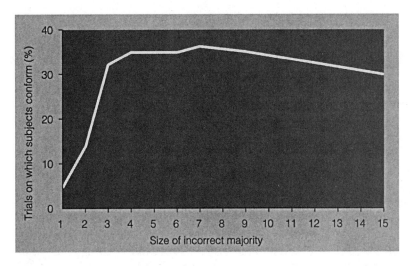

Figure 2 Conformity, group size, and cohesiveness: Asch found that conformity became more frequent as group size increased up to about three and then leveled off. But when subjects had an "ally," conformity decreased considerably.

There are several techniques for increasing the likelihood that people will comply with a request. (These are worth knowing about so that you can avoid being tricked into doing something you don't want to do.) One technique is to make a modest request at first and then follow it up with a much larger second request. This is called the foot-in-the-door technique. When Jonathan Freedman and Scott Fraser asked suburban residents in Palo Alto, California, to put a small "Drive Safely" sign in their window, most of them agreed to do so. A couple of weeks later, other researchers asked the same residents to let them set up a large, unsightly "Drive Safely" billboard in their front yard for 10 days. They made the same request to a group of residents whom the first group of researchers had not approached. Of those who had already been asked to display the small sign, 76% agreed to let them set up the billboard. Only 17% of the others agreed. Even agreeing to make such a small commitment as signing a petition to support a cause significantly increases the probability that people will later donate money to that cause.

Another technique for gaining compliance is the door-in-the-face technique. In this technique, someone follows an outrageous initial request with a much more reasonable second one. Imagine, for example, that someone comes to your door and asks you to donate $50 to the fund to Protect Endangered Species of Ticks. You refuse. Then she says, "Okay. But would you at least buy a box of oatmeal cookies? Part of the money goes to support the cause." You feel a little guilty about refusing her first request and now she is asking so little. Even if you don't particularly like oatmeal cookies, how can you possibly refuse?

Robert Cialdini and his colleagues demonstrated the power of the door-in-the-face technique with a clever experiment. They asked college students to agree to spend two hours a week for two years working as counselors to juvenile delinquents. Not surprisingly, every student refused. Then the researchers asked, "If you won't do that, would you chaperone a group from the juvenile detention center for one trip to the zoo?" Half the subjects complied with this more modest request, as compared to only 17% of the subjects who had not first been asked to make the larger commitment.

Why did presenting the larger request first make the students more willing to comply with the smaller request? Apparently they felt that the researchers were conceding a great deal and that it was only fair to meet them halfway.

Another approach is the that's-not-all technique. In this one, someone makes an offer and then, before the other person has a chance to reply, makes a better offer. The television announcer says, "Here's your chance to buy this amazing combination paper shredder and coffee maker for only $39.95. But wait, there's more! We'll throw in a can of dog deodorant! And this handy windshield-wiper cleaner and a subscription to *Modern Lobotomist!* And if you act now, you can get this amazing offer, which usually costs $39.95, for only $19.95! Call this number!" People who hear the first offer and then the "improved" offer are more likely to comply than are people who begin with the "improved" offer.

Obedience to Authority

Obedience means following a direct command from someone in authority: a parent, boss, teacher, or government official. When are people most likely to obey commands? When are they not?

When the Nazi concentration camps were exposed after the Second World War, those who had committed the atrocities defended themselves by saying they were only obeying orders. International courts rejected that defense, and outraged people throughout the world told themselves, "If I had been there, I would have refused to follow such orders" and "It couldn't happen here."

What do you think? Could it happen here? Stanley Milgram set up an experiment to discover under what conditions people would obey apparently dangerous orders. Here is how the experiment worked: Two adult male subjects arrived at the experimental room—the real subject and a confederate of the experimenter pretending to be a subject. The experimenter told them that this was an experiment on learning and that one subject would be the "teacher" and the other the "learner." The teacher would read lists of words through a microphone to the learner, who would sit in a nearby room. The teacher would then test the learner's memory for the words. Every time the learner made a mistake, the teacher was to deliver an electric shock as punishment.

The experiment was rigged so that the real subject was always the teacher and the confederate was always the learner. The teacher watched as the learner was strapped into the shock device, so he knew that the learner could not escape. In one version of the experiment, the learner was a middle-age man who said he had a heart condition. The learner never actually received any shocks, but the teacher was led to believe that he did.

The experiment began uneventfully. The teacher read the words and tested the learner's memory for them. The learner made many mistakes. The teacher sat at a shock generator that had levers to deliver shocks ranging from 15 volts up to 450 volts, in 15-volt increments. The experimenter instructed the teacher to deliver a shock every time the learner made a mistake, beginning with the 15-volt switch and raising the voltage by 15 volts for each successive mistake.

As the voltage went up, the learner in the next room cried out in pain and even kicked the wall. Typically, the teachers grew upset as they delivered what they believed were more and more painful shocks, but the experimenter kept ordering them to continue. If a teacher asked who would take responsibility for any harm to the learner, the experimenter replied that he would take responsibility, but he insisted that "while the shocks may be painful, they are not dangerous." When the shock reached 150 volts, the learner called out in pain and begged to be let out of the experiment, complaining that his heart was bothering him. Beginning at 270, he responded to shocks with agonized screams. At 300 volts he shouted that he would no longer answer any questions. After 330 volts he made no response at all. Still, the experimenter ordered the teacher to continue asking questions and delivering shocks. (Remember, the learner was not really being shocked; the screams of pain were played on a tape recorder.)

How many subjects, if any, would you guess continued to deliver shocks? Of 40 subjects, 25 continued to deliver shocks all the way up to 450 volts. Milgram replicated his results in somewhat modified experiments: He conducted the experiment in a rundown office in a rundown office building in Bridgeport, Connecticut, instead of on the campus of Yale University. He recruited a different man to play the role of learner and had women serve as teachers. In each case, about half the teachers continued to give shocks all the way to 450 volts.

Many students who hear about this experiment exclaim, "There must have been something wrong with those people! Maybe they were sadists." They were not. They were normal adults, recruited from the community through newspaper ads. (They were not college students.) They were paid a few dollars for their services, and those who asked were told that they could keep the money even if they quit. (Not many asked.) People from all walks of life obeyed the experimenter's orders, including blue-collar workers, white-collar workers, and professionals. Most of them grew quite upset and agitated while they were supposedly delivering shocks to the screaming learner, but they kept right on.

What may have promoted obedience in this experiment? One factor is that the teacher was in another room and could not see the learner. In another version of the experiment, both were in the same room and the teacher could see the learner's expressions of pain as well as hear his cries. Under those conditions, fewer subjects (40%) obeyed. In yet another version, Milgram asked the teacher to force the learner's hand down on a shock plate when he tried to quit. Obedience then dropped to 30% (It may be easier to press a button to fire a missile that will kill a million people you don't see than to plunge a bayonet into one person you do see.)

In further experiments, Milgram added the pressure to conform to the pressure to obey. Now the real subject acting as teacher was joined by two other teachers who were Milgram's confederates. Each one had a specific duty to perform, such as reading the list of words or flipping the switches on the shock generator. So long as the two confederates followed the orders without protest, 93% of the real subjects followed suit. But when the confederates rebelled and refused to go on, only 10% of the real subjects continued to obey orders. Figure 3 shows the results under a variety of conditions.

Diffusion of Responsibility

Who do you think would be more likely to go to the aid of someone in distress: someone in a group or a lone individual? Late one night in March, 1964, Kitty Genovese was stabbed to death near her apartment in Queens, New York. For 30 minutes, 38 of her neighbors listened to her screams. A few stood at their windows watching. None of them came to her aid or called the police. Why?

Bibb Latané and John Darley proposed that one reason the neighbors failed to help was diffusion of responsibility—the fact that we feel less responsibility for helping when other people are around than when we know that no one else can help. Latané and Darley suggest that no one helped Kitty Genovese because everyone knew that there were many other people on the scene who *could* help her.

In an experiment designed to test this hypothesis, a young woman ushered either one student or two students into a room and asked them to wait a few minutes for the start of a market research study. She then went into the next room, closing the door behind her. There she played a tape recording that made it sound as if she had climbed onto a chair and had fallen off. For about two minutes she could be heard crying and moaning, "Oh . . . my foot . . . I can't move it. Oh . . . my . . . ankle. . . ." Of the subjects who were

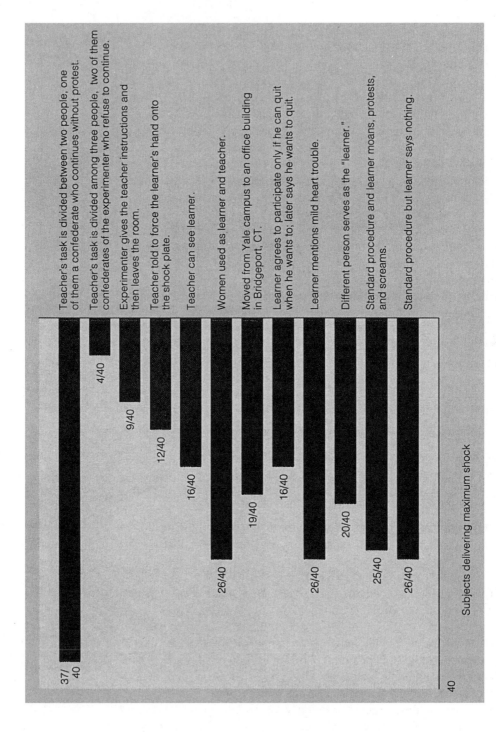

Teacher's task is divided between two people, one of them a confederate who continues without protest.

Teacher's task is divided among three people, two of them confederates of the experimenter who refuse to continue.

Experimenter gives the teacher instructions and then leaves the room.

Teacher told to force the learner's hand onto the shock plate.

Teacher can see learner.

Women used as learner and teacher.

Moved from Yale campus to an office building in Bridgeport, CT.

Learner agrees to participate only if he can quit when he wants to; later says he wants to quit.

Learner mentions mild heart trouble.

Different person serves as the "learner."

Standard procedure and learner moans, protests, and screams.

Standard procedure but learner says nothing.

37/40
4/40
9/40
12/40
16/40
26/40
19/40
16/40
26/40
20/40
25/40
26/40

Subjects delivering maximum shock

40

Figure 3 *Compliance in various forms of Milgram's experiment on obedience. Note that unlike Nazi soldiers, who might have been shot for not following orders, these people simply risked displeasing some strangers.*

waiting alone, 70% went next door and offered to help. Of the subjects who were waiting with someone else, only 13% offered to help.

Diffusion of responsibility is one possible explanation. Each person thinks, "It's not my responsibility to help any more than it is the other person's. And if we get blamed for not helping, it's as much that person's fault as it is mine." A second possible explanation is that the presence of another person changes the way we react to an ambiguous situation: Does that woman need help or not? I'm not really sure. This other person isn't doing anything, so maybe she doesn't."

Note the similarity between the results of this study and the results of Milgram's obedience experiment: In both cases, people followed social pressures instead of their own conscience.

 Step 3   *Analyze What You Read—Create a Study Guide*

Objective Questions

Go back and underline what you believe will be on a test. Then write self-test notes in the margin. If you prefer, you may use flash cards instead.

Essay Questions

A. *Predict Questions*

There are four topics that may be on a test. Write the topics here.

1. _____

2. _____

3. _____

4. _____

B. *Make Graphic Organizers*

1. Fill in the blanks in the outline for conformity.

Conformity

I. _____

II. _____

III. Asch experiment

     A. _____

     B. _____

     C. _____

         1. _____

         2. _____

     D. _____

         1. _____

         2. _____

             a. _____

             b. _____

             c. _____

2. Fill in the map for compliance.

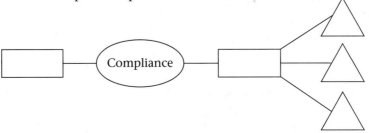

3. Fill in the map for obedience to authority.

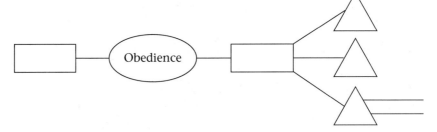

4. Fill in the map for diffusion of responsibility.

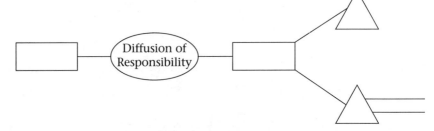

Step 4   Remember What's Important

Self-test using the marginal notes and graphic organizers. Use mnemonic devices as needed.

 Step 5   Make Use of What you Read

Your instructor will give you a mastery test for this article.

Step 6   Evaluate Your Active Critical Thinking Skills

After your mastery test is graded, use the checklist in the appendix to evaluate your skills.

Reading 17

How We Listen to Music

Vocabulary Preview

engender (en jen′dər) to bring into being; cause

apropos (ap′rə pō′) fitting the occasion; relevant; apt

usurp (yōo surp′) to take or assume (power, a position, property, rights, etc.) and hold in possession by force or without right

integral (in′tə grəl) necessary for completeness; essential

intransigent (in tran′sə jənt) refusing to come to a compromise, come to an agreement, or be reconciled.

abetted (ə bet′id) incited, sanctioned, or helped, esp. in wrongdoing

exuberance (eg zōo′bər əns, -zyōo′) a state of high spirits; liveliness

fugue (fyōog) a musical composition for a definite number of parts of voices, in which a subject is announced in one voice, imitated in succession by each of the other voices, and developed by playing different voices at the same time

engross (en grōs′) to take the entire attention of; occupy wholly; absorb

correlation (kôr′ə lā′shən) mutual relationship or connection

---

fat, āpe, cär; ten, ēven; is, bīte; gō, hôrn, tōol, look; oil, out; up, fur; chin, she; thin, *then*; zh, leisure; ŋ, ring; ə for *a* in *ago;* ′ as in *able* (ā′b'l)

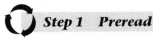 **Step 1   Preread**

Preread the following article by reading the title, the author's name, and the first sentence of each paragraph. In this case, the author's name is important because he was an internationally famous composer. Answer the following questions without looking back.

1. What is the subject of the article? _____

    _____

2. What is the main idea of the article? _____

    _____

3. On how many planes does Copland believe that music exists? _____

    _____

4. What kind of listening does Copland believe the listener should strive for?

    _____

5. Take a moment to think about how we listen to music. Think about what you know from your experience, what you don't know, and what you might find out from reading this article. Make up three questions that might be answered by reading the article.

    a. _____

    b. _____

    c. _____

 Step 2   Read

Now read the article without underlining.

How We Listen to Music

Aaron Copland

We all listen to music according to our separate capacities. But, for the sake of analysis, the whole listening process may become clearer if we break it up into its component parts, so to speak. In a certain sense we all listen to music on three separate planes. For lack of a better terminology, one might name these: (1) the sensuous plane, (2) the expressive plane, (3) the sheerly musical plane. The only advantage to be gained from mechanically splitting up the listening process into these hypothetical planes is the clearer view to be had of the way in which we listen.

The simplest way of listening to music is to listen for the sheer pleasure of the musical sound itself. That is the sensuous plane. It is the plane on which we hear music without thinking, without considering it in any way. One turns on the radio while doing something else and absent-mindedly bathes in the sound. A kind of brainless but attractive state of mind is engendered by the mere sound appeal of the music.

You may be sitting in a room reading this book. Imagine one note struck on the piano. Immediately that one note is enough to change the atmosphere of the room—proving that the sound element in music is a powerful and mysterious agent, which it would be foolish to deride or belittle.

The surprising thing is that many people who consider themselves qualified music lovers abuse that plane in listening. They go to concerts in order to lose themselves. They use music as a consolation or an escape. They enter an ideal world where one doesn't have to think of the realities of everyday life. Of course they aren't thinking about the music either. Music allows them to leave it, and they go off to a place to dream, dreaming because of and apropos of the music yet never quite listening to it.

Yes, the sound appeal of music is a potent and primitive force, but you must not allow it to usurp a disproportionate share of your interest. The sensuous plane is an important one in music, a very important one, but it does not constitute the whole story.

There is no need to digress further on the sensuous plane. Its appeal to every normal human being is self-evident. There is, however, such a thing as becoming more sensitive to the different kinds of sound stuff as used by various composers. For all composers do not use that sound stuff in the same way. Don't get the idea that the value of music is commensurate with its sensuous appeal or that the loveliest sounding music is made by the greatest composer. If that were so, Ravel would be a greater creator than Beethoven. The point is that the sound element varies with each composer, that his usage of sound forms an integral part of his style and must be taken into account when listening. The reader can see, therefore, that a more conscious approach is valuable even on this primary plane of music listening.

The second plane on which music exists is what I have called the expressive one. Here, immediately, we tread on controversial ground. Composers have a way of shying away from any discussion of music's expressive side. Did not Stravinsky himself proclaim that his music was an "object," a "thing," with a life of its own, and with no other meaning than its own purely musical existence? This intransigent attitude of Stravinsky's may be due to the fact that so many people have tried to read different meanings into so many pieces. Heaven knows it is difficult enough to say precisely what it is that a piece of music means, to say it definitely, to say it finally so that everyone is satisfied with your explanation. But that should not lead one to the other extreme of denying to music the right to be "expressive."

My own belief is that all music has an expressive power, some more and some less, but that all music has a certain meaning behind the notes and that that meaning behind the notes constitutes, after all, what the piece is saying, what the piece is about. This whole problem can be stated quite simply by asking, "Is there a meaning to music?" My answer to that would be, "Yes." And "Can you state in so many words what the meaning is?" My answer to that would be, "No." Therein lies the difficulty.

Simple-minded souls will never be satisfied with the answer to the second of these questions. They always want music to have a meaning, and the more concrete it is the better they like it. The more the music reminds them of a train, a storm, a funeral, or any other familiar conception the more expressive it appears to be to them. This popular idea of music's meaning—stimulated and abetted by the usual run of musical commentator—should be discouraged wherever and whenever it is met. One timid lady once confessed to me that she suspected something seriously lacking in her appreciation of music because of her inability to connect it with anything definite. That is getting the whole thing backward, of course.

Still, the question remains, How close should the intelligent music lover wish to come to pinning a definite meaning to any particular work? No closer than a general concept, I should say. Music expresses, at different moments, serenity or exuberance, regret or triumph, fury or delight. It expresses each of these moods, and many others, in a numberless variety of subtle shadings and differences. It may even express a state of meaning for which there exists no adequate word in any language. In that case, musicians often like to say that it has only a purely musical meaning. They sometimes go farther and say that *all* music has only a purely musical meaning. What they really mean is that no appropriate word can be found to express the music's meaning and that, even if it could, they do not feel the need of finding it.

But whatever the professional musician may hold, most musical novices still search for specific words with which to pin down their musical reactions. That is why they always find Tschaikovsky easier to "understand" than Beethoven. In the first place, it is easier to pin a meaning-word on a Tschaikovsky piece than on a Beethoven one. Much easier. Moreover, with the Russian composer, every time you come back to a piece of his it almost always says the same thing to you, whereas with Beethoven it is often quite difficult to put your finger right on what he is saying. And any musician will tell you that that is why Beethoven is the greater composer. Because music which always says the same thing to you will necessarily become dull music, but music whose meaning is slightly different with each hearing has a greater chance of remaining alive.

Listen, if you can, to the forty-eight fugue themes of Bach's *Well Tempered Clavichord.* Listen to each theme, one after another. You will soon realize that each theme mirrors a different world of feeling. You will also soon realize that the more beautiful a theme seems to you the harder it is to find any word that will describe it to your complete satisfaction. Yes, you will certainly know whether it is a gay theme or a sad one. You will be able, in other words, in your own mind, to draw a frame of emotional feeling around your theme. Now study the sad one a little closer. Try to pin down the exact quality of its sadness. Is it pessimistically sad or resignedly sad; is it fatefully sad or smilingly sad?

Let us suppose that you are fortunate and can describe to your own satisfaction in so many words the exact meaning of your chosen theme. There is still no guarantee that anyone else will be satisfied. Nor need they be. The important thing is that each one feel for himself the specific expressive quality of a theme or, similarly, an entire piece of music. And if it is a great work of art, don't expect it to mean exactly the same thing to you each time you return to it.

Themes or pieces need not express only one emotion, of course. Take such a theme as the first main one of the *Ninth Symphony,* for example. It is clearly made up of different elements. It does not say only one thing. Yet anyone hearing it immediately gets a feeling of strength, a feeling of power.

It isn't a power that comes simply because the theme is played loudly. It is a power inherent in the theme itself. The extraordinary strength and vigor of the theme results in the listener's receiving an impression that a forceful statement has been made. But one should never try to boil it down to "the fateful hammer of life," etc. That is where the trouble begins. The musician, in his exasperation, says it means nothing but the notes themselves, whereas the nonprofessional is only too anxious to hang on to any explanation that gives him the illusion of getting closer to the music's meaning.

Now, perhaps, the reader will know better what I mean when I say that music does have an expressive meaning but that we cannot say in so many words what that meaning is.

The third plane on which music exists is the sheerly musical plane. Besides the pleasurable sound of music and the expressive feeling that it gives off, music does exist in terms of the notes themselves and of their manipulation. Most listeners are not sufficiently conscious of this third plane. . . .

Professional musicians, on the other hand, are, if anything, too conscious of the mere notes themselves. They often fall into the error of becoming so engrossed with their arpeggios and staccatos that they forget the deeper aspects of the music they are performing. But from the layman's standpoint, it is not so much a matter of getting over bad habits on the sheerly musical plane as of increasing one's awareness of what is going on, insofar as the notes are concerned.

When the man in the street listens to the "notes themselves" with any degree of concentration, he is most likely to make some mention of the melody. Either he hears a pretty melody or he does not, and he generally lets it go at that. Rhythm is likely to gain his attention next, particularly if it seems exciting. But harmony and tone color are generally taken for granted, if they are thought of consciously at all. As for music's having a definite form of some kind, that idea seems never to have occurred to him.

It is very important for all of us to become more alive to music on its sheerly musical plane. After all, an actual musical material is being used. The intelligent listener must be prepared to increase his awareness of the musical material and what happens to it. He must hear the melodies, the rhythms, the harmonies, the tone colors in a more conscious fashion. But above all he must, in order to follow the line of the composer's thought, know something of the principles of musical form. Listening to all of these elements is listening on the sheerly musical plane.

Let me repeat that I have split up mechanically the three separate planes on which we listen merely for the sake of greater clarity. Actually, we never listen on one or the other of these planes. What we do is to correlate them—listening in all three ways at the same time. It takes no mental effort, for we do it instinctively.

Perhaps an analogy with what happens to us when we visit the theater will make this instinctive correlation clearer. In the theater, you are aware of the actors and actresses, costumes and sets, sounds and movements. All these give one the sense that the theater is a pleasant place to be in. They constitute the sensuous plane in our theatrical reactions.

The expressive plane in the theater would be derived from the feeling that you get from what is happening on the stage. You are moved to pity, excitement, or gayety. It is this general feeling, generated aside from the particular words being spoken, a certain emotional something which exists on the stage, that is analogous to the expressive quality in music.

The plot and plot development is equivalent to our sheerly musical plane. The playwright creates and develops a character in just the same way that a composer creates and develops a theme. According to the degree of your awareness of the way in which the artist in either field handles his material you will become a more intelligent listener.

It is easy enough to see that the theatergoer never is conscious of any of these elements separately. He is aware of them all at the same time. The same is true of music listening. We simultaneously and without thinking listen on all three planes.

In a sense, the ideal listener is both inside and outside the music at the same moment, judging it and enjoying it, wishing it would go one way and watching it go another—almost like the composer at the moment he composes it; because in order to write his music, the composer must also be inside and outside his music, carried away by it and yet coldly critical of it. A subjective and objective attitude is important in both creating and listening to music.

What the reader should strive for, then, is a more *active* kind of listening. Whether you listen to Mozart or Duke Ellington, you can deepen your understanding of music only by being a more conscious and aware listener—not someone who is just listening, but someone who is listening *for* something.

 ## Step 3   *Analyze What You Read—Create a Study Guide*

Objective Questions

Go back and underline what you believe will be on the test. Then write self-test notes in the margin. If you prefer, use flash cards instead.

Essay/Application Questions

A. *Predict Questions*

Write the most important topic to study for this article. _____

B. *Make Graphic Organizers*

1. Draw a study map to show Copland's three planes.

2. Copland compares his three planes with a visit to the theater. In the following space, use the three planes to explain how to read a poem.

   a. Plane 1 _____

   b. Plane 2 _____

   c. Plane 3 _____

Step 4   Remember What's Important

Test yourself using the notes or flash cards and graphic organizers. Use mnemonic devices as needed.

Step 5   Make Use of What You Read

Your instructor will give you a mastery test for this article.

Step 6   Evaluate Your Active Critical Thinking Skills

After the mastery test is graded, use the checklist in the appendix to evaluate your skills.

Reading 18

Arguments, Premises, and Conclusions

Vocabulary Preview

formulate (fôr′myo͞o lāt′) to work out or form in one's mind; devise, develop

prevailed (prē vāld′) won

subsequent (sub′si kwənt) coming after; following in time, place, or order

restructure (rē struk′chər) to plan or provide a new structure or organization for

implicitly (im plis′it lē) suggested or to be understood though not plainly expressed; implied

fat, āpe, cär; ten, ēven; is, bīte; gō, hôrn, to͞ol, look; oil, out; up, fʉr; chin, she; thin, *then*; zh, leisure; ŋ, ring; ə for *a* in *ago;* ' as in *able* (ā′b'l)

Step 1   Preread

The following article does not contain headings and subheadings. Survey it by reading the title, the first sentence of each paragraph, the words in boldface, and the illustration. When you have finished, answer the following questions without looking back at the article.

1. What is the subject of the article? _____

_____

2. What is the main idea of the article? _____

_____

225

3. What is the difference between a premise and a conclusion? _____

_____

4. Give an example of a conclusion indicator. _____

_____

5. Take a moment to think about logical arguments. Think about what you know, what you don't know, and what you might find out by reading this article. Make up three questions that might be answered by reading the article.

a. _____

b. _____

c. _____

 Step 2   Read

Now read the article without underlining.

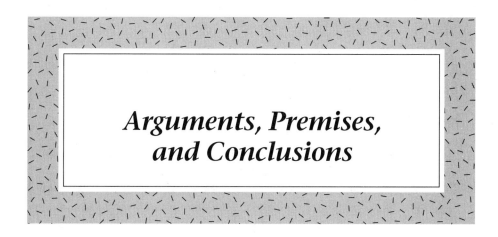

Arguments, Premises, and Conclusions

Patrick J. Hurley

Logic may be defined as the science that evaluates arguments. All of us encounter arguments in our day-to-day experience. We read them in books and newspapers, hear them on television, and formulate them when communicating them with friends and associates. The aim of logic is to develop a system of methods and principles that we may use as criteria for evaluating the arguments of others and as guides in constructing arguments of our own. Among the benefits to be expected from the study of logic is an increase in confidence that we are making sense when we criticize the arguments of others and when we advance arguments of our own.

An **argument,** as it occurs in logic, is a group of statements, one or more of which (the premises) are claimed to provide support for, or reasons to believe, one of the others (the conclusion). All arguments may be placed in one of two basic groups: those in which the premises really do support the conclusion and those in which they do not, even though they are claimed to. The former are said to be good arguments, the latter bad arguments. The purpose of logic, as the science that evaluates arguments, is thus to develop methods and techniques that allow us to distinguish good arguments from bad.

As is apparent from the above definition, the term "argument" has a very specific meaning in logic. It does not mean, for example, a mere verbal fight, as one might have with one's parent, spouse, or friend. Let us examine the features of this definition in greater detail. First of all, an argument is a group of statements. A **statement** is a sentence that is either true or false—in other words, typically a declarative sentence. The following sentences are statements:

Aluminum is attacked by hydrochloric acid.
Broccoli is a good source of vitamin A.
The *Lusitania* was sunk by the British navy.
Napoleon prevailed at Waterloo.

The first two are true, the second two false. Truth and falsity are called the two possible **truth values** of the statement. Thus, the truth value of the first two statements is true, and the truth value of the second two is false.

Unlike statements, many sentences cannot be said to be either true or false. Questions, proposals, suggestions, commands, and exclamations usually cannot, and so are not classified as statements. The following sentences are not statements:

What is the atomic weight of carbon?	(question)
Let's go to the park today.	(proposal)
We suggest that you travel by bus.	(suggestion)
Turn to the left at the next corner.	(command)
Right on!	(exclamation)

The statements that make up an argument are divided into one or more premises and one and only one conclusion. The **premises** are the statements that set forth the reasons or evidence, and the conclusion is the statement that the evidence is claimed to support or imply. Here is an example of an argument:

All crimes are violations of the law.
Theft is a crime.
Therefore, theft is a violation of the law.

The first two statements are the premises; the third is the conclusion. (The claim that the premises support or imply the conclusion is indicated by the word "therefore.") In this argument the premises really do support the conclusion, and so the argument is a good one. But consider this argument:

Some crimes are misdemeanors.
Murder is a crime.
Therefore, murder is a misdemeanor.

In this argument the premises do not support the conclusion, even though they are claimed to, and so the argument is not a good one.

Argument

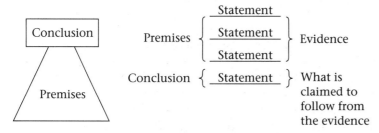

One of the most important tasks in the analysis of arguments is being able to distinguish premises from conclusion. If what is thought to be a conclusion is really a premise, and vice versa, the subsequent analysis cannot possibly be correct. Frequently, arguments contain certain indicator words that provide clues in identifying premises and conclusion. Some typical **conclusion indicators** are:

therefore	hence	whence
wherefore	thus	so
accordingly	consequently	it follows that
we may conclude	we may infer	implies that
entails that	it must be that	as a result

Whenever a statement follows one of these indicators, it can usually be identified as the conclusion. By process of elimination the other statements in the argument are the premises. Example:

Corporate raiders leave their target corporation with a heavy debt burden and no increase in productive capacity. Consequently, corporate raiders are bad for the business community.

The conclusion of this argument is "Corporate raiders are bad for the business community," and the premise is "Corporate raiders leave their target corporation with a heavy debt burden and no increase in productive capacity."

If an argument does not contain a conclusion indicator, it may contain a premise indicator. Some typical **premise indicators** are

since	in that	seeing that
as indicated by	may be inferred from	for the reason that
because	as	inasmuch as
for	given that	owing to

Any statement following one of these indicators can usually be identified as a premise. Example:

Expectant mothers should never use recreational drugs, since the use of these drugs can jeopardize the development of the fetus.

The premise of this argument is "The use of these drugs can jeopardize the development of the fetus," and the conclusion is "Expectant mothers should never use recreational drugs."

One premise indicator not included in the above list is "for this reason." This indicator is special in that it comes immediately *after* the premise it indicates. "For this reason" (except when followed by a colon) means for the reason (premise) that was just given. In other words, the premise is the statement that occurs immediately *before* "for this reason." One should be careful not to confuse "for this reason" with "for the reason that."

Sometimes a single indicator can be used to identify more than one premise. Consider the following argument:

The development of high-temperature superconducting materials is technologically justified, for such materials will allow electricity to be transmitted without loss over great distances, and they will pave the way for trains that levitate magnetically.

The premise indicator "for" goes with both "Such materials will allow electricity to be transmitted without loss over great distances" and "They will pave the way for trains that levitate magnetically." These are the premises. By process of elimination, "The development of high-temperature superconducting materials is technologically justified" is the conclusion.

Sometimes an argument contains no indicators. When this occurs, the reader/listener must ask himself or herself such questions as: What single statement is claimed (implicitly) to follow from the others? What is the arguer trying to prove? What is the main point in the passage? The answer to these questions should point to the conclusion. Example:

The space program deserves increased expenditures in the years ahead. Not only does the national defense depend upon it, but the program will more than pay for itself in terms of technological spinoffs. Furthermore, at current funding levels the program cannot fulfill its anticipated potential.

The main point of this argument is that the space program deserves increased expenditures in the years ahead. All the other statements provide support for this statement. This example reflects the pattern of most (but not all) clear-cut arguments that lack indicator words: The conclusion is the first statement. When the argument is restructured according to logical principles, however, the conclusion is always listed *after* the premises:

P$_1$: The national defense is dependent upon the space program.

P$_2$: The space program will more than pay for itself in terms of technological spinoffs.

P₃: At current funding levels the space program cannot fulfill its anticipated potential.

C: The space program deserves increased expenditures in the years ahead.

When restructuring arguments such as this, one should remain as close as possible to the original version, while at the same time attending to the requirement that premises and conclusion be complete sentences that are meaningful in the order in which they are listed.

Note that the first two premises are included within the scope of a single statement in the original argument. For the purposes of this text, compound arrangements of statements in which the various components are all claimed to be true will be considered as separate statements.

Passages that contain arguments sometimes contain statements that are neither premises nor conclusion. Only statements that are actually intended to support the conclusion should be included in the list of premises. If a statement has nothing to do with the conclusion or, for example, simply makes a passing comment, it should not be included within the context of the argument. Example:

> Socialized medicine is not recommended because it would result in a reduction in the overall quality of medical care available to the average citizen. In addition, it might very well bankrupt the federal treasury. This is the whole case against socialized medicine in a nutshell.

The conclusion of this argument is "Socialized medicine is not recommended," and the two statements following the word "because" are the premises. The last statement makes only a passing comment about the argument itself and is therefore neither a premise nor a conclusion.

 Step 3   Analyze What You Read—Create a Study Guide

Objective Questions

Go back and underline what you believe will be asked on a test and write marginal self-test items. You may use flash cards if you prefer.

Problem-Solving Questions

The best way to see whether you understand the concepts in this article might be to solve problems using the concepts. Create five arguments on topics of your choice. Each argument must have at least three statements, including one premise and a conclusion. Each argument must have a premise indicator and a conclusion indicator.

Step 4   Remember What's Important

Use the marginal notes or flash cards for self-testing on the objective portion. For the problem-solving portion, it might be helpful to work with other students. Try to identify in each argument the premise(s), premise indicator(s), conclusion, and conclusion indicator.

Step 5   Make Use of What You Read

Your instructor will give you a mastery test on this article.

Step 6   Evaluate Your Active Critical Thinking Skills

After your mastery test is graded, use the checklist in the appendix to evaluate your skills.

Reading 19

Principles of Genetics

Vocabulary Preview

genetics (jə net′iks) the branch of biology that deals with heredity and variation in similar or related animals and plants

nucleus (n‾oo′klē əs) the central, usually spherical or oval mass of protoplasm present in most plant and animal cells, containing most of the hereditary material and necessary to such functions as growth, reproduction, etc.

ultimate (ul′tə mit) final

predispose (prē dis pōz′) to make receptive beforehand; make susceptible

recessive (ri ses′iv) designating or relating to that one of any pair of hereditary factors which, when both are present in the germ plasm, remains latent; opposed to dominant

---

fat, āpe, cär; ten, ēven; is, bīte; gō, hôrn, t‾ool, look; oil, out; up, fʉr; chin, she; thin, *then*; zh, leisure; ŋ, ring; ə for *a* in *ago;* ′ as in *able* (ā′b'l)

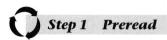

Step 1   Preread

Preread the following article by reading the headings, italics, illustrations, and the first sentence of each paragraph. You should be able to answer the following questions without looking back at the article.

1.   What is the subject of the article? _____

_____

233

2. What is the main idea of the article? _____

_____

3. How many chromosomes do human cells have? _____

_____

4. What is the difference between homozygous and heterozygous pairs of chromosomes? _____

5. Take a moment and think about genetics. Think about what you know about the subject, what you don't know, and what you might find out from reading the article. Make up three questions that might be answered by reading the article.

a. _____

b. _____

c. _____

 ## Step 2   Read

Read the article without underlining.

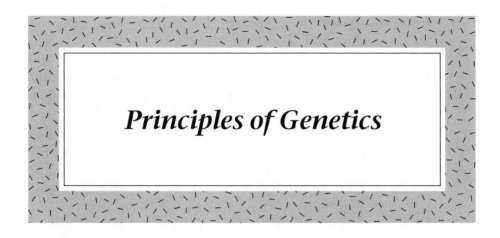

Principles of Genetics

James W. Kalat

You may have studied genetics in a biology class, but here we will explore concepts of genetics from the viewpoint of psychology, as well as biology.

Nearly every cell of every plant and animal contains a *nucleus,* which in turn contains strands called chromosomes (see Figure 1). Chromosomes, which consist of the chemical deoxyribonucleic acid, or DNA, provide the chemical basis of heredity. Humans have 23 pairs of chromosomes; they receive one chromosome of each pair from the mother and one from the father (see Figure 2).

Sections along each chromosome are known as genes—DNA segments that exert an indirect control on development. The chemical structure of the DNA that makes up the chromosomes and genes controls the formation of another chemical, called *ribonucleic acid,* or *RNA,* which in turn controls the body's production of chemicals called *proteins.* Certain proteins serve as structural units in the body; others control chemical reactions that take place in the body. A change in the body's chemical reactions, especially a change that occurs early in development, can have a profound effect on an individual's structure and function. Figure 3 summarizes this chain of events.

Occasionally a mutation (a random change) occurs in the structure of one of the genes, causing that gene to produce RNA molecules different from those the original gene produced. The ultimate result is an alteration in the appearance or activity of the organism. Most mutations are disadvantageous, although an occasional mutation will enable the body to produce proteins that are more advantageous than those it would otherwise have produced.

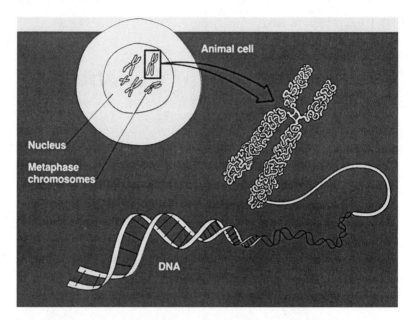

Figure 1 *Chromosomes, which reside in the nucleus of animal cells, are made of helical DNA. During metaphase the DNA is very tightly coiled, but when the cell needs access to it during cell growth, the DNA unfolds into long, delicate strands.*

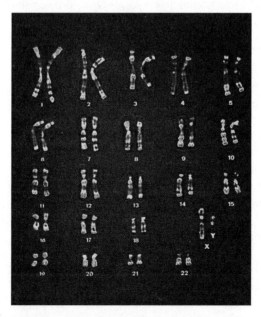

Figure 2 *The nucleus of each human cell contains 46 chromosomes, 23 from the sperm and 23 from the ovum united in pairs.*

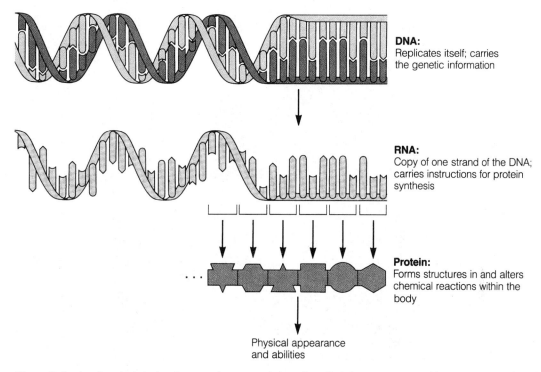

DNA:
Replicates itself; carries the genetic information

RNA:
Copy of one strand of the DNA; carries instructions for protein synthesis

Protein:
Forms structures in and alters chemical reactions within the body

Physical appearance and abilities

Figure 3 *In the chemical chain of events that controls heredity, the information carried by DNA is transferred to RNA and then translated into proteins.*

We can locate and identify certain genes by examining chromosomes under a microscope, though most genes cannot be located so readily. If we know that a particular gene is close to some other gene that we have already located on a chromosome, then we can use that other gene as a marker. For example, if you have a particular gene that we know your father and his mother also had, then you probably also have certain other genes that are close to that gene on their chromosomes. By using such reasoning, we can identify people who have a gene that predisposes them to a particular disease even before the symptoms have become evident.

The Transmission of Genes from One Generation to Another

Because people have two of each chromosome, they have two of each type of gene, one on each of the chromosomes. They have two genes for eye color, two for hair color, two for every characteristic. The two genes for hair color may be either the same or different. When both genes of a given pair are the same, the person is said to be homozygous (HO-mo-ZI-gus) for that gene. When the two genes are different, the person is heterozygous (HET-er-o-ZI-gus) for that gene (see Figure 4).

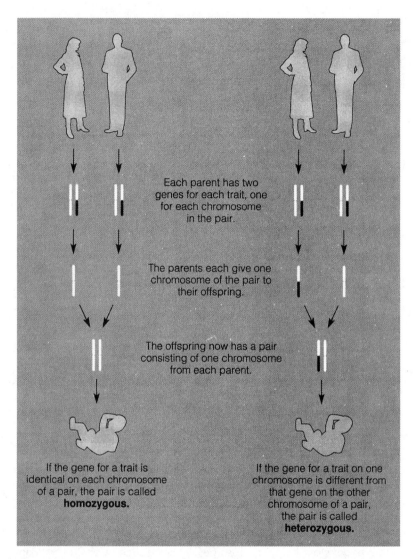

Each parent has two genes for each trait, one for each chromosome in the pair.

The parents each give one chromosome of the pair to their offspring.

The offspring now has a pair consisting of one chromosome from each parent.

If the gene for a trait is identical on each chromosome of a pair, the pair is called **homozygous.**

If the gene for a trait on one chromosome is different from that gene on the other chromosome of a pair, the pair is called **heterozygous.**

Figure 4 *In a pair of homozygous chromosomes, the gene for a trait is identical on both chromosomes. In a heterozygous pair, the chromosomes contain different genes for a trait.*

Certain genes are labeled dominant genes because they can mask the effects of other genes. Very few human behaviors depend on a single gene, but here is one example: The gene for the ability to curl the tongue lengthwise (Figure 5) is a dominant gene; all people who have that gene can curl their tongue, regardless of whether they are homozygous or heterozygous for that gene. The gene for the inability to curl the tongue is said to be a

Figure 5 *Curling the tongue lengthwise is a behavior that depends on a single gene.*

recessive gene. Only people who are homozygous for a recessive gene show its effects. In other words, if you cannot curl your tongue, you must be homozygous for the inability to curl gene (not exactly a serious handicap).

A person who is heterozygous for a particular gene will show the effects of the dominant gene, but may still pass the recessive gene to a son or a daughter. If parents who are heterozygous for the tongue-curling genes both pass the recessive gene to a child, the child will not develop the ability to curl his or her tongue.

Sex-Linked and Sex-Limited Genes

Some characteristics are more common in men; others are more common in women. Why? There can be many explanations, and a genetic explanation is not always a likely one. Still, genes do account for some of the differences, and it is valuable to know how genes could produce differences between the sexes.

One pair of human chromosomes are known as sex chromosomes because they determine whether a child will develop as a male or as a female. The other 22 pairs of chromosomes found in humans are known as autosomal chromosomes, from the Greek words *auto,* meaning "self," and *soma,* meaning "body." The autosomal chromosomes control the development of the body other than the genitals.

The sex chromosomes are of two types, known as X and Y (see Figure 6). A female has two X chromosomes in each cell; a male has one X chromosome and one Y chromosome. The female contributes one X chromosome to each child, and the male contributes either an X or a Y chromosome.

Genes located on the X chromosome are known as X-linked genes or as sex-linked genes, because the probability of their influence is linked to the sex of the individual. For example, the most common type of color blindness depends on a recessive gene the X chromosome carries. That gene is more likely to make its effects felt in males than in females. Why? Because every female has two X chromosomes, a female must be homozygous for this re-

Figure 6 *An electron micrograph of X and Y chromosomes shows the difference in length.*

cessive gene in order for it to show its effects. A male, however, has only one X chromosome and consequently any gene on that chromosome exerts its effects; it cannot be overruled by a recessive gene on another chromosome.

Genetically controlled differences between the sexes do not necessarily depend on sex-linked genes. For example, adult men generally have deeper voices and more facial hair than women do. Those characteristics are not controlled by genes on the X or Y chromosome. They are controlled by genes that are present in women as well as men, but these genes are activated only in men. Sex-limited genes are those that affect one sex only or affect one sex more strongly than the other. The genes that control breast development in women are also sex-limited genes.

Why are men more likely to get into fistfights than women are? We do not have enough evidence to determine whether genes are responsible, but if the difference is because of their genes, the responsible genes are probably sex-limited genes rather than sex-linked genes. That is, males and females have the same genes that promote aggressive behavior, but male hormones activate those genes more strongly.

 Step 3   *Analyze What You Read—Create a Study Guide*

Objective Questions

Go back and underline what you believe will be on a test. Make your own marginal notes that you can use to test yourself on what you have underlined. If you prefer, you may put the marginal note on the front of a flash card, and what you have underlined on the back.

Essay/Application Questions

A. *Predict Questions*

Three topics from this article are most likely for essay questions. Write them here:

1. _____
2. _____
3. _____

B. *Make Graphic Organizers*

Draw diagrams for the following concepts:

1. the structure of a cell
2. the transmission of genes from parent to offspring
3. sex of offspring and sex-linked genes

Step 4   *Remember What's Important*

Self-test using the marginal notes and graphic organizers. Use mnemonic devices as needed.

Step 5   *Make Use of What You Read*

Your instructor will give you a mastery test for this article.

Step 6   *Evaluate Your Active Critical Thinking Skills*

After you mastery test is graded, use the checklist in the appendix to evaluate your skills.

Reading 20

Free Will and Social Science

Vocabulary Preview

preordained (prē′or dānd′) ordained or decreed beforehand

capricious (kə prē′shəs) tending to change abruptly and without apparent reason; erratic; flighty

ironic (ī rän′ik) meaning the opposite of what is expressed; directly opposite of what is or might be expected

efface (ə fās′) to rub out, as from a surface; erase; wipe out

postulate (päs′työo lāt′) to assume without proof to be true, real, or necessary, esp. as a basis for argument

---

fat, āpe, cär; ten, ēven; is, bīte; gō, hôrn, tool, look; oil, out; up, fur; chin, she; thin, *then*; zh, leisure; ŋ, ring; ə for *a* in *ago;* ′ as in *able* (ā′b'l)

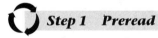 **Step 1   Preread**

Preread the following article by reading the title and the first sentence of each paragraph. Answer the following questions without looking back.

1. What is the subject of the article? _____

_____

2. What is the main idea of the article? _____

_____

3. What is the relation of free will to social science? _____

_____

4. Take a moment to think about free will. Think about what you know from your experience, what you don't know, and what you might find out from reading this article. Make up three questions that might be answered by reading the article.

a. _____

b. _____

c. _____

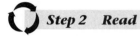

Step 2   Read

Now read the article without underlining.

Free Will and Social Science

Rodney Stark

For many centuries a major dispute in theology concerned individual responsibility. According to the doctrine of religious determinism (or fatalism), all human actions are preordained, determined by the gods or God; humans are helpless to alter their fates. But, if this were so, how could humans be asked to observe moral codes? If our actions are not ours to choose, how can we be blamed for our evil deeds? Early Christian theologians dealt with this problem by declaring that each individual possesses free will. God did make the world and create humans, they argued, but He did not create robots required to do His bidding. Instead, He gave humans the capacity to choose freely among alternatives, and He can therefore reward those who choose good and condemn those who choose evil.

This was a very powerful religious idea. God was no longer to be regarded as capricious, unjust, and terrible, as He must be if He is responsible for what we do, whether good or evil. Instead, it was possible to conceive of a God of mercy, justice, and absolute virtue—a God who gave humans life and choice and asked only virtue in return.

But what does the doctrine of free will have to do with social science? It mistakenly led to the conclusion that because humans possess free will, it is impossible to construct scientific theories to predict and explain their behavior! Thus, it was assumed that if it were possible to achieve social science, then humans must not possess free will; if their behavior is lawful and predictable, then it is inescapable and preordained. If we can predict who will commit crimes, then criminals can't choose good over evil and therefore bear no personal responsibility for their deeds.

While philosophers and theologians often used this argument to "prove" that social science was impossible, since it violated the principle of free will, ironically many social scientists have used much the same argument to "prove" that humans do not possess free will. Thus, Quételet claimed that the stability of crime and suicide rates not only challenged the doctrine of free will; it also demonstrated that humans do not really choose among courses of action but are essentially puppets dancing to the beat of society. As he put it: "The greater the number of individuals observed, the more do individual peculiarities, whether physical or moral, become effaced, and allow the general forces to predominate."

Another version of this view underlies claims by some psychotherapists that there are no "bad" people in prison, only "sick" people. But . . . sociological theories of crime do not assume that criminals have no choices. Instead, they concentrate on how different people have a different basis for making choices and different alternatives from which to choose. This is contrary to an image of human robots programmed to steal and kill.

Similarly, the first assumption of virtually all social science theories is the same: Humans possess the ability to reason and therefore to select among different lines of action. Social science proceeds from this starting point by postulating that the choices people make can be predicted and explained by assuming that they will *attempt* to do the most reasonable thing, given their circumstances, information, and preferences. That is, *people will seek to maximize their rewards and minimize their costs.* . . . This simple assumption about human behavior quickly leads to explanations of why and how codes of morality come to exist and why these, in turn, shape individual calculations about what choices are rewarding. Here, let us concentrate on the fact that it is *only* because people's choices *are* predictable that it is possible to claim that people have free will.

If people's behavior is not predictable, it must be random. That is, if knowledge of their past actions and their present situation tells us nothing about what people will do next, then the human mind does not reason but operates like a slot machine or a pair of dice. For only then can there be no consistent patterns between past and future behavior, no link between circumstance and action. Such people would indeed be unpredictable and would frustrate all attempts at social science. But such people would not be human. And surely they could not be judged for their acts or be said to possess free will, for they would have no capacity to choose and no reasoning power at all.

Let's approach this matter in another way. Suppose I set up a money store and offered to sell genuine $20 bills for 35¢ each. As soon as people made sure that there was no hidden gimmick, that they really could buy money from me at a huge discount, I'm sure I would have more customers than I could handle. When I predict that people will opt for a good deal, I am not reducing them to predetermined robots lacking the power of choice. I am merely saying that by assuming people can select reasonable choices, it is often easy to predict what they will choose to do.

Free will is the essential assumption of social science. Or, as W. E. B. Du Bois put it, sociology "is the science of free will." We do not assume that humans are puppets but that they are reasoning, feeling organisms who learn from experience, who respond to the world around them, who have the power to love, hope, dream, and plan. The goal of social science is to understand why and how humans have these capacities. Moreover, it is because humans can include the findings of social science in making their choices that social science is worthwhile. Social science is not dehumanizing. Rather, it is in some ways the most humanizing of disciplines: It asks what the nature of humanity is and how human life can be enhanced.

 ## Step 3 Analyze What You Read—Create a Study Guide

Objective Questions

Go back and underline what you believe will be on the test. Then write self-test notes in the margin. If you prefer, you may use flash cards instead.

Essay Questions

A. *Predict Questions*

There are two major subtopics in this article. Write them here:

1. _____

2. _____

B. *Make a Graphic Organizer*

Make a chart comparing religious determinism with the doctrine of free will in which you compare each theory's view of God and morality and each theory's effects on social science.

Step 4   Remember What's Important

Self-test using the marginal notes and graphic organizers. Use mnemonic devices as needed.

 Step 5   Make Use of What You Read

Your instructor will give you a mastery test for this article.

 Step 6   Evaluate Your Active Critical Thinking Skills

After your mastery test is graded, use the checklist in the appendix to evaluate your skills.

Unit Four

Advanced
Application
of ACT

The purpose of Unit Four is to give you practice in applying ACT on your own, the way you should while studying for your other classes. We provide ten articles, some persuasive and some informative. Follow the six steps of ACT for each article.

Using ACT Independently

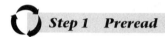

Step 1   Preread

Before you read each article, preview to find the subject and the main idea or point of view. The type of preview you do depends on the article's structure. Sometimes it is enough to read the title, headings, and illustrations. Sometimes the first and last paragraphs give you the information you need. If that doesn't work, read the first sentence of each paragraph, because the first sentence usually contains the main idea.

After the prereading, activate your background knowledge and your intellectual curiosity. Think about what you know about the topic, what you don't know, and what you would like to find out. If you can apply the information to your own life, that's even better. Generate a few questions to engage your mind as you read.

The prereading step will increase your comprehension, memory, and speed.

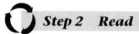

Step 2   Read

Read at whatever speed enables you to comprehend the ideas. Don't worry about what to underline for the memory step.

Step 3   Analyze What You Read

If the article is persuasive, note the point of view and the arguments in the margin and underline the supporting details for the arguments. If the article is informative, underline what you believe you will need to remember and write self-test notes in the margin. If the article is both persuasive and informative, use both techniques.

To prepare for essay questions, predict the questions and create one or more graphic organizers. If the article requires problem solving or application, prepare the problems and make a plan for practice.

Your instructor may choose to target certain types of objectives. For example, he or she may ask you to prepare for an objective or essay test, complete a written assignment, or join in a class discussion. If your instructor hasn't given you specific instructions, assume that you are preparing for a general quiz like the ones for the other articles in this book.

Step 4   *Remember What's Important*

Review your underlining, marginal notes, graphic organizers, or problems, and self-test until you feel you have mastered the information.

Step 5   *Make Use of What You Read*

Your instructor will give you a test or other assignment covering this material.

Step 6   *Evaluate Your Active Critical Thinking Skills*

An active critical thinker is always adapting to new situations, subtly changing techniques to be as efficient as possible. Asking yourself critical questions about the feedback you receive from your instructor will help you evaluate how well you've accomplished your reading and study objectives. By analyzing the questions you missed on a test, the comments and grades you received on written assignments, and the oral or written feedback your instructor gave you on speeches or discussions, you can revise your reading and study strategies before your next similar experience, continuing to improve your thinking skills with each new challenge. To aid you in evaluating your effectiveness, a checklist appears in the appendix.

Reading 21

Rubbish

Vocabulary Preview

herbicide (hur′bə sīd) any chemical substance used to destroy plants, especially weeds

insuperable (in sōō′pər ə b'l) cannot be overcome

disproportionate (dis prə pôr′shə nət) not in proportion

biodegrade (bī′ō di grād′) readily decompose by biological means, especially bacterial action

inert (in urt′) having few or no active properties

---

fat, āpe, cär; ten, ēven; is, bīte; gō, hôrn, tōōl, look; oil, out; up, fur; chin, she; thin, *then*; zh, leisure; ŋ, ring; ə for *a* in *ago;* ' as in *able* (ā′b'l)

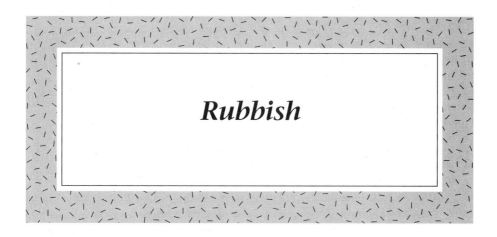

Rubbish

William L. Rathje

Newspapers. Telephone books. Soiled diapers. Half-empty cans of paint, motor oil and herbicide. Broken furniture and forsaken toys. Americans produce a lot of garbage. Recently, the press has paid much attention to the filling up (and closing down) of landfills and to the apparent inadequacy of our recycling efforts. The word *crisis* has become routine. For all the publicity, however, it may be that misinformation constitutes the real garbage crisis.

Since the early 1970s, the University of Arizona's Garbage Project has been looking at landfills and garbage fresh out of the can. As director of the program, I have talked extensively with people who talk about garbage every day—city officials, junkyard owners, landfill operators, civil engineers, microbiologists. Our garbage woes turn out to be serious, but not exceptional. And they can be dealt with by disposal methods that are safe and already available.

How much garbage is there? I have seen figures ranging from 2.9 to eight pounds discarded per person per day. But Garbage Project studies of refuse reveal that even three pounds of garbage per person per day may be too high an estimate for much of the country. Americans are wasteful, but we think of ourselves as more wasteful than we are.

What's more, we forget everything we no longer see; as much as 1200 pounds per year of wood or coal ash that every American generated at home at the turn of the century; the tens of thousands of dead horses that once had to be disposed of every year; the food waste that modern packaging has prevented. Consider the difference in terms of garbage generation between making orange juice from concentrate and orange juice from scratch, keeping in mind that producers of the concentrate sell the leftover rinds as feed, while households don't. In reality, Americans, as individuals, are not suddenly producing more garbage. Per capita our record seems to be one of relative stability.

Landfills

In the northeastern United States, there is an acute shortage of sanitary landfills. Nationwide some 3000 landfills reached capacity and were shut down between 1982 and 1987. Articles on the subject often warn that 50 percent of the landfills now in use will likely close down within five years. But that has always been true because most landfills are designed to be in use for only about ten years. The real problem is that in many areas old landfills are not being replaced. Texas, for example, awarded some 250 permits a year for municipal solid-waste landfills in the mid-'70s, but only 13 last year.

The landfill movement that matured after World War II intended not only to dispose of mountains of garbage but also to reclaim thousands of acres of "waste" land. Its proponents argued that the ideal sites for landfills were the very places that most scientists now believe to be the worst: along rivers or in wetlands. It is in unlined landfills in places like these that chemical "leachates"—solubles removed by percolating water—have posed a grave concern.

Environmental scientists now know enough to design and locate safe landfills. Places such as Long Island, N.Y., where the water table is high, should never have landfills again and should continue to ship garbage elsewhere. But the country at large still has room aplenty.

The obstacles to the sanitary landfill these days are monetary (transporting the garbage) and psychological: no one wants a garbage dump in his back yard. But these problems are not insuperable. Few nations have the enormous, and enormously safe, landfill capabilities that America has.

Fast Foods and Diapers

Another idea that persists about landfills is that certain products are disproportionately responsible for filling them up. I recently ran across articles in an Oregon newspaper that blame disposable diapers. An editorial in the New York *Times* singled out fast-food packaging, almost everyone's villain of choice, for straining the capacity of the nation's landfills. I have asked many people who have never seen the inside of a landfill to estimate what percentage consists of fast-food packaging. Most estimated either 20 or 30 percent.

The reality is considerably different. Over the past two years, the Garbage Project team has dug into seven landfills: two outside Chicago, two in the San Francisco Bay Area, two in Tucson and one in Phoenix. In eight tons of garbage and dirt cover, there were fewer than 16 pounds of fast-food packaging—about a tenth of one percent of the landfills' contents by weight. Less than one percent by weight was disposable diapers. Things made from plastic accounted for less than five percent by weight.

The real "culprit" in every landfill is plain old paper—non-fast-food paper—which accounts for 40 to 50 percent by weight. Yet, in all the hand-wringing, has a single voice been raised against the proliferation of telephone books? Each two-volume set of these books distributed in Phoenix last year—to be thrown out this year—weighed 7.95 pounds, for a total of more than 5000 tons of wastepaper. Dig a trench through a landfill and you will see layers of phone books, like geological strata. Just as conspicuous are newspapers, which, according to my research, make up ten to 18 percent of a typical municipal landfill by volume. During a recent dig in Phoenix, I found newspapers dating back to 1952 that looked so fresh you might read one over breakfast.

Biodegrading

The notion that paper rapidly biodegrades inside lined landfills is largely a myth. This may be a blessing, because if paper did degrade quickly, the result would be an enormous amount of ink and paint that could leach into ground water.

The fact that plastic hardly biodegrades at all, often cited as one of its great defects, may actually be a great virtue. Being inert, it doesn't introduce toxic chemicals into the environment. The senior staff scientist of the National Audubon Society, Jan Beyea, contends that plastics in landfills are no problem. The plastics that marine animals sometimes swallow or become enmeshed in generally come from ocean dumping.

Recycling

There is a big split between those who would recycle to make money and those who would recycle to do good. When I described the city of Tucson's successful newspaper-recycling program to a wastepaper dealer, he looked at me in horror. "You're telling me how well the competition is doing—the ones who are subsidized by the taxpayers to take away our livelihood," he said. "Don't you understand? There never has been a shortage of recycled newspapers. There just isn't enough demand. The more Tucson recycles, the less business I do."

Recycling by anyone should be encouraged. But it is important to understand what kind of recycling works and what kind may do more harm than good. Newsprint illustrates one potential problem. Only about ten percent of old newspapers are recycled into new newspapers. What newspapers are really good for is making cereal boxes and other containers (if the box is gray on the inside, it's from recycled stock), the insides of automobiles (the average car contains about 60 pounds of recycled paperboard containing newsprint), wallboard and insulation. All these end uses seem to be near saturation.

What happens when the market is suddenly flooded with newsprint? Two years ago the state of New Jersey began implementing legislation requiring every community to separate at curbside and collect at least three categories of recyclables. As a result, the price of used newspaper in some parts of New Jersey has plummeted from as much as $40 a ton to minus $25 a ton—in other words, you have to pay to have it taken away. If legislation like this became widespread, without measures to increase demand for recycled-paper products, the effects could be precisely the opposite of those intended.

The fact is that we are currently recycling about as much paper as the market can bear. The demand for recyclable plastic and aluminum has not been fully met, but Americans have been doing a pretty good job of returning their aluminum cans. And whatever people say about their willingness to recycle, the only reliable predictor of recycling is the price paid at buy-back centers. The Garbage Project's research showed that as prices rose for, say, newsprint, the number of newspapers found in local refuse declined.

Source Reduction

Not long ago I stopped at the University of California at Berkeley, where a ban was being considered on expanded-polystyrene foam—the substance used in coffee cups, hamburger boxes and meat trays. It was lunch time, and Sproul Plaza was filled with some 700 or 800 students, virtually all of whom held large foam clamshells containing hot food. I asked one group of lunchers what they thought about a ban on polystyrene. Great idea they said between mouthfuls and without irony.

Source reduction is to garbage what preventive medicine is to health—a means of eliminating a problem before it can happen. But the utility of legislated source reduction is in many respects an illusion. Most consumer industries already have made products as compact and light as possible for ease of distribution and to conserve costly resources. In 1970 a typical plastic soda bottle weighed 60 grams; today it weighs 48 grams and is more easily crushed. And source-reduction measures don't eliminate much garbage; hamburgers, eggs, and VCRs still have to be put in something.

America *can* manage its garbage. Safely designed landfills should be employed where there is still room for them. Incinerators with appropriate safety devices can be sited anywhere, but make the most sense in the Northeast. States and municipalities need to cut deals with wastepaper and scrap dealers on splitting the money to be made from recycling.

Additional steps could be taken to reduce the biggest component of garbage: paper. Freight rates could be revised to make the transport of paper for recycling cheaper than the transport of wood for pulp to make new paper. And to increase the demand for recycled paper, the federal government—which uses far more paper than any other institution in America—could insist that most federal paper work be done on recycled paper.

Finally, we need to expand our knowledge. Many of us are better informed about Neptune than we are about this country's garbage.

But even if present trends continue, I am not worried that we will be buried in our garbage. Perhaps the biggest challenge we face is to recognize that the conventional wisdom about garbage is often wrong.

Reading 22

Assertiveness

Vocabulary Preview

self-disclosure (self′dis klō′zhər) making something known about oneself

entails (in tālz′) makes necessary

verbalizing (vʉr′bə līz iŋ) putting into words

coercive (kō ʉr′siv) forceful; compelling; using force

tirade (tī′rād) long, angry speech

---

fat, āpe, cär; ten, ēven; is, bīte; gō, hôrn, to͞ol, look; oil, out; up, fʉr; chin, she; thin, *then*; zh, leisure; ŋ, ring; ə for *a* in *ago;* ' as in *able* (ā′b'l)

Assertiveness

Rudolph F. Verderber

As we have seen, describing feelings means putting your feelings into words. Assertiveness, another self-disclosure skill, entails verbalizing your position on an issue for purposes of achieving a specific goal. Assertiveness may involve describing feelings, giving good reasons for a belief or feeling, or suggesting a behavior or attitude you think is fair, without exaggerating for dramatic effect or attacking the other individual verbally.

Suppose you have been unable to pin your professor down about setting up a specific time for discussion of the mistakes you made on your first paper, yet you need to talk with him before you turn in the second paper, which is due at the end of the week. In this case your *goal* is to get an appointment before the end of the week. One way of being assertive would be to say to your professor, "I'm really feeling anxious about not getting to talk with you about my paper—I'm afraid that if we don't talk I'm likely to make the same kinds of mistakes again. Could we please meet to talk about my writing before Thursday?" This wording builds from a description of feelings. Another way of being assertive would be to stop your professor after class and say, "I really need to talk to you before I turn in my next paper—I don't want to make the same mistakes I made last time. Can we please get together before Thursday?" This wording focuses on the reason for requesting the meeting. Note, too, that both this approach and the previous one represent reasonable behavior that neither exaggerates for dramatic effect nor represents an "attack" on the other individual.

Contrasting Methods of Coping with Adversity

When people believe they have been wronged, they are likely to behave in one of three ways: passively, aggressively, or assertively.

Passive Behavior

When people behave passively, they do not try to influence the behavior of others. People who behave passively are reluctant to state opinions, share feelings, or assume responsibility for their actions. Thus, they often submit to the demands of others, even when doing so is inconvenient or against their best interests.

For example, when Bill uncrates the new color television set he purchased at a local department store, he notices a large, deep scratch on the left side of the cabinet. If he behaved passively, Bill would be angry about the scratch, but he would keep the set and do nothing to influence the store clerk from whom he purchased it to replace it.

Aggressive Behavior

When people behave aggressively, they lash out at the source of their discomfort with little regard for the situation or for the feelings of those they are attacking. Unfortunately, too many people confuse aggressiveness with assertiveness. Unlike assertiveness, aggressive behavior is judgmental, dogmatic, fault-finding, and coercive.

To exemplify aggressive behavior and to extend the contrast we are making, let's return to Bill's problem. If Bill behaved aggressively, after discovering the scratch on the cabinet of his new television set, he might brashly display his anger. He might storm back to the store, loudly demand his money back, and accuse the clerk of intentionally selling him damaged merchandise. During his tirade, he might threaten the store with a lawsuit. Such aggressive behavior might or might not get Bill a new television set; it would certainly damage the interpersonal relationships he had with those to whom he spoke.

Assertive Behavior

When people behave assertively, they state what they believe to be true for them, describe their feelings fully, give good reasons for their beliefs or feelings, suggest the behavior or attitude they think is fair, avoid exaggerating for dramatic effect, and take responsibility for their actions and feelings without personal attacks on others. If Bill behaved assertively, he would be angry about bringing home a damaged set—the feeling of anger is common to each of these three contrasting response behaviors. The difference between assertive behavior and the other two response styles is not the feeling but the behavior of the person as a result of that feeling. If Bill responded assertively, he might call the store and ask to speak to the clerk from whom he had purchased the set. When the clerk answered, Bill would describe his anger that resulted from discovering a large scratch on the cabinet when he uncrated the set. He would then say that he was calling to find out what to do to return the damaged set and get a new one.

While both the aggressive and the assertive behaviors might achieve Bill's purpose of getting a new television set, the assertive behavior would achieve the same result at lower emotional costs to both Bill and those with whom he talked.

In order to emphasize the contrast among the response styles, let's examine another situation in which the issue is the quality of an interpersonal relationship. Betty works in an office with both male and female employees. Whenever the boss has an especially interesting job to be done, he assigns it to a male employee whose desk is next to Betty's. The boss has never said anything to Betty or to the male employee that would indicate that the boss thinks less of Betty or her ability. Nevertheless, Betty is hurt by the boss's behavior.

If Betty behaved passively, she would say nothing to the boss. If Betty behaved aggressively, she would call her boss on his behavior by saying something like "Why the hell do you always give Tom the plums and leave me with the garbage! I'm every bit as good a worker and I'd like a little recognition!"

In contrast, if Betty behaved assertively, she would go back to the boss's office and describe his behavior and her feelings about that behavior to him. She might say, "I don't know whether you are aware of it, but during the last three weeks every time you had a really interesting job to do, you gave the job to Tom. To the best of my knowledge, you believe that Tom and I are equally competent—you've never given me any evidence to suggest that you thought less of my work. But when you 'reward' Tom with jobs that I perceive as plums and continue to offer me routine jobs, it really hurts my feelings. Do you understand my feelings about this?"

If you were Betty's boss, which of her responses would be most likely to achieve her goal of getting better assignments? Probably the assertive behavior. Which of her responses would be most likely to get her fired? Probably the aggressive behavior. Which of her behaviors would be least likely to "rock the boat"? Undoubtedly the passive behavior—but then she would continue to get the boring job assignments.

To be assertive, then, you should (1) identify what you are thinking or feeling and (2) state it in the most interpersonally sound way possible.

You must also understand that being assertive may not achieve your goals. Every skill we have discussed in this section is designed to increase the chances of interpersonal effectiveness. But there will still be times when what you attempt won't work or may even backfire. Just as with self-disclosure and describing feelings, being assertive involves risks. For instance, in the preceding example Betty's boss might become so defensive that he fires Betty. But if being treated unfairly is a concern to Betty—and

I believe it should be—then Betty can accept the risk of such an undesirable outcome, knowing that if she uses the skill properly, getting fired would be very unlikely. If you are truly assertive and not aggressive, you are far more likely to achieve your goals than you would be if you behaved in some other way.

Reading 23

Improving Your T.Q.

Vocabulary Preview

astronomical (as'trə näm'i kəl) very large, as the numbers used in astronomy

aptitude (ap'tə to͞od') a natural tendency, inclination, or ability

divulging (də vulj'iŋ) making known; revealing

proctors (präk'tərz) college officials who maintain order, supervise examinations, etc.

disclaimer (dis klā'mer) a denial; refusal to accept responsibility

---

fat, āpe, cär; ten, ēven; is, bīte; gō, hôrn, to͞ol, look; oil, out; up, fʉr; chin, she; thin, *th*en; zh, leisure; ŋ, ring; ə for *a* in *ago;* ' as in *able* (ā'b'l)

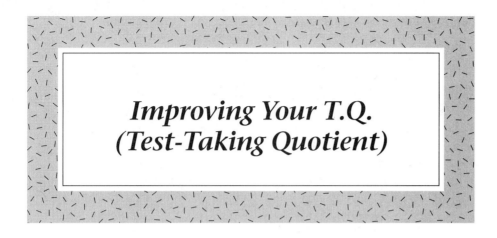

Improving Your T.Q. (Test-Taking Quotient)

Perry W. Buffington

You will have one hour to complete this test. All answers must be marked on the answer sheet. Make no marks on the test booklet. Using a No. 2 pencil, place your name . . . . Ready? Begin."

They're off! Each test-taker working at a different pace; each using a different technique and strategy; all wishing they were somewhere else.

Ours is a test-taking culture. And whether you are an adult job-hunter, license-applicant or student, tests always provoke uncertainty, especially if life decisions are attached to them.

In 12 years of your elementary and secondary education, you completed a conservative estimate of 2,600 weekly quizzes. College midterm and final examinations over a four-year period account for another 100, and each year of advanced professional training adds another 25 major exams.

People do not realize that classroom examinations represent only a small segment of testing experience. School systems administer approximately 2 million standardized tests in addition to regular classroom tests.

The total number administered by business, government, industry and clinics, however, is astronomical, dwarfing the total number of school tests.

People tend to take tests without really understanding them. One sure way to improve your performance is to familiarize yourself with the different types of examinations. Simply understanding the test format promotes self-confidence.

Can familiarity with test-taking boost your test scores? Yes, along with 15 other "tricks." Read on.

All tests—whether simple classroom quizzes, tests for a driver's license or statistically oriented aptitude tests—have one major point in common: A test is a measure of a person's behavior at *one* point in time.

A long-held myth has led most people to conclude that test scores are forever. This is simply not true.

Scores change from one test-taking to the next. In fact, there are numerous reported cases of intelligence quotients (IQs) fluctuating as much as 30 or 40 points between test administrations.

Another source of score fluctuation is a result of the test-taker's uncertainty with different types of tests.

Overall there are two specific types: maximal- and typical-performance tests. Maximal tests attempt to measure an individual's best possible performance accurately. Included in this type of test are intelligence tests, academic or classroom (achievement) tests and aptitude tests. Of these, IQ tests are the most widely known and the least understood.

It's amazing how so much confusion over those two little letters, IQ, has proliferated since the testing movement began in the early 1900s. The first intelligence tests were conceived by Alfred Binet, a French psychologist, who was asked to develop a procedure to predict which children were unable to learn in a classroom setting. Today there are approximately 350 intelligence tests on the market.

Myths surrounding the IQ test have grossly contaminated the public's understanding; people want the IQ test to do more than it is capable of doing. It is best used to measure school success: to assess mental skills and the ability to adapt in new situations and learn academically.

Another maximal-performance test is an admissions test (technically a form of aptitude testing). These tests are designed to measure the degree of skill of people when they are attempting to perform to the limit of their ability. But people allow these tests to intimidate them, and that puts them under a great deal of tension. If you've taken one of these exams previously, chances are your score will increase in subsequent testing.

Two important points here: First, put the practice rule to work for you (familiarity, again). Second, ask friends who have taken the test what they remember about it, and then check your local bookstore for manuals that will prepare you for the test. Books currently on the market that raise scores do so not by divulging knowledge, but by giving you familiarity with the items and test formats.

Typical performance tests do not promote as much anxiety as maximal-performance tests, for they are designed to assess interests, personality traits, attitudes and other similar characteristics. There is little preparation needed and no "right" or "wrong" answers.

Now for the 15 other tricks:

1. When it is possible to prepare for a test, do so! In fact, "overlearn" the material.

Research consistently shows that overlearning the material reduces anxiety and raises test scores.

Also, it has been found that consistent studying over a period of time is more effective than cramming just before a test. Going to the movies the night before an exam can be therapeutic. How do you know when over-learning takes place? When you feel you have mastered the subject, study one or two hours more.

2. Show up on time, but not early. If you must get there early, stand alone, away from the crowd. If you pay attention to others' worries, your anxiety level will increase, too.

3. Know in advance if the test has a correction formula. For example, for every four items you answer incorrectly, one right one might be deducted from your total score. If you answer 50 items correctly, but miss 20, after the correction formula, your score would be 45. This is an attempt to correct for guessing.

4. Eliminate alternatives. If the item is a four-choice, multiple-choice format, the odds are one in four you could guess the right one. If you can eliminate any two of the four, your odds are 50–50. If you cannot eliminate any of the alternatives, you have no idea which one is correct, and if there is no correction for guessing, then pick the longest answer and proceed to the next test question.

Test authors tend to make the correct answer the longest.

5. Test authors also tend to make one of two parallel statements the correct answer. For instance, if two of the four choices have major differences in wording, and if the other two are almost identical in structure and wording, chances are one of the parallel statements is right.

Probably the longer statement will get you points.

6. Read directions carefully. Many points are lost because people don't understand what they are supposed to do. If you have not finished reading the directions or don't understand them, ask the proctors for assistance.

7. If the test is multiple-choice, requiring you to read a "stem" and then select one correct response from four alternatives, attempt to answer the question before you read the possible choices. After you formulate your answer, match your ideas to the possibilities and pick the one most similar. By doing this, you are using not only recognition but recall.

8. Pace yourself so you complete as many items as possible.

Sometimes the items at the end of a test are weighted more because fewer people answer them.

9. If the test requires you to read long passages and then answer questions about the reading, read the questions first. By doing this, you will know what you are looking for as you read, and you'll be in a much better position to answer. If the test is timed, this technique also increases your speed and efficiency.

10. Skip items you are unsure of, items about material you've seen before but can't remember the answer immediately. Chances are your brain

will be searching for and retrieving the information while you are working on other items. When the answer comes to you, go back and mark it.

11. Do not change your answers on multiple-choice tests unless you are very uncertain about your initial answer. Research has shown that only when you have strong doubts is your second answer more likely to be correct.

12. Read the questions carefully. On essay tests, note such key words as compare, contrast, discuss, evaluate, analyze, define and describe. If you are unsure about an essay question, your response will come across as wordiness. Do what the questions asks, be direct, make your point and support it. On multiple-choice tests, look out for such negative disclaimers as, "Which of the following could *not* be . . . ?"

As you read the test questions, underline the key words. This will re-check your thinking.

13. There is some evidence that if you are slightly cool you will do better on a test. Informal observations certainly support this point. For instance, if you are too warm, you may become sleepy and lose your focus.

14. Re-check your work. Make clerical corrections only.

15. Finally, ask to see your corrected test and scores. By reviewing a test, you become test-wise.

Tests are necessary to determine levels of knowledge and to help make placement decisions. They are capable of motivating via feedback. So it is important to develop a healthy, positive attitude toward examinations.

As tests are mastered, they serve as "trial runs" for other, more difficult life tests.

Reading 24

Fake News

Vocabulary Preview

logo (lō′gō) a distinctive company signature, trademark, symbol, etc.

pharmaceutical (fär′mə sōōt′i kəl) of or by drugs

tainted (tānt′id) spoiled; made morally corrupt

transponder (tran spän′dər) a radio or radar transceiver that automatically transmits electrical signals when activated by a specific signal

authenticity (ô′thən tis′ə tē) believability; genuineness

---

fat, āpe, cär; ten, ēven; is, bīte; gō, hôrn, tōōl, look; oil, out; up, fʉr; chin, she; thin, *then*; zh, leisure; ŋ, ring; ə for *a* in *ago;* ′ as in *able* (ā′b'l)

Fake News

TV Guide

The *CBS Evening News* appeared to have put a lot of work into its June 13, 1991 segment on the hazards of automatic safety belts. The shoulder straps, announced correspondent Mark Phillips, are "a labor-saving device that may be costing lives instead of saving them." Proof: videotape of a car being tipped on its side, the door opening and the strap allowing a dummy to fall out and be crushed beneath the car.

A good piece, apparently showing the lengths to which CBS News would go to verify a report.

Trouble is, the videotape was not by CBS. Not that you'd have known it from the newscast: CBS's famous "eye" logo ran throughout the piece and there was no indication to the viewer as to who performed the demonstration. In fact, the tape was part of a "video news release" created by the Institute for Injury Reduction (IIR), a swell-sounding name for a lobby group largely supported by lawyers whose clients often sue auto companies for crash-related injuries. Indeed, say the group's opponents, IIR lawyers often show reports like the CBS segment in court to win cases, increase their client's payments and fatten their fees. After all, juries find reports aired by CBS more credible than, say, some taped test by a group with an obvious ax to grind.

Score another hit for the fast-growing world of fake news.

Fake? Yes, to viewers who think of news as the work of independent journalists who broadcast their own reporting and camera work. But that's not what we see when reporters air the handiwork of PR firms out to plug a product, polish an image, or ensure that a particular political spin is spun.

Over the last few years, fake news has grown into a big business. Every day, PR pros supply the country's 700-plus local TV outlets and the national networks with news-like reports and features. In some cases, they offer stations prepaid satellite interviews with celebrities and newsmakers. Most material, however, arrives as a "video news release" (VNR). This is a collection of pictures and words, delivered free of charge by satellite or cassette, which usually includes everything from background shots that can be edited into a story to a fully produced piece ready to air.

Some other recent examples from around the television dial:

- The audience for WJBK-TV's newscast in June 1991 saw a colorful report on Cheerios' 50th anniversary. But the Detroit station didn't have to send its news crews to the Minneapolis headquarters of General Mills. The company transmitted videos of its product via satellite to WJBK—and virtually every other TV station across the country—and eventually into the homes of about 17 million viewers.
- On Nov. 21 last year, a Frenchman was the first person to row across the Pacific Ocean. A great human-interest story, covered by ABC, CBS, NBC, and CNN. But much of the videotape used by three of the networks was provided by Sector Sport Watches, sponsor of the trip, which sent footage shot by its own crews to every major newsroom in the country. Conveniently, the company's logo was plastered all over the boat and appeared throughout the video. Result: three of the four national newscasts were momentarily transformed into commercials (NBC apparently didn't use the footage).

Most VNR material looks so realistic that it's hard for viewers to tell the difference. But don't blame the PR pros for doing their jobs. If you're confused about what news is real, and what's fake, the fault lies with the newscasters. The vast majority ignore the pleas of their own trade group—the Radio-Television News Directors Association (RTNDA)—to include a label on the screen that identifies material supplied by nonnews outfits. "When that isn't done, even if it's without malicious intent, then there's a problem," says RTNDA president David Bartlett.

If it's so easy to justify with a simple label, why don't stations do it more often? The answer is: newscasters have their own images to protect. Eugene Secunda, a professor of marketing at Baruch College in New York City, points to the essential irony of the problem: "If you are a news director, why would you do anything that might in any way compromise the believability of your program?"

As a result, although most viewers don't realize it, on any given night—especially on a local broadcast—there's a good chance that some of the news they see will be fake. Not that it's necessarily inaccurate. Just that it was made to plug something else. And it's something the PR community has grown skillful at providing, as many top-notch former TV correspondents and producers join their ranks. These veterans know how to slip the client's name into the video without making the package seem too commercial for newscasters to air.

In one sense, all of this may not seem overly alarming. After all, viewers love to see behind-the-scenes shots from a new Hollywood flick . . . a tape of a local high-school band marching at Disney World (a prolific producer of VNRs) . . . or a first look at a pharmaceutical company's latest wonder drug. Freebie videos commonly appear in stories about medicine, science, business or consumer affairs, and entertainment. Often enough, it's just a way to get some media attention. . . .

Then what's the great harm?

Well, sometimes, if the stakes are high enough, decisions of life and death can be affected. When Kuwait was invaded, it was a public-relations firm and its camera crews—not news organizations—that distributed much of the news and film about atrocities in the occupied country and whipped up war fever.

But a more common reason for concern is that when VNRs are well-made, they attack the Achilles' heel of serious TV news: Since viewers prefer pieces that are "picture-rich," VNRs often knock out (or at least reduce the available time for) important stories that are "picture-poor." A fluffy feature with a strong VNR, then, may drive out a serious story about the economy. At other times, the slick PR pictures may persuade a producer to favor one story over another.

Elections can be affected. . . . Presidential candidates are increasingly using a VNR-like technique for increasing the amount of airtime they get in important cities. Instead of spending all their time seeking out TV reporters and staging photo opportunities, they stay put and purchase time on a satellite. From where they are, they beam into stations to be interviewed by local anchors. In fact, of course, the process is tainted, because it is the candidate, not the station, that is paying for the airtime—and at a far cheaper rate than a commercial would cost. Meanwhile, local anchors get to play Ted Koppel for a day—and often air every minute of their interviews.

It's easy to see why the candidates like this technique. "If you want to cover a lot of places in the country very quickly, this allows you to do it in a cost-effective way," says Clinton media adviser Frank Greer. A satellite transponder, he says, costs a mere $600 an hour to rent. And, says Steve Rabinowitz, whose Washington, D.C.–based firm provides satellite services for Sen. Bob Kerrey, "It's much easier for a Presidential candidate to get a local station to interview him than to get a network to do so." Unspoken is another advantage for the candidates: Local anchors Rock and Roxanne are unlikely to be as tough to handle as a national reporter—a Sam Donaldson—who covers the campaign regularly.

This, too, is a form of fake news. The RTNDA's Bartlett says stations should treat a campaign-supplied interview as though it were a VNR—and tell viewers what's happening. The audience should be able to know whether an anchor is "wimping out because the candidate paid for the time."

VNRs and satellite media tours probably wouldn't be as popular as they are if the news business wasn't under so much stress. New competition from cable and independent TV, plus the recession, has forced many news operations to lay off correspondents, producers and crews. Yet at the same time, programmers are adding time for news shows: they're usually less expensive (and more profitable) than entertainment shows. Larry Pintak, a former CBS correspondent who now makes VNRs at Pintak Communications International, says frankly, "The news industry has been so gutted over the last few years that they don't have a choice (but to use VNRs)."

And that's just fine with a lot of corporations, interest groups, and politicians. They'll pay for VNRs and satellite interviews because viewers will believe a news segment far more willingly than a paid commercial. (Also, it costs an average of $20,000 to produce and distribute a VNR nationwide—a bargain compared with the $50,000 it costs just to air a 30-second spot on a national newscast.) In addition, many lobby groups and politicians often are barred from buying commercial time during newscast periods. Stations say they don't want viewers to confuse the ads with the programming, or to think that their correspondents are financially beholden to a political sponsor.

But these same stations won't ban VNRs.

How, and how extensively, are VNRs used? Consider a few statistics:

- Roughly 80 percent of the country's news directors acknowledge that they employ VNR material at least several times a month, according to a survey by Nielsen Media Research. If anything, this statistic probably understates how commonly the PR-produced material airs. These days, news stories and video flow freely between stations and networks. As a result, newscasters may carry a piece produced by someone else, without knowing that the original story included VNR footage.
- About 4000 VNRs were made available to newscasters in 1991, up from around 700 in 1988, according to Laurence Moskowitz, president of a New York–based firm, Medialink, which distributes nearly half of these video packages.
- And more than 46 percent of the country's news directors predict that national newscasters—including network, cable and syndicated shows—will increase their use of VNRs over the next five years, according to a new Nielsen survey commissioned by Medialink, using questions supplied by *TV Guide.* Only 10 percent anticipated any decline.

In justifying their use, some news directors insist they are not being manipulated. A smart reporter, they say, can still craft balanced stories using pictures from biased sources. They characterize the VNR as a cousin of the printed press release, which nearly every news organization uses to prepare stories. If VNRs are so different, they ask, then where do you draw the line?

Should newscasters not use NASA's films from space? Should they banish Pentagon-supplied file shots of missiles being launched?

The answer lies in Truth in Advertising—labeling. But newscasters, concerned about their own credibility, don't like to own up to their freebies. So a smooth outfit like Medialink, which understands this weakness, can be open about its aims. In a tape promoting the use of VNRs, the company assures its PR clients that TV stations will "use the supplied narration, or, by using the [company-supplied script], voice the story themselves." To encourage that, a Medialink pamphlet supplies hints to VNR producers: They shouldn't show anyone who looks like a correspondent on-screen ("Stations do not want a reporter appearing in their newscast who is not on their staff") and they can achieve news-like authenticity on the soundtrack ("Always have your announcer sign off with a standard outcue: 'This is John Doe reporting'").

The harsh truth is that newscasters need to be aware of manipulation more than ever, says former NBC correspondent David Hazinski, who now teaches telecommunications at the University of Georgia. "They're selling television news shows, and they're selling the credibility they spent 30 years building up."

Some of the lines between news and commercials have become so blurred that the Federal Food and Drug Administration, which oversees pharmaceutical aids, said it might step in. In July, the FDA said it is preparing "a comprehensive policy of VNRs—and told drug companies that until the rules are drawn up, the releases would be treated as ad messages, which have to be submitted to the agency."

Interestingly, on this, the RTNDA rears back and says it opposes the FDA's action as "inappropriate government interference" in the First Amendment–protected news business. "A video news release is a matter between the issuer and the newsroom," says the RTNDA's Bartlett.

Not quite. It's also a matter between the television newsroom, an institution more trusted than most, and the viewer. As long as newscasters pretend out of pride that what they broadcast is real news, instead of labeling it for what it is, this trust—and the integrity of the news itself—will continue to erode.

Reading 25

Building a House:
Culture and Adaptation

Vocabulary Preview

adaptive (ə dap′tiv) able to change

material (mə tir′ē əl) of matter; of substance; physical

anthropologist (an′thrō päl′ə jist) a person who specializes in the study of humanity

verandah (və ran′də) an open porch, usually roofed, along the outside of a building

tinkered (tiŋ′kʉrd) made clumsy attempts to mend something

---

fat, āpe, cär; ten, ēven; is, bīte; gō, hôrn, to̅o̅l, look; oil, out; up, fʉr; chin, she; thin, *then*; zh, leisure; ŋ, ring; ə for *a* in *ago;* ′ as in *able* (ā′b′l)

Building a House:
Culture and Adaptation

Serena Nanda

The emphasis on culture as adaptive is more easily seen in some areas of culture than in others. The ways in which humans satisfy their basic needs for food, shelter, and safety, for example, while part of a culturally constructed reality, are more directly adaptive to the requirements of the physical environment than, say, art. The material culture of societies with simple technologies is based on adaptive strategies that have developed slowly over long periods of trial and error and are finely suited to their physical environments, even when the people in the society cannot say why things are done in a certain way.

Anthropologist James Hamilton found this out the hard way, when he tried to build a house for himself while doing fieldwork among the Pwo Karen of northwestern Thailand. To learn about house construction, Hamilton observed carefully the details of the building of a house. Karen houses are essentially wooden-post structures, raised about six feet off the ground, with bamboo walls, peaked roofs, and a verandah. There are no windows: The space between the thatch of the roof and the height of the walls serves for light and ventilation. The kitchen is in the house, with a water-storage area on one side of the verandah. This is an important feature of the house because Karen customs of sociability require that visitors and guests be offered water.

There were some features of the Karen house with which Hamilton, as an American, did not feel comfortable and which he tried to alter in building his own house. First of all, he insisted that, because the climate was very hot, his house be in a shaded area under some tall trees. The Karen villagers suggested that this was a bad location, but this didn't dissuade him. Like most Americans, Hamilton also liked the "lawn"—the wide grassy area in front of his house—and protested when the villagers started pulling up the grass.

He wasn't, he said, concerned about the snakes and scorpions that might be in the grass; besides, he had a flashlight and boots in case he had to go out at night.

In a traditional Karen house, a person cannot stand up straight as the side walls are less than five feet high. In order to allow for the American view that people ought to be able to stand up in their houses, Hamilton lowered the floor on his house to about two feet off the ground, to give the house more height. Furthermore, because the Karen house is dark, and, to Americans, rather small, Hamilton decided to have his kitchen outside the house, in spite of the grumbling of the Karen that this was not the proper way to build a house. He built an extension on one side of the house with a lean-to roof covering made of leaves—this became his kitchen. Finally, when the Karen started to cut off the long overhanging thatch from the roof, Hamilton asked that they let it remain, as it gave him some privacy from eyes peering over the wall, which did not meet the top of his house.

After the house was finished and Hamilton had lived in it for a while, he found out why the Karen had not liked the alterations he had made in his house. This part of Thailand has a heavy rainy season, and because the house was under the trees, the roof could not dry out properly and it rotted. In addition, so many twigs and branches fell through the roof that it was like a sieve. The slope of the lean-to over the kitchen was not steep enough; instead of running off, the water came through the roof. So the whole side of the house roof had to be torn off and replaced with a steeper roof, made of sturdier (and more expensive) thatch.

The nice "lawn" combined with the reachable thatch of the roof was too great a temptation for the local cows, who tried to make their meal out of it. One morning Hamilton woke up to find his lawn covered with piles of cow dung, with hundreds of dung beetles rolling little balls of dung all around the "yard." He cut off the thatch overhang that was left under the trees and pulled up all the grass.

Because the house had been built too low to the ground (by Karen standards) in a shady, cool, wet area, there was insufficient ventilation and drying in and around the house to prevent mildew. This meant that Hamilton had to sweep walls and wipe all leather objects once a week and tightly seal all his anthropological tools—field notes, camera, film, tape recorder, and typewriter.

The Karen house, like houses everywhere, has symbolic meanings and reflects the social organization and world view of a people. But there is no getting around the fact that it must also be built within the constraints posed by the physical environment. While some alterations have been made in the Karen house over the last eighty years, reflecting some changes in social organization, the materials and house construction are not so easily tinkered with.

The house of James Hamilton, with its characteristic features of Karen (Thailand) architecture. (Courtesy James Hamilton)

Reading 26

Emptying the Cages

Vocabulary Preview

patronage (pā′trən ij) goodwill, favor, courtesy, etc., toward those considered inferior; condescension

avant-garde (ä vänt′gärd′) of new or unconventional ideas; of the vanguard

abolitionist (ab′ə lish′ən ist) in favor of abolishing some custom or law

hierarchy (hī ə rär′kē) a group of persons or things arranged in order of rank, grade, etc.

niche (nich) an especially suitable place or position

infamous (in′fə məs) having a very bad reputation; notorious

mandated (man′dāt id) ordered or commanded

amenities (ə men′ə tēz) things that add to one's comfort or convenience

gratuitous (grə tōō′ə təs) uncalled for

sentient (sen′shənt) of, having, or capable of feeling or perception; conscious

---

fat, āpe, cär; ten, ēven; is, bīte; gō, hôrn, tōōl, look; oil, out; up, fʉr; chin, she; thin, *then*; zh, leisure; ŋ, ring; ə for *a* in *ago;* ' as in *able* (ā′b'l)

Emptying the Cages:
Does the Animal Kingdom
Need a Bill of Rights?

Jerry Adler and Mary Hart

If animals really do think, what do you suppose they think about?

Do they feel fear? Locked in a laboratory, do they mourn their freedom? Do they hear the footsteps in the corridor and wonder whose cage they will stop at this time?

Once, it would have been inconceivable to entertain these questions seriously—but then, it once was considered idle to ask similar questions about human slaves. Today they are central to one of the fastest-growing causes in America, one that seeks to overthrow the principles that have governed relations among the species since Adam: animal rights.

To those who use animals in medical research, the questions above are not just irrelevant but mischievous, the products of superstition and egalitarianism gone berserk. Where, they wonder, will the next generation of medical miracles come from? Will science be reduced to trying to cure cancer in vegetables?

To both sides, it is an issue of great passion and urgency. Congress has received more mail on the subject of animal research than any other topic, according to Dr. Charles McCarthy, head of the Office for Protection from Research Risks at the National Institutes of Health; the mail runs 100 to 1 against the use of animals. Just last month, in the midst of World Laboratory Animal Liberation Week, as about 150 protesters marched on the NIH, a counterdemonstration was called by 60 health organizations to emphasize the need for animals in medical research. One side makes its case by showing pictures of baboons with their skulls cemented into helmets for an experiment on head trauma; the other brings out the mother of seven-year-old Lilah Koch, the youngest child ever to receive a pacemaker, spokesperson of the Incurably Ill for Animal Research.

The concept of humane treatment of animals is not new in Western society. The English Parliament passed the first anti-cruelty act in 1822, followed by most other civilized nations, followed eventually by the United States. But the laws were intended to protect animals from specific acts of cruelty, a concern that animal-rights activists now regard as hopelessly out of date. "Humane treatment is simply sentimental, sympathetic patronage," says Michael W. Fox, director of the Center for Respect for Life and Environment at the Humane Society of the United States. The avant-garde position is that human beings have no inherent right to utilize other animal species. "The animal-rights philosophy is abolitionist rather than reformist," states Tom Regan, an intellectual leader of the movement. "It's not better cages we work for, but empty cages. We want every animal out."

Activists like Regan are quick to seize on evidence of animal intelligence. "If it is true that animals are fundamentally like us and differ in degree, not in kind," Regan explains, "what one minimally wants is not to allow treatment of them that differs in kind to the treatment we give one another. Yet our culture is based on just that. We do to them things we would not do to each other. We chop them up in laboratories, we fricassee them on the skillet." But the movement has deeper philosophic roots. It draws inspiration from current thinking about evolution, which has moved away from belief in a hierarchy of species, with man at the top. "Animals evolved along with humans," says Dr. Neal Barnard, a George Washington University psychiatrist who heads the Physicians Committee for Responsible Medicine. "Each has a niche. Dogs have more sensitive hearing and sense of smell. We have a more developed problem-solving ability. Every species has its own capability that allows us to exist."

"Lower Animals"

Framing the issue in terms of "rights" is a heritage of the various rights movements that preceded it. The modern movement may be dated to the 1975 publication of "Animal Liberation" by Australian philosopher Peter Singer. He coined the term "speciesism," by analogy to "racism," to describe mankind's traditional attitude toward so-called lower animals. Yet activists are careful—most of the time, anyway—not to equate animals with oppressed human minorities. "When I say animals should have rights, that does not mean animals should have the same rights as people," says Joyce Tischler, executive director of the Animal Legal Defense Fund. Pigs will never be interested in freedom of religion, but they might have an interest in due process—if it meant remaining alive and not being chained to the floor.

The most basic right, presumably, is the right not to be eaten. But the struggle for now is centered mainly on the 20 million animals in America's laboratories, for several reasons. Much research and testing is of necessity gruesome, like the infamous Draize test, in which substances such as cosmetics are applied to the sensitive corneas of rabbits, causing varying degrees of damage. Research also is less central to our culture than eating, as

Tischler was reminded recently while talking at a school, when a sixth grader turned to his classmates and announced: "You realize she's talking about our hamburgers here." And there is an informal hierarchy of animals based on public-relations value. A group called the Animal Liberation Front won attention last February when it stole—or "liberated"—13 beagles from a California laboratory. It is hard to imagine evoking much sympathy with a freedom raid on, say, a Perdue broiler house.

The research establishment, after years of ignoring the issue, has begun to take notice and fight back. "The movement is slowly strangling research to death," warns Frankie Trull, head of the Foundation for Biomedical Research, an organization that defends the use of experimental animals. She says new federal rules, mandated by Congress in 1985 but not yet implemented, will cost $1 billion to provide such amenities as exercise runs for laboratory animals.

It ought to go without saying that the motivation for using animals is not the gratuitous infliction of pain. Researchers have a long list of medical advances that would not have been possible without animals. Among them are kidney dialysis and the artificial heart, polio vaccine and the antiviral drug acyclovir. At least a few investigations—such as the head-trauma research involving baboons—have been dropped in the face of criticism.

But not all laboratory animals are used for research, and not all research is vital. "The [animal-rights] phenomenon certainly has raised awareness about our responsibilities to the animals as sentient beings," says Dennis Stark, a veterinarian who is working to develop alternatives to animals for some research. "It has made people bother to think about what they are doing." Scientists are looking for substitutes for the Draize test and have worked out ways to test drugs for toxicity that involve less slaughter than the "LD-50" standard (finding a dose that kills 50 percent of a sample of animals).

Social Contract

But perhaps it is time for the medical establishment to confront the animal-rights establishment on its own terms and propose its own version of the social contract. It might start with the observation that animals derive certain benefits from their association with human beings including their use in medical research; it was researchers working with cats, after all, who devised the vaccine against feline leukemia. In exchange, humane society requires animals for certain vital purposes and one cannot reasonably expect them to volunteer. When society faced a similar situation with respect to young men in war time, the solution was the draft. For that matter, horses were, in effect, drafted to fight in the Civil War. Was the use of cavalry to fight slavery immoral? Is the war against AIDS or coronary disease any less important? Can we recognize and protect the interests of different species—and still call on them to do their duty?

Better Temper That Temper!

Vocabulary Preview

tenacious (tə nā′shəs) holding firmly

secular (sek′yə lər) not connected with a church; worldly

exorcisms (ek′sôr si z′ms) rituals used to expel evil spirits

empathy (em′pə thē) intellectual or emotional identification with another

admonish (əd män′ish) warn; caution

cathartic (kə thär′tik) relieving of the emotions

conciliatory (kən sil′ē ə tôr′ē) tending to soothe the anger of; winning over; making friendly

choleric (käl′ər ik) easily angered; bad tempered

sedentary (sed′'n ter′ē) involving much sitting

bellicose (bel′ə kōs) quarrelsome or warlike

maxim (mak′sim) a rule of conduct that is brief and to the point

abrasive (ə brā′siv) tending to provoke anger, ill will, etc.; aggressively annoying; irritating

shtetl (shtet′əl) any of the former Jewish village communities of Eastern Europe, esp. in Russia

placid (plas′id) tranquil; calm

polemical (pə lem′ik əl) argumentative

---

fat, āpe, cär; ten, ēven; is, bīte; gō, hôrn, tōōl, look; oil; out; up, fʉr; chin, she; thin, *th*en; zh, leisure; ŋ, ring; ə for *a* in *ago;* ' as in *able* (ā′b'l)

Better Temper
That Temper!

John Carey

Woman No. 1: You'll feel better if you get your anger out.
Woman No. 2: Anger? Why am I angry?
1: Because he left you, that's why.
2: Left me? What are you talking about? He died. He was an old man.
1: Yes, but underneath you are blaming him for not keeping his obligation to protect you forever.
2: Margaret . . . we both knew he was dying, and we had time to make our peace. I don't feel angry, I feel sad. I miss him.
1: Why are you so defensive? Why are you denying your true feelings?
2: Margaret, you are driving me crazy. *I don't feel angry, dammit!*
1: (*smiling*): So why are you shouting?

    This exchange, overheard in a New York café, illustrates one of the most tenacious myths of popular psychology: that admitting and venting anger are the necessary first steps to health and happiness. Authorities from Konrad Lorenz to Ann Landers, from psychoanalysts to est instructors, warn of the dangers of bottled-up rage. Unreleased anger, frustration, and hostility, warn these secular priests of behavior, can cause sadness and depression, high blood pressure and heart disease, eating binges, ulcers, migraines, impotence, and even child abuse. "In short," claims a recent popular article, "by repressing your God-given talent for anger, you're killing yourself."

    But the notion that letting off steam is good for you has a fatal flaw, according to psychologist Carol Tavris. "People are not teapots," she says. In a . . . controversial book, "Anger: The Misunderstood Emotion," Tavris argues that in most cases, getting mad actually creates more problems than it solves, escalating the hostility and anxiety rather than clearing the air. She also maintains that some of the recommended exorcisms for anger, such as pouring out one's fury to a sympathetic ear or channeling it into a game of racquetball, are frequently ineffective. Tavris fears for a nation that needs to get everything off its chest. "A ventilationist society pays no attention to the social glue of kindness and empathy and is in danger of disintegrating from within," she says.

Primal Scream

People have not always been urged to vent their rage. "Be not hasty in thy spirit to be angry: for anger resteth in the bosom of fools," admonishes the Bible. The idea that getting mad is beneficial dates back to Freud and the early animal behaviorists, who believed that there is a fixed reservoir of aggressive energy in the body. Block that energy in one direction and it flows out in another, usually as anger. Although Freud later backed away from the belief that anger has a cathartic function, says Yale psychoanalyst Albert Rothenberg, the notion found ready acceptance in the more permissive society of the 1960s and 1970s, which spawned primal-scream therapy. "People wanted to hear that you could indulge yourself and your feelings," says Rothenberg.

In fact, some early studies did show that expressing anger was cathartic. When Jack Hokanson of Florida State University allowed male college students to retaliate with anger against fellow students who had frustrated them, their blood pressure dropped up to eight times faster than if they contained their anger. Subsequent experiments, however, shook Hokanson's belief in the cathartic theory. Blood pressure, he found, did not drop more quickly when volunteers vented their rage against an authority figure, such as a teacher, who had angered them. Nor did it help to yell at innocent bystanders or to fantasize about taking revenge.

Hokanson's biggest surprise came when he brought women into his lab. He discovered that their blood pressure dropped much more rapidly when they responded to their tormentors with friendship rather than anger. "The finding raised major questions about the cathartic theory," he says. "It suggested that the responses we make while angry are the ones we have learned are effective." The psychologist then tested whether there are innate differences in this area between men and women: he designed experiments that rewarded aggressive anger in women and friendliness in men. The original gender difference was reversed; venting rage turned out to be cathartic for women while being conciliatory actually lowered blood pressure in men. "The myth that ventilating anger brings down tension is long gone," Hokanson says.

Hostility

Talking about anger appears to be equally ineffective. Psychologists at the University of California at San Diego asked 100 laid-off aerospace workers how they felt about their companies and their supervisors. Then they had each man fill out a report describing his feelings. The psychologists discovered that the men who let out anger in conversation expressed even more hostility in their reports. Fuming to a third party may make people feel better because it serves to legitimize their rage, Tavris concludes, but it perpetuates, even increases, feelings of anger by rehearsing the emotion.

Active sports have commonly been viewed as effective substitutes for punching a tyrannical boss or attacking an enemy. They do make choleric people feel less angry, says Leonard Berkowitz of the University of Wisconsin, but only because concentrating on—and physically enjoying—the activity takes their minds off their grievances. "Anger will dissolve equally well during a sedentary chess game," he says. The popular notion that violent sports like football and ice hockey function as safety valves for aggression in society, that people who play hard make less war, also seems to be wrong. When anthropologist Richard Sipes compared 10 peaceful cultures—including Lapp herdsmen, Bushmen hunter/gatherers and American Hutterites—with 10 constantly warring societies, such as the belligerent Aztecs and quarrelsome Thais, he discovered that the pacific peoples played far fewer combative games than the bellicose cultures.

Although letting anger out does not necessarily make people feel better, many psychologists and psychoanalysts still believe that holding it back is unhealthy, too. "Ninety-nine percent of the cases of severe anxiety I see are related to repressed anger," says psychoanalyst Theodore Rubin. Tavris counters that anger is more often a symptom than a cause of distress; she points out that depressed people often express more anger as they get more depressed. "The clinical maxim for depression was always, 'Go after the underlying anger,'" explains Rothenberg. "But when patients express anger, it does not solve their problems."

Contrary to popular belief, argues Tavris, clamping a lid on obviously boiling rage is not worse for you than letting it all out. In fact, the evidence suggests that both strategies can be unhealthy. Psychologists led by Ernest Harburg of the University of Michigan asked hundreds of men and women in four neighborhoods in Detroit how they would respond to such situations as an unjust boss, a prejudiced neighbor or an abrasive policeman. Both people who said they would explode in anger as well as those who said they would feel anger but would not express it had significantly higher blood pressure than respondents who had said they would try to reason with offenders. Other studies have implicated both suppressed anger and frequent angry outbursts in heart disease. The danger that rage poses to health, suggests Tavris, comes not from expressing it or suppressing it, but from letting it linger and fester, spawning anxiety and feelings of impotence.

Certainly, letting anger out may be just what the doctor ordered. Take the case of Sonia Johnson, who was eventually excommunicated from the Mormon Church for supporting the Equal Rights Amendment. After a humiliating church meeting, she locked herself in a room and "for two solid hours I raged at God at the top of my lungs," she wrote recently. "When my vocal cords and lungs finally gave out . . . I discovered to my amazement that I felt wonderful—absolutely euphoric." Violent anger, Tavris argues, is most effective, cathartic and healthy when it meets three conditions: when it is a legitimate cry for justice, when it is directed against the offending target and when at worst it leads to no retaliation or at best brings about the desired change. Without righteous and violent anger there would still be moneylenders in the temple, blacks in the back of the bus, and women in the kitchen.

Liability

Ire is an instinctive physical and emotional response when things don't go the way they are supposed to. But its expression, from the constant bickering of the !Kung-san Bushmen to the colorful Yiddish curses born amid the hardships of the Russian *shtetl,* is a matter of social and political choice. Some cultures, like the Utkuhikhalingmiut Eskimos, shun anyone with a volatile temper; others, like the Gururumba of New Guinea and our own, often accept passionate anger as an excuse for irresponsible and even criminal acts. Just as methods of expressing anger help us understand different cultures, they also highlight individual differences. Using personality tests and an anger scale, Mary Biaggio of the University of Idaho found that college students who were easily aroused to anger were more narrow-minded, less tolerant, less perceptive about other people and less socially responsible than their more placid colleagues. Being overly quick to anger can be a social liability as well as a fast track to disease.

Tavris's book will be attacked for its polemical tone and its tendency to highlight evidence that supports the author's arguments. Yet both Tavris and her critics reach basically the same conclusions and the same prescriptions for dealing with anger. When your heart races, your blood boils and you want to strangle someone, *stop.* Figure out why you are angry and who you are angry at. Then decide if rage is the right response. Most grievances, Tavris believes, are not worthy of anger and the best solution may simply be avoiding the cause. But if you do express anger, be assertive and courteous, not aggressive and threatening. If the advice sounds familiar, that's because it is. Ultimately, says Tavris, "my book is just a plea for a little common sense."

Reading 28

The Ultra Mega Vita Guide

The Ultra Mega Vita Guide

Bonnie Liebman

How much of what do I need?

That's the toughest question most shoppers face as they squint at the tiny print on multi-vitamin-and-mineral supplement labels.

Don't feel bad if you don't know the answer. No one does. Even the committee that sets the official Recommended Dietary Allowances (RDAs) admits that it doesn't know how much of each nutrient promotes *optimal* health.

So how could we write this Ultra Mega Guide? Call it educated guessing. While many of our rules are based on incomplete science, that's more than most people have when they face a shelf full of vitamins.

1. Get the most beta-carotene and the least vitamin A palmitate or acetate. "With beta-carotene," says the label on Theragran-M. The question is, how much?

You're better off with a supplement that's rich in beta-carotene. While high doses of vitamin A can be toxic, beta-carotene isn't. The body turns it into vitamin A, but stops when you've got enough.

What's more, only beta-carotene—not vitamin A—is an antioxidant. Studies using 25,000 to 50,000 IU of beta-carotene per day are currently under way to see if it reduces the risk of cancer, heart disease, and cataracts.

The problem is: some labels list the total "International Units" (IU) supplied by vitamin A and beta-carotene *together,* but don't say how much comes from each.

For example, GNC's Stress Vita-Pak and its Women's Ultra Mega both have 15,000 IU of "vitamin A." But the Vita-Pak gets 10,000 of the 15,000 IU from beta-carotene, while the Ultra Mega gets only 5,000.

You don't need *any* non-beta-carotene vitamin A (it's listed as "acetate," "palmitate," or "fish oil"). And if your supplement *does* have any, it shouldn't be more than the USRDA, which is 5,000 IU. That's especially true for a "women's" tablet, since high doses have been linked to birth defects.

2. Ignore high doses of thiamin, riboflavin, and niacin. Think of them as the "three Bs you probably don't need." Thiamin (vitamin B-1), riboflavin (B-2), and niacin (B-3) are plentiful in the food supply, largely because they're added to the "enriched" white flour that goes into bread, pasta, crackers, cereals, and dozens of other grain products.

But judging from "high-potency" supplement labels, you'd think there was a national shortage. In fact, multis load up on these Bs because they're cheap and don't take up much room.

3. Look for extra vitamin C unless it's expensive. Vitamin C is an antioxidant. Whether studies will conclusively show that it reduces the risk of cancer, heart disease, cataracts, and colds is unclear.

The USRDA is 60 mg. It's worth taking more—say 250 mg to 500 mg—but it's not worth paying a premium price for a high-potency multi when you can buy your C separately for a few pennies a tab. More than 1,000 mg a day causes diarrhea in some people.

4. Many women should get the USRDA for vitamin D in winter. Postmenopausal women who live in northern latitudes may get too little vitamin D from the sun between October and March.

In one study, postmenopausal women who took 400 IU (the USRDA) in a supplement—along with enough calcium to bring their daily calcium intake to 800 mg—lost less bone than women who took only calcium (or nothing).

Most multis have 400 IU of vitamin D. But several made by Bronson—including its Women's Formula #2—Your Life Daily Pack for Women, Unicap Senior, and AARP Formula #502 have 200 IU or less. (So much for "women's" and "senior" formulas.)

High doses of vitamin D can be toxic, so don't exceed 400 IU a day.

5. Look for 100 to 400 IU of vitamin E. Researchers have reported that supplements containing at least 100 IU of vitamin E are linked to a lower risk of heart disease. In one study, a multi containing 44 IU halved the incidence of infections in older people. And in another study, 400 IU of vitamin E a day improved some immune-system functions. The USRDA is only 30 IU.

It's too early to conclude that vitamin E boosts the immune system—or that it reduces the risk of cancer or cataracts, as some studies suggest. Like vitamin C and beta-carotene, it's usually cheaper to take separately than to purchase as part of a high-potency multi.

6. Many women should get the USRDA for folic acid. All females who are capable of becoming pregnant should get 400 micrograms (mcg) of folic acid to reduce the risk of neural tube birth defects, which can occur before a woman finds out that she is pregnant.

The easiest way to make sure you get enough is to take a multi—that is, unless (and until) the government requires companies to add folic acid to foods.

Postmenopausal women and older men might be better off with no more than 50 percent of the USRDA, according to some vitamin B-12 experts, who fear that folic acid will mask B-12 deficiencies.

7. Vegans need vitamin B-12. If you consume no animal or dairy products, take a supplement with the USRDA for B-12. A deficiency can cause *irreversible* neurological damage, so don't take chances.

Because some older people don't absorb B-12 well, they're more likely to be deficient. Some are even misdiagnosed as having Alzheimer's.

If you're concerned, get a blood test for serum B-12. If it's "low-normal," it may be worth having your methyl malonate and homocysteine checked, according to a not-yet-published study by Ralph Green of the Cleveland Clinic Foundation.

8. Iron shouldn't exceed the USRDA. Can iron harm your heart? According to one recent study, high blood levels of stored iron may increase the risk of heart disease.

That study needs to be confirmed. But in the meantime, there's no reason to take more than the USRDA for iron. In fact, less is better—unless your doctor says otherwise. That's especially true for men and postmenopausal women, who don't lose iron by menstruating, and who are also at risk for iron overload (hemochromatosis).

Unfortunately, some brands—like Nature's Plus Power-Plex, GNC Women's Vita Pak, and Geritol Complete—supply two to three times the USRDA. Avoid 'em.

9. Don't take high doses of zinc without copper. High doses of zinc can make it harder for your body to absorb copper. Yet some people take extra zinc in addition to a multi that has no copper.

Copper, on the other hand, is an oxidant. What with all the research suggesting that *anti*oxidants promote health, you want the USRDA, but no more.

10. Don't expect to get all your calcium and magnesium in one swallow. Most people assume that a multi provides 100 percent of the USRDA for all nutrients. But you can't squeeze that much calcium or magnesium into a single tablet. So unless each daily dose consists of two or more tablets, you're probably getting no more than 25 percent of the USRDA for either.

Most women don't get enough calcium from food to reach the recommended level—1,200 mg a day until age 25 and 800 mg thereafter. If you will eat several daily servings of dairy products, canned fish without bones, tofu made with calcium sulfate, or leafy green vegetables like kale, you don't need a supplement.

Calcium is less important for men, but magnesium isn't.

11. Don't forget chromium and selenium. Some studies suggest that too little chromium can lead to glucose intolerance, an early sign of diabetes. And there is sketchy evidence that selenium may reduce the risk of cancer (as an antioxidant).

The problem is both selenium and chromium are often left out of multis. A supplement should have at least 50 mcg—but no more than 200 mcg—of each.

12. Don't worry about most other ingredients. Until we know more, you can ignore most other ingredients in multis. Almost all people get enough phosphorus, chloride, pantothenic acid, manganese, and molybdenum in their diets. Nickel, tin, and silicon are what the RDA committee calls "nutrients essential for some higher animals but not proved to be required by normal humans."

Boron is also on that list, but there is growing evidence that we may need less. The same goes for choline, but there is not much evidence that anyone gets too little.

13. Don't overpay. If you're paying more than $10 a month for all your supplements, you're paying too much.

Reading 29

Minorities and Stardom

Vocabulary Preview

Hispanic (hi span′ik) of Spanish, Portuguese, or Latin American origin

assessed (ə sest′) evaluated

aspire (ə spīr′) to seek after something grand or lofty

theoretical (thē′ə ret′ə kəl) limited to or based on theory; hypothetical

proposition (präp′ə zish′ən) a subject or statement to be discussed or debated

---

fat, āpe, cär; ten, ēven; is, bīte; gō, hôrn, to͞ol, look; oil, out; up, fʉr; chin, she; thin, *then*; zh, leisure; ŋ, ring; ə for *a* in *ago;* ′ as in *able* (ā′b′l)

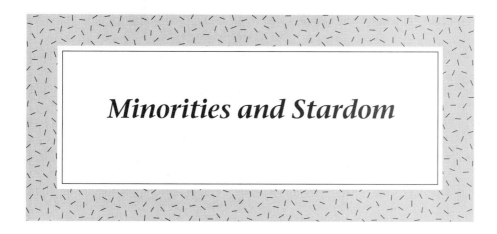

Minorities and Stardom

Rodney Stark

The majority of players on every team in the National Basketball Association are black. White boxing champions are rare. A far greater proportion of professional football players are black than would be expected based on the size of the black population. Furthermore, blacks began to excel in sports long before the Civil Rights Movement broke down barriers excluding them from many other occupations. This has led many people, both black and white, to conclude that blacks are born with a natural talent for athletics. How else could they have come to dominate the ranks of superstars?

The trouble with this biological explanation of blacks in sports is that it ignores an obvious historical fact: It is typical for minorities in North America to make their first substantial progress in sports (and, for similar reasons, in entertainment). Who today would suggest that Jews have a biological advantage in athletics? Yet at the turn of the century, the number of Jews who excelled in sports far exceeded their proportion in the population. And late in the nineteenth century, the Irish dominated sports to almost the same extent as blacks have done in recent decades.

By examining an encyclopedia of boxing, for example, we can draw accurate conclusions about patterns of immigration and at what period which ethnic groups were on the bottom of the stratification system. The Irish domination of boxing in the latter half of the nineteenth century is obvious from the names of heavyweight champions, beginning with bare-knuckle champ Ned O'Baldwin in 1867 and including Mike McCoole in 1869, Paddy Ryan in 1880, John L. Sullivan in 1889, and Jim Corbett in 1892. The list of champions in lower-weight divisions during the same era is dominated by fighters named Ryan, Murphy, Delaney, Lynch, O'Brien, and McCoy.

Early in the twentieth century, Irish names became much less common among boxing champions, even though many fighters who were not Irish took Irish ring names. Suddenly, champions had names like Battling Levinsky, Maxie Rosenbloom, Benny Leonard, Abe Goldstein, Kid Kaplan, and Izzy Schwartz. This was the Jewish era in boxing. Then Jewish names dropped out of the lists, and Italian and Eastern European names came to the fore: Canzoneri, Battalino, LaMotta, Graziano, and Basilio; Yarosz, Lesnevich, Zale, Risko, Hostak, and Servo. By the 1940s, fighters were disproportionately black. Today, black domination of boxing has already peaked, and Hispanic names have begun to prevail.

The current overrepresentation of blacks in sports reflects two things: first, a *lack of other avenues to wealth and fame* and, second, the fact that minority groups can overcome discrimination most easily in occupations where *the quality of individual performance is most easily and accurately assessed.* These same factors led to the overrepresentation of other ethnic groups in sports earlier in history.

It is often difficult to know which applicants to a law school or a pilot training school are the most capable. But we can see who can box or hit a baseball. The demonstration of talent, especially in sports and entertainment, tends to break down barriers of discrimination. As these fall, opportunities in these areas for wealth and fame open up, while other opportunities remain closed. Thus, minority groups will aspire to those areas in which the opportunities are open and will tend to overachieve in these areas.

In an important theoretical contribution to racial and ethnic relations, H. M. Blalock was one of the first to explain why minorities more rapidly overcome discrimination in sports. Let's consider several of his propositions.

First, Blalock argued, work groups differ in the extent to which an outstanding individual can bring success to the whole group. A worker on an assembly line, for example, does not increase the earnings of other workers by working faster. But a great quarterback or a great hitter can transform an average team into champions. Thus, Blalock theorized, the more an individual can increase the benefits of all work-group members, the less that group will discriminate against minority members. This will be particularly so when it is easy to judge how much a person could add to the group's success.

To illustrate Blalock's point, consider a baseball team. All players are white, and many of them are prejudiced against blacks. However, they also want to win the pennant and the World Series, but they need a better power hitter to do so. Such a team will be inclined to ignore their prejudice against blacks if they have a chance to get a star hitter who is black.

Blalock also suggested that when employers compete intensely for talented people, they will be much less likely to discriminate. Because such competition is the essence of management in sports, highly talented minority players will be an irresistible temptation for owners and managers. Discrimination should cease in sports long before it does in most other high-status occupations. Blalock's proposition also implies that less successful teams would take the lead in ending discrimination, whereas the most successful teams would resist it. In fact, during the many years when they routinely won the pennant and the World Series, the New York Yankees were the least integrated team in baseball.

Thus, the overrepresentation of an ethnic or racial minority in sports often signals that group's early progress in struggling up from the bottom of society. However, the real signal that a group is making it comes when their overrepresentation in sports begins to decline, for it means that young people of this racial or ethnic background have other possible roads to success. This is not to suggest that it is better for people to become lawyers or dentists than to become linebackers. (I much prefer to watch a linebacker fill a hole than a dentist.) But no group should face such limited opportunities that playing sports is their only escape from poverty and prejudice. The overrepresentation of a racial or ethnic minority in sports does not reflect inborn athletic talent any more than their underrepresentation in science reflects an inborn lack of academic talent. Instead, both reflect limited opportunities.

These same principles apply to overrepresentation in the entertainment world. The early success of blacks in music, for example, led to the belief that they were born with a "natural sense of rhythm." Again, when opportunities are few, people will concentrate their efforts. Blacks who could play musical instruments, dance, sing, or write music dedicated themselves to perfecting their skills, as did other ethnic groups when their opportunities were limited. Like athletic talent, entertainment skills are very visible and easily demonstrated. Bill "Bojangles" Robinson could have become a star just by dancing on a street corner (which he often did even after he was world famous). Louis Armstrong's trumpet playing was as obviously inspired as Michael Jordan's dunk shots. To claim that Fats Waller couldn't play the piano would have been as silly as to say Joe Louis couldn't punch. As in sports, barriers of discrimination tend to fall early in the entertainment industry.

Reading 30

When Aristotle Fails, Try Science Fiction

Vocabulary Preview

Homeric (hō mər′ik) large-scale; massive; enormous; like the poems of Homer

oratorical (ôr′ə tôr′i kəl) a style showing skill in public speaking

eloquent (el′ə kwənt) fluent, forceful, and persuasive

pontificate (pän tif′i kāt′) to speak or act in a pompous or dogmatic way

verity (ver′ə tē) truth; reality

appalling (ə pôl′iŋ) causing horror, shock, or dismay

ludicrous (lōō′di krəs) so absurd, ridiculous, or exaggerated as to cause or merit laughter

voluminous (və lōōm′ə nəs) consisting of, or forming enough material to fill volumes

verbiage (vʉr′bē ij′) style of expression; diction

affluence (af′lōō əns) wealth

---

fat, āpe, cär; ten, ēven; is, bīte; gō, hôrn, tōōl, look; oil, out; up, fʉr; chin, she; thin, _then_; zh, leisure; ŋ, ring; ə for _a_ in _ago;_ ′ as in _able_ (ā′b'l)

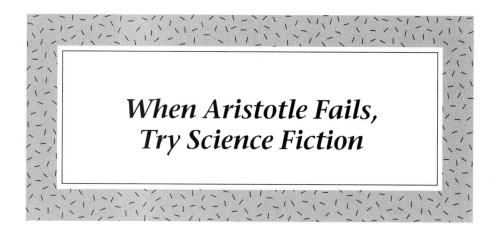

When Aristotle Fails, Try Science Fiction

Isaac Asimov

It is odd to be asked whether science fiction is a literature of ideas. Far from doubting that it is, I would like to suggest that it is the *only* literature of relevant ideas, since it is the only literature that, at its best, is firmly based on scientific thought.

Of the products of the human intellect, the scientific method is unique. This is not because it ought to be considered the only path to Truth; it isn't. In fact, it firmly admits it isn't. It doesn't even pretend to define what Truth (with a capital T) is, or whether the word has meaning. In this it parts company with the self-assured thinkers of various religious, philosophical, and mystical persuasions who have drowned the world in sorrow and blood through the conviction that they and they alone own Truth.

The uniqueness of science comes in this: the scientific method offers a way of determining the False. Science is the only gateway to proven error. There have been Homeric disputes in the history of science, and while it could not be maintained that either party was wholly right or had the key to Truth, it could be shown that the views of at least one were at variance with what seemed to be the facts available to us through observation.

Pasteur maintained alcoholic fermentation to be the product of living cells; Liebig said no. Liebig, in the mid-nineteenth-century context of observation, was proved wrong; his views were abandoned. Newton advanced a brilliantly successful picture of the universe, but it failed in certain apparently minor respects. Einstein advanced another picture that did not fail in those respects. Whether Einstein's view is True is still argued and may be argued for an indefinite time to come, but Newton's view is False. There is no argument about the latter.

Compare this with other fields in which intellectuals amuse themselves. Who has ever proved a school of philosophy to be False? When has one religion triumphed over another by debate, experiment and observation?

What rules of criticism can settle matters in such a way that all critics will agree on a particular work of art or literature?

A man without chemical training can speak learnedly of chemistry, making use of a large vocabulary and a stately oratorical style—and he will be caught out almost at once by any bright teenager who has studied chemistry in high school.

That same man, without training in art, can speak learnedly of art in the same way, and while his ignorance may be evident to some real expert in the field, no one else would venture to dispute him with any real hope of success.

There is an accepted consensus in science, and to be a plausible fake in science (before any audience not utterly ignorant in the field) one must learn that consensus thoroughly. Having learned it, however, one has no need to be a plausible fake.

In other fields of intellectual endeavor there is, however, no accepted consensus. The different schools argue endlessly, moving in circles about each other as fad succeeds fashion over the centuries. Though individuals may be unbelievably eloquent and sincere, there is, short of the rack and the stake, no decision ever. Consequently, to be a plausible fake in religion, art, politics, mysticism, or even any of the "soft" sciences such as sociology (to anyone not utterly expert in the field), one need only learn the vocabulary and develop a certain self-assurance.

It is not surprising, then, that so many young intellectuals avoid the study of science and so many old intellectuals are proud of their ignorance of science. Science has a bad habit of puncturing pretension for all to see. Those who value their pretension to intellect and are insecure over it are well advised to avoid science.

To be sure, when a scientist ventures outside his field and pontificates elsewhere, he is as likely to speak nonsense as anyone else. (And there may be those unkind enough to say I am demonstrating this fact in this very article.) However, since nonsense outside science is difficult or impossible to demonstrate, the scientist is at least no worse than anyone else in this respect.

If we consider Literature (with a capital L) as a vehicle of ideas, we can only conclude that, by and large, the ideas with which it is concerned are the same ideas that Homer and Aeschylus struggled with. They are well worth discussing, I am sure; even fun. There is enough there to keep an infinite number of minds busy for an infinite amount of time, but they weren't settled and aren't settled.

It is these "eternal verities" that are precisely what science fiction doesn't deal with. Science fiction deals with change. It deals with the possible advance in science and with the potential changes—even in those damned eternal verities—this may bring about in society.

As it happens, we are living in a society in which all the enormous changes—the *only* enormous changes—are being brought about by science and its application to everyday life. Count up the changes introduced by the automobile, by the television set, by the jet plane. Ask yourself what might happen to the world of tomorrow if there is complete automation, if robots become practical, if the disease of old age is cured, if hydrogen fusion is made a workable source of energy.

The fact is that no previous generation has had to face the possibility and the potentialities of such enormous and such rapid change. No generation has had to face the appalling certainty that if the advance of science isn't judged accurately, if the problems of tomorrow aren't solved before they are upon us, that advance and those problems will overwhelm us.

This generation, then, is the first that can't take as its primary concern the age-old questions that have agitated all deep thinkers since civilization began. Those questions are still interesting, but they are no longer of first importance, and any literature that deals with them (that is, any literature but science fiction) is increasingly irrelevant.

If this thought seems too large to swallow, consider a rather simple analogy: the faster an automobile is moving, the less the driver can concern himself with the eternal beauties of the scenery and the more he must involve himself with the trivial obstacles in the road ahead.

And that is where science fiction comes in.

Not all science fiction, of course. Theodore Sturgeon, one of the outstanding practitioners in the field, once said to a group of fans, "Nine-tenths of science fiction is crud." There was a startled gasp from the audience and he went on, "But why not? Nine-tenths of everything is crud." Including mainstream literature, of course.

It must be understood, then, that I am talking of the one-tenth (or possibly less) of science fiction that is not crud.

This means you will have to take my word for what follows, if you are not yourself an experienced science-fiction fan. The nonfan or even the mild fan with occasional experience in the field is almost certain to have been exposed only to the crud, which is, alas, of high visibility. He sees the comic strips, the monster movies, the pale TV fantasies. He never sees the better magazines and paperbacks where the science-fiction writers of greatest repute are to be found.

So let's see—

In 1940 there was endless talk about Fascism, Communism, and Democracy, talk that must have varied little in actual content concerning the conflicts of freedom and authority, of race, religion, and patriotism, from analogous discussions carried on in fifth and fourth centuries B.C. Greece. In 1940, when the Nazis were everywhere victorious, such talk might well have been considered important. It might plausibly have been argued that these discussions dealt with the great issues of the century.

And what was science fiction talking about? Well, in the May 1941 issue of *Astounding Science Fiction,* there appeared a story called "Solution Unsatisfactory" by Anson MacDonald (real name, Robert A. Heinlein), which suggested that the United States might put together a huge scientific project designed to work out a nuclear weapon that would end World War II. It then went on, carefully and thoughtfully, to consider the nuclear stalemate into which the world would consequently be thrown. At about the same time, John W. Campbell, Jr., editor of the magazine, was saying, in print, that the apparent issues of the war were, in a sense, trivial, since nuclear energy was on the point of being tamed and that this would so change the world that what then seemed life-and-death differences in philosophy would prove unimportant.

Well, who were the thinkers who, in 1940, were considering the nuclear stalemate? What generals were planning for a world in which each major power had nuclear bombs? What political scientists were thinking of a situation in which no matter how hot the rhetoric between competing great powers, any war between them would have to stay cold—not through consideration of fine points of economics or morals, but over the brutal fact that a nuclear stalemate cannot be broken, short of world suicide?

These thoughts, which were, after all, the truly relevant ideas on 1940's horizon, were reserved to science-fiction writers.

Nowadays, articles on ecology are in great demand, and it is quite fashionable to talk of population and pollution and of all the vast changes they may bring about. It is easy to do so now. Rachel Carson started it, most people would say, with her *Silent Spring.* But did anyone precede her?

Well, in the June, July, and August 1952 issues of *Galaxy,* there appeared a three-part serial, "Gravy Planet," by Frederik Pohl and Cyril Kornbluth, which is a detailed picture of an enormously overpopulated world from almost every possible aspect. In the February 1956 issue of *Fantasy and Science Fiction,* there appeared "Census Takers" by Frederik Pohl in which it is (ironically) suggested that the time will come when one of the chief duties of census takers will be to shoot down every tenth (or fourteenth, or eighth, depending on the population increase in the past decade) person they count, as the only means of keeping the population under control.

What sociologist (not now, but twenty years ago) was clamoring in print over the overwhelming effect of population increase? What government functionary (not now, but twenty years ago) was getting it clearly through his head that there existed no social problem that did not depend for its cure, *first of all,* on a cessation of population growth? (Surely not President Eisenhower, who piously stated that if there was one problem in which the government must not interfere, it was the matter of birth control. He changed his mind later; I'll give him credit for that.) What psychologist or philosopher (not now, but twenty years ago) was pointing out that if population continued to increase, there was no hope for human freedom or dignity under any circumstances?

Such thoughts were pretty largely reserved, twenty years ago, to science-fiction writers.

There are many people (invariably those who know nothing about science fiction) who think that because men have reached the moon, science has caught up with science fiction and that science fiction writers have "nothing to write about."

They would be surprised to know that the mere act of reaching the moon was outdated in science fiction in the 1920s and that no reputable science-fiction writer has been excited by such a little thing in nearly half a century.

In the July 1939 issue of *Astounding Science Fiction,* there appeared a story called "Trends," written by myself while I was still a teenager. It did indeed deal with the first flights to the moon, which I put in the period between 1973 and 1978. (I underestimated the push that would be given rocket research by World War II.) My predictions on the details of the beginnings of space exploration were ludicrously wrong, but none of that represented the point of the story, anyway.

What made the story publishable was the social background I presented for the rocket flights. In my story, I pictured strong popular opposition to the notion of space travel.

Many years later it was pointed out to me that in all the voluminous literature about space travel, either fictional or nonfictional, no such suggestion had ever before been broached. The world was always pictured as wildly and unanimously enthusiastic.

Well, where in 1939 was there the engineer or the industrialist who was taking into serious account the necessity of justifying the expense and risk of space exploration? Where was the engineer or the industrialist who was soberly considering the possibility of space exploration?

Such thoughts were largely reserved for the science-fiction writer and for a few engineers, who in almost every case were science-fiction fans—Willy Ley and Wernher von Braun, to name a couple.

And where does science fiction stand today?

It is more popular than ever and has gained a new respectability. Dozens of courses in it are being given in dozens of colleges. Literary figures have grown interested in it as a branch of the art. And, of course, the very growth in popularity tends to dilute and weaken it.

It has grown sufficiently popular and respectable, since the days of Sputnik, for people to wish to enter it as a purely literary field. And once that becomes a motive, the writers don't need to know science anymore. To write purely literary science fiction, one returns to the "eternal verities" but surrounds them with some of the verbiage of science fiction, together with a bit of the new stylistic experimentation one comes across in the mainstream and with some of the explicit sex that is now in fashion.

And this is what some people in science fiction call the "new wave."

To me, it seems that the new wave merely attempts to reduce real science fiction to the tasteless pap of the mainstream.

New-wave science fiction can be interesting, daring, even fascinating, if it is written well enough, but if the author knows no science, the product is no more valuable for its content of relevant ideas than is the writing outside science fiction.

Fortunately, the real science fiction—those stories that deal with scientific ideas and their impact on the future as written by someone knowledgeable in science—still exists and will undoubtedly continue to exist as long as mankind does (which, alas, may not be long).

This does not mean that every science-fiction story is good prediction or is necessarily intended to be a prediction at all, or that very good science-fiction stories might not deal with futures that cannot reasonably be expected to come to pass.

That does not matter. The point is that the habit of looking sensibly toward the future, the habit of assuming change and trying to penetrate beyond the fact of change to its effect and to the new problems it will introduce, the habit of accepting change as now more important to mankind than those dreary eternal verities, is to be found only in science fiction or in those serious nonfictional discussions of the future by people who, almost always, are or have been deeply interested in science fiction.

For instance, while ordinary literature deals merry-go-round-wise with the white-black racial dilemma in the United States, I await the science-fiction story that will seriously consider the kind of society America might be attempting to rebuild *after* the infinitely costly racial war we are facing—a war that may destroy our world influence and our internal affluence. Perhaps such a story, sufficiently well thought out and written, may force those who read it into a contemplation of the problem from a new and utterly relevant angle.

To see what I mean, ask yourself how many of those, north and south, who blithely talked abolition and secession in the 1850s in terms of pure rhetoric might not have utterly changed their attitudes and gotten down to sober realities if they could have foreseen the exact nature of the Civil War and of the Reconstruction that followed and could have understood that none of the torture of the 1860s and 1870s would in the least solve the problem of white-and-black after all.

So read this magazine and others of the sort by all means, and follow the clash of stock ideas as an amusing intellectual game. Or read Plato or Sophocles and follow the same clash in more readable prose. But if you want the real ideas, the ideas that count today and may even count tomorrow, the ideas for which Aristotle offers little real help, or Senator X or Commissar Y either, then read science fiction.

Appendix

Evaluation Checklist

1. Score on total test _____

2. Which section was your weakest: objective, essay, application, problem solving? _____

3. Objective section:
   a. Do you understand why your wrong answers were wrong? _____
   b. Did your underlining and marginal notes cover the correct information?

   _____

   c. Did you review them enough to remember them? _____

4. Essay/application:
   a. Do you understand why you got the score you did? _____
   b. Did your graphic organizer(s) cover the correct information? _____
   c. Did you review them enough to remember them? _____

5. Problem solving:
   a. Did you provide the right kind of practice problems? _____
   b. Did you provide enough practice problems so that you could understand and remember the information? _____

6. Test-taking skills:
   a. Did you use the time available to maximize your score? _____
   b. Did you follow the directions? _____
   c. Did you answer the easy questions first? _____
   d. If you changed any answers, did it improve your score? _____
   e. Did you leave anything blank? _____

Credits

Footnotes (pages 3–17)

[1] Adapted from Joan Ferrante, *Sociology: A Global Perspective* (Belmont, CA: Wadsworth, 1992), p. 303.

[2] Philip C. Starr, *Economics Principles in Action,* 5th ed. (Belmont, CA: Wadsworth, 1988), pp. 204–205.

[3] Ferrante, p. 463.

[4] Starr, p. 176.

[5] Ferrante, p. 45.

[6] Ibid., p. 463.

[7] Robert Winer, *Music for Our Time* (Belmont, CA: Wadsworth, 1992), p. 49.

[8] Ferrante, p. 386.

[9] Ibid., p. 335.

[10] G. Tyler Miller, Jr. *Living in the Environment,* 7th ed. (Belmont, CA: Wadsworth, 1992), p. 25.

[11] Ibid., p. 228.

[12] Ibid., p. 160.

[13] Ibid., p. 10.

[14] Ibid., pp. 79–80.

[15] Adapted from Miller, p. 636.

Credits

Page 29: John Leo, "Homeless Rights, Community Wrongs." Copyright © July 24, 1989. *U.S. News & World Report.* Reprinted by permission.

Page 37: James D. Wright, "The Worthy and Unworthy Homeless." Reprinted by permission of Transaction Publishers from *Society,* July/August 1988, Vol. 25, No. 5. Copyright © 1988 by Transaction Publishers.

Page 49: *Human Events,* "Female Troops Desert Feminist Ranks." Reprinted with permission from *Human Events,* December 22, 1990. Copyright © 1990 by Human Events, Inc.

Page 59: Jeanne M. Holm, "Women in Combat: The New Reality." Reprinted by permission of the author.

Page 75: Raul Tovares, "How Best to Solve the Drug Problem: Legalize," *National Catholic Reporter,* December 22, 1989. Reprinted with permission, National Catholic Reporter, P.O. Box 419281, Kansas City, MO 64141.

Page 85: William Bennett, "Should Drugs Be Legalized?" *Reader's Digest,* March 1990, pp. 90–94. Reprinted with permission from the March 1990 *Reader's Digest.* Copyright © 1990 by the Reader's Digest Assn., Inc.

Page 99: Fleming Meeks and James Drummond, "The Greenest Form of Power." Reprinted by permission of *Forbes* magazine, June 11, 1990. Copyright © Forbes Inc., 1990.

Page 109: From the Union of Concerned Scientists pamphlet, "Nuclear Power: Past and Future." Reprinted with permission of the Union of Concerned Scientists.

Page 121: Steven Goldberg, "So What If the Death Penalty Deters?" Copyright © 1989 by *National Review,* Inc., 150 East 35th St., New York, NY 10016. Reprinted by permission.

Page 129: From *An Eye for an Eye: The Morality of Punishing by Death,* by Stephen Nathanson, pp. 15–20, 24–26, 29–31. Copyright © 1987 by Rowman and Littlefield, Savage, MD.

Page 149: Rudolph F. Verderber, "Remembering What You Hear," in *Communicate,* 6th ed. (Belmont, CA: Wadsworth, 1990), pp. 121–124.

Page 159: Philip C. Starr, "Working with Graphs," in *Economics: Principles in Action,* 5th ed. (Belmont, CA: Wadsworth, 1988), pp. 60–69.

Page 173: Michael A. Seeds, "The Venusian Greenhouse," in *Foundations of Astronomy,* 2nd ed. (Belmont, CA: Wadsworth, 1988), pp. 459–460.

Page 179: Karl J. Smith, "Early Numeration Systems," in *The Nature of Mathematics,* 6th ed. (Monterey, CA: Brooks/Cole, 1991), pp. 201–213. Reprinted by permission.

Page 191: Cecie Starr, "Human Population Growth," in *Biology: Concepts and Applications,* pp. 498–503. Copyright © 1991, Wadsworth, Inc.

Page 205: James W. Kalat, "Interpersonal Influence," in *Introduction to Psychology,* 2nd ed. (Belmont, CA: Wadsworth, 1990), pp. 628–635.

Page 219: Aaron Copland, "How We Listen to Music," in *What to Listen for in Music,* Chapter 4. Copyright © 1957 by McGraw Hill, Inc.

Page 227: Patrick J. Hurley, "Arguments, Premises, and Conclusions," from *A Concise Introduction to Logic.* Copyright © 1991 by Wadsworth, Inc., pp. 1–5. Reprinted by permission of Wadsworth Publishing Company, Belmont, CA 94002.

Page 235: James W. Kalat, "Principles of Genetics," from *Introduction to Psychology,* 2nd ed., pp. 57–60. Copyright © 1990 Wadsworth, Inc. Reprinted by permission of the publisher.

Page 245: Rodney Stark, "Free Will and Social Science," in *Sociology,* 4th ed. (Belmont, CA: Wadsworth, 1992), pp. 26–28.

Page 253: William L. Rathje, "Rubbish," in *Reader's Digest,* March 1990, pp. 171–174. Copyright 1986 by The Reader's Digest Association, Inc. Reprinted by permission of the author. Copyright © 1989 by William L. Rathje, *The Atlantic* (December 1989), 8 Arlington Street, Boston, MA 02116.

Page 259: Rudolph Verderber, "Assertiveness," *Communicate,* 6th ed., pp. 155–158. Copyright © Wadsworth, Inc. Reprinted by permission of the publisher.

Page 265: Perry W. Buffington, "Improving Your T.Q. (Test-Taking Quotient)," *Friendly Exchange,* Winter 1962, pp. 34, 36. Copyright © Farmers Insurance Group of Companies. Reprinted by permission of the author.

Page 271: *TV Guide,* "Fake News." Reprinted with permission from *TV Guide*® Magazine. Copyright © 1992 by News America Publications, Inc.

Page 277: Serena Nanda, "Building a House: Culture and Adaptation." Reprinted in *Cultural Anthropology,* 4th ed. (New York: Van Nostrand, 1991), pp. 60–62. Reprinted by permission of Wadsworth Publishing Company, Belmont, CA.

Page 281: Jerry Adler and Mary Hart, "Emptying the Cages," *Newsweek,* May 23, 1988. Copyright © 1988 Newsweek, Inc. All rights reserved. Reprinted by permission.

Page 285: John Carey, "Better Temper that Temper!," *Newsweek,* January 3, 1983, pp. 42–43. Copyright © 1983 by Newsweek, Inc. All rights reserved. Reprinted by permission.

Page 291: Bonnie Liebman, "The Ultra Mega Vita Guide," *Nutrition Action Healthletter,* January/February 1993. Copyright © 1993 CSPI. Reprinted from Nutrition Action Healthletter (1875 Connecticut Ave., NW, Ste. 300, Washington, D.C. 20009).

Page 297: Rodney Stark, "Minorities and Stardom," in *Sociology,* 4th ed. (Belmont, CA: Wadsworth, 1992), pp. 328–329.

Page 301: Isaac Asimov, "A Literature of Ideas" (orig. "When Aristotle Fails, Try Science Fiction"). Copyright © 1973 by Isaac Asimov. From *Today and Tomorrow and . . .* by Isaac Asimov. Reprinted by permission of Doubleday, a division of Bantam Doubleday Dell Publishing Group, Inc.